American Public Support for U.S. Military Operations from Mogadishu to Baghdad

Eric V. Larson

Bogdan Savych

Prepared for the Arroyo Center

RAND ARROYO CENTER

The research described in this report was sponsored by the United States Army under Contract No. DASW01-01-C-0003.

Library of Congress Cataloging-in-Publication Data

Larson, Eric, 1957–
American public support for U.S. military operations from Mogadishu to Baghdad / Eric Larson, Bogdan Savych.
p. cm.
Includes bibliographical references.
"MG-231."
ISBN 0-8330-3672-6 (pbk.)
1. United States—Foreign relations—1989—Public opinion. 2. United States—Military policy—Public opinion. 3. Intervention (International law)—Public opinion. 4. War—Public opinion. 5. Public opinion—United States. 6. United States—History, Military. I. Savych, Bogdan. II. Title.

E885.L368 2004
355.4'773—dc22

2004016643

Published 2005 by the RAND Corporation
1776 Main Street, P.O. Box 2138, Santa Monica, CA 90407-2138
1200 South Hayes Street, Arlington, VA 22202-5050
201 North Craig Street, Suite 202, Pittsburgh, PA 15213-1516
RAND URL: http://www.rand.org/
To order RAND documents or to obtain additional information, contact
Distribution Services: Telephone: (310) 451-7002;
Fax: (310) 451-6915; Email: order@rand.org

Preface

The support of the American public is widely held to be a critical prerequisite for undertaking military action abroad. As shown in this report, however, the absence of support for military operations from a majority of Americans has not hindered presidents from undertaking those operations in the past, nor does it seem likely to prove much of a barrier in the future.

The purpose of the present study is to describe American public opinion toward wars and other large military operations over the last decade, to delineate the sources of support and opposition for each war or operation, to identify the principal fault lines in support, and to illuminate those factors that are consistent predictors of support for and opposition to military operations.

This research was sponsored by Chief, National Security Policy Division, Office of the Deputy Chief of Staff, G-3, Department of the Army. It was conducted in RAND Arroyo Center's Strategy, Doctrine, and Resources Program. RAND Arroyo Center, part of the RAND Corporation, is a federally funded research and development center sponsored by the United States Army.

For more information on RAND Arroyo Center, contact the Director of Operations (telephone 310-393-0411, extension 6419; FAX 310-451-6952; email Marcy_Agmon@rand.org), or visit Arroyo's web site at http://www.rand.org/ard/.

Contents

Figures

Tables

Summary

While it is not at all clear that public opinion is a dominant factor in decisions on whether or not to undertake military operations, there is ample evidence that the public opinion environment shapes the way military operations are justified and even, in some cases, the way they are conducted. And, as shown in the Vietnam War, Lebanon, and Somalia, presidents can find that an unfavorable public opinion environment ultimately constrains the range of politically acceptable policies for successfully concluding a military operation.

This report describes American public opinion toward military operations from the final stage of the Somalia intervention through the global war on terrorism (GWOT), and it identifies the key factors that are associated with—and can be used to predict—support or opposition for military operations conducted under the umbrella of the GWOT. The study builds upon the insights of an earlier RAND study that identified the factors associated with support or opposition—and the willingness to tolerate casualties—in a wide range of military operations, including World War II, the Korean War, the Vietnam War, the first Gulf War, and the U.S. interventions in Panama and Somalia (Larson, 1996a).

Based upon our analyses of the available public opinion data, including bivariate and multivariate analyses of individual-level data from polling datasets, the most important predictors of support or opposition for military actions in the peace operations of the 1990s—and the GWOT as well—are a small set of key beliefs that are linked to support or opposition in a very sensible fashion:

- **Importance of the stakes.** Beliefs about the importance of the United States' stakes in a situation are systematically associated with support and opposition for military operations there: those who believe the United States has important stakes—whether in terms of vital national interests, security interests, or moral or humanitarian interests—are more likely to support the operation than those who don't believe the United States has important stakes involved.
- **Prospects for success.** Beliefs about the prospects for a successful outcome in the operation are also systematically associated with support or opposition: those who are more confident in a successful outcome are more likely to support the operation than those who are less confident.
- **Expected and actual casualties and other costs.** Beliefs about the likely costs, especially in casualties, are also associated with support: those who expect few casualties typically are more likely to support the operation than those who expect many casualties.
- **Partisan leadership and "followership."** These beliefs, and support and opposition as well, are in turn related to partisan leadership and what we call "followership"—the inclination to follow one's "natural" party or ideological leaders: individuals who are members of the president's party are more likely to support a president's use of force than those who are not, and within each party, those who are the best informed are more likely to take the same positions as their partisan leaders than those who are less well informed.

Using respondent-level datasets from polls done on various operations (Haiti, Bosnia, Kosovo, Operation Enduring Freedom in Afghanistan, and Operation Iraqi Freedom), our bivariate analyses consistently demonstrated a statistically significant relationship between support and these variables, and between key beliefs about the military operation and membership in the president's party. And, using a family of statistical techniques called probit regression, we were able to correctly predict support or opposition for about 60 to 85 percent of the respondents based upon these key variables.

Our multivariate analyses suggested that the perceived importance of the stakes was the most important belief predicting support for the operation.

We also were able to develop a cogent and empirically supported explanation for another phenomenon: when support is lost, those who oppose an operation may do so either because they want to cut their losses and withdraw or because they believe that greater effort is warranted. Beliefs about the importance of the stakes and prospects for success also predict individuals' positions on the matter: those who believe that the stakes are important and the prospects favorable are more likely to support escalation, while those holding the opposite beliefs tend to prefer withdrawal. Our modeling of respondent-level public opinion data on Somalia after the October firefight correctly predicted the preferences for escalation and withdrawal of over 60 percent of the respondents. By comparison, continued support for the U.S. intervention in Iraq after the early November deaths in the shoot down of a CH-46 Chinook helicopter was, because of the perception of greater stakes in Iraq, far more stalwart.

The robustness of this simple model—whether in terms of its ability to predict outcomes during specific military operations, its ability to predict outcomes in datasets based upon models estimated using other datasets, its reliability over time and across cases, and its ability to explain multiple phenomena—allowed us to analyze and diagnose the public opinion on GWOT-related military operations by concentrating on a small set of conceptually meaningful variables.

The Peace Operations of the 1990s

To establish the robustness of our model for analyzing the public opinion on the GWOT, we first assessed a number of peace operations from the 1990s: the U.S. peace operations in Somalia, Haiti, Bosnia, and Kosovo.

Somalia

Newly available data from a poll done by ABC News just before the October 3–4, 1993 firefight in Mogadishu showed that Americans preferred pulling out of Somalia by a nearly two-to-one margin *even before the firefight*, and following the firefight, this sentiment increased. A review of all of the available public opinion data on withdrawal and escalation sentiment confirmed that this result was a robust one: the overwhelming preference of Americans following the firefight was an orderly withdrawal from Somalia, i.e., a withdrawal following the recovery of U.S. servicemen held hostage. Our statistical models correctly predicted escalation or withdrawal preferences for slightly more than 60 percent of the respondents, and suggested that the reason that most preferred withdrawal was the widespread belief that the United States had only modest stakes in the situation. By comparison, the deaths of 16 U.S. service personnel in Iraq in early November 2003 led to a very different response: majority support for the U.S. mission in Iraq held, and there was even evidence of a stiffening in resolve. The reason for the difference was the more prevalent belief that the United States had important stakes in Iraq.

As a result of these analyses, we conclude that the frequently heard academic arguments that most Americans preferred an increased commitment in Somalia, or that President Clinton could have drawn upon a deep well of support for continuing the operation there, are on exceedingly dubious empirical ground. Our analyses also suggest that the argument that members of the public are more "defeat-phobic" than "casualty-phobic" is not true in cases where the United States' stakes are judged to be relatively unimportant; none of the peace operations of the 1990s (Somalia, Haiti, Bosnia, Kosovo) were judged particularly important by most members of the public, and avoidance of casualties turned out to be a more important consideration than avoidance of defeat in these cases.

Haiti, Bosnia, and Kosovo

In Haiti, Bosnia, and Kosovo, only about four in ten typically supported the use of U.S. ground troops in a combat role, and in Haiti and Bosnia, fewer than half typically supported the use of U.S. troops at all. In the case of Kosovo, there was typically majority support for the air campaign as well as the use of U.S. troops as peacekeepers once peace had actually been established, but most opposed the use of ground troops in a combat role.

The main reason for this reluctance to commit ground troops was that few believed the stakes were sufficiently important to risk the lives of U.S. servicemen:

- Only about three in ten of those polled before the intervention in Haiti typically believed that the United States had vital interests involved, or found very convincing the argument that the United States should contribute troops to a UN intervention for moral reasons.
- Only about three in ten of those polled before the operation in Bosnia felt that the United States had a moral obligation to intervene there, and fewer than four in ten Americans believed that Bosnia engendered particularly important U.S. interests.
- While 60–70 percent typically said that the United States had a moral obligation in Kosovo, fewer than half thought the United States had vital interests there. More than half supported an air war, while about four in ten supported the use of combat troops.

This low level of support for using ground troops in combat in peace operations involving only modest U.S. stakes was also evident in the public opinion data on Lebanon and, more recently, Liberia.

Focusing on the key beliefs described above, and on such individual-level characteristics as party, gender, and race, our statistical modeling correctly predicted support for 75 percent of the respondents in polling on Haiti, over 80 percent in polling on Bosnia, and 66–73 percent in polling on Kosovo. The modeling also consistently suggested that the perceived importance of the stakes was the most important belief in determining support or opposition.

These results suggested that our basic conceptual model of support, developed using an earlier set of cases, was quite robust and would also be suitable for use in understanding the sources of and fault lines in support for military operations undertaken under the umbrella of the war on terrorism.

Attitudes Toward the Global War on Terrorism

Our analysis of the public opinion data on military operations undertaken in the war on terrorism shows that there has been much higher support—and a higher willingness to use ground troops and even accept casualties—in actions related to the GWOT than was observed in the peace operations of the 1990s that preceded it.

The principal reason is the post–September 11 view that most Americans believed this new war to involve nearly existential stakes. Americans polled after 9/11 who were asked which event was the more historically significant—the attacks on the World Trade Center and Pentagon or the attack on Pearl Harbor—chose 9/11 by a nearly three-to-one margin. The 9/11 attacks also resonated with long-standing fears about the threat of terrorism and weapons of mass destruction, each of which had been identified by eight in ten or more Americans for a number of years as critically important threats that needed to be addressed.

The result has been high support for the use of ground troops in spite of the strong possibility of high casualties, and in spite of beliefs that the GWOT is likely to be a long, difficult war. And although most Americans continue to believe that the GWOT will involve additional military actions, they nevertheless continue to support the war, especially as it relates to capturing or killing Osama bin Laden and eliminating the Al Qaeda organization. Indeed, since about September 2002, six in ten have said that bin Laden must be killed or captured for the GWOT to be considered a success.

Operation Enduring Freedom in Afghanistan

The average level of support for the U.S. military action in Afghanistan approached the eight in ten that typically supported World War II.

Using the key predictors described above, our statistical modeling predicted support or opposition for 79–86 percent of the respondents in datasets from three separate polls. As suggested by the discussion of the GWOT above, the principal predictors of support were the perceived importance of the stakes and prospects for success; beliefs about casualties, and membership in the president's party, were also statistically significant but less important predictors.

Polling organizations have not polled very heavily on Afghanistan since the rout of the Taliban and Al Qaeda in late 2001 and early 2002, but the last available data suggested that majority support for the U.S. military effort in Afghanistan was holding up. Although confidence in the war on terrorism was buoyed by the victory in Iraq, the public appears to be having a difficult time judging progress, in large measure due to the failure to capture or kill bin Laden and the inability to judge the importance of various arrests and military engagements in continued action in Afghanistan.

Operation Iraqi Freedom

Public support for the war in Iraq was also high by historical standards, but not quite as high as support for Afghanistan or the first Gulf War. Support and opposition on Iraq were most influenced by beliefs about the importance of the United States' security interests, but also by the perceived prospects for success, likely casualties, and membership in the president's party; based upon these factors, our statistical models were able to predict support or opposition for about 75 percent of the respondents in the two poll datasets we analyzed.

In spite of widespread predictions that Americans would not support the war without UN authorization, the fact that seven in ten ultimately would support the war should not have been terribly surprising in light of the public opinion record since the first Gulf War. This record showed that in the more than 100 times the question was asked, the percentage of Americans supporting reintroduction of U.S. ground troops in an effort to overthrow Saddam Hussein never fell below a majority. The prevalence of beliefs about the importance of the stakes and, to a lesser extent, the high probability of success were the key sources that buoyed support; as a result, although casualty expectations were much higher than in the peace operations we examined, the willingness to tolerate casualties in a war in Iraq also was much higher.

While there is some evidence that majorities of the public continue to view the success of postconflict stability, "nation building," and democracy building operations in Iraq as very important, there are some worrisome trends in postwar attitudes on Iraq. While some measures of support for U.S. action in Iraq have held up reasonably well (e.g., six in ten continue to say the war was the right thing to do), others have not. There has also been a deterioration among the numbers who feel the war in Iraq was worth its costs, in spite of Saddam Hussein's capture, in part because of the failure to find weapons of mass destruction.

That said, the October 2003 passage of United Nations Security Council Resolution 1511, which provided political cover for other nations to provide troops, and financial contributions made at an international donors conference offered the prospect of buoying support for the war in Iraq. If the United States were still to discover weapons of mass destruction or credible evidence of connections between Iraq and Al Qaeda, or if there was a reduction or cessation of attacks or more visible evidence that Iraq is moving toward stability and a viable democracy, those developments would also be expected to buoy support.

Our analyses suggest that the main fault lines on Iraq are largely partisan in nature. Democratic critics of the administration's Iraq policy have sought, first, to suggest that other problems (Al Qaeda or North Korea) were in fact more important than Iraq, and then to question the administration's credibility on the justification for war (first weapons of mass destruction, then Iraqi connections to Al Qaeda). Recent administration speeches on Iraq appear to have done little to staunch the erosion in support for Iraq, and the presidential campaign has only sharpened these divisions, which will in turn only weaken overall support for operations in Iraq.

Another fault line is that the willingness of Americans to support military operations, including using ground troops and accepting casualties, rests on beliefs that the stakes remain high and, to a lesser extent, that progress is being made: if most Americans were to come to believe that the stakes in Iraq were no more important than those in the peace operations of the 1990s, for example, or that the situation closely resembled the quagmires of Vietnam, Lebanon, and Somalia, remaining support and the willingness to accept casualties could quickly erode. The public's reaction to the 16 deaths incurred in the helicopter shoot down in Iraq in early November 2003 and the deaths of four civilians in April 2004 provide evidence that the greater robustness of support for operations in Iraq than in Somalia is mainly attributable to the greater importance Americans have attached to Iraq. It also is worth pointing out, however, that the characteristics of the sort of war we are waging in the GWOT—mostly in the shadows, with only occasional evidence of success—make it a significant challenge to sustain public optimism about the outcome.

Implications

We now turn to the main implications of this research for the Army and national political leaders.

The main implication for the Army is that Americans have proved themselves far more willing to use ground troops—to put "boots on the ground"—and to accept casualties in operations conducted under the GWOT than in any of the military operations in the decade that preceded it. This suggests more support for an Army role than was observed in the peace operations of the 1990s, at least to the extent that the specific military operations that are proposed under the GWOT are judged to be relevant to the GWOT, and that they have good prospects for a successful outcome.

To the extent that the public believes that proposed new military operations are part of the GWOT, national leaders should expect a relatively permissive public opinion environment for taking military action, including the use of ground forces. It seems likely, however, in light of questions that have arisen about the existence and nature of any connections between Iraq and Al Qaeda, that it is no longer a foregone conclusion that Americans will unquestioningly accept arguments making these connections.

More broadly, the immediate aftermath of 9/11 initially seemed to show that a post–Cold War consensus on the focus of national security and defense policies had finally emerged among national leaders in the executive and legislative branches: for the foreseeable future, it seemed at the time, leaders in both parties supported a focus for U.S. national security on terrorist groups with global reach, their sponsors, and those providing them refuge.

The U.S. action in Afghanistan generally received overwhelming bipartisan support from national leaders, and public support accordingly was preternaturally high. Bipartisan support for the war in Iraq was slightly weaker, and as a result, public support, while still high, was somewhat lower than that observed for Afghanistan. Bipartisan consensus on postconflict stability operations in Iraq, however, now appears elusive at best.

It is still too early to say whether or how this breakdown in consensus might color support for other military actions taken under the banner of the GWOT. Nevertheless, it raises the specter that, as a result of the reappearance of leadership divisions, future operations in the GWOT also may suffer from lower and/or more highly conditional support.

While national leaders argue their differences on national security, they need to remain mindful that a failure to agree on the ends, ways, and means for ensuring the nation's security in the face of these new threats can actually weaken the credibility of deterrence and coercive diplomacy—and beliefs in the United States' ability to stay the course in its war on terrorism—and ultimately encourage the nation's enemies.

The United States has always been a noisy democracy when it comes to issues of war and peace—witness the partisan divisions over the peace operations of the 1990s. Unlike these earlier operations, however, where the U.S. stakes were relatively modest, and the consequences of failure equally so, the outcome of the GWOT greatly matters. The only way to sustain the public's support for this war—arguably a requirement for its success—will be for national leaders to forge policies that reflect a new consensus on the matter. Absent such a consensus, the nation's ability to reduce this grave threat may be placed in jeopardy.

Acknowledgments

We would like to thank the following for their assistance over the course of this project: COL James Boling and MAJ Todd Key, Headquarters, DAMO-SSP, G-3, Department of the Army; Gary Langer, Director, ABC News' Polling Unit; Maura Strausberg, The Gallup Organization; John Mueller, Woodrow B. Hayes Professor of National Security, The Mershon Center, Ohio State University; and The Pew Research Center for People and the Press. We would like to thank Professor Charles Ostrom of Michigan State University and RAND Corporation colleague Kevin McCarthy for their helpful reviews, as well as the above-mentioned John Mueller for his helpful comments on an earlier draft. Within RAND, we would like to thank Lauri Zeman and Tom Szayna, Program Director and Assistant Program Director for RAND Arroyo Center's Strategy, Doctrine, and Resources Program (SD&R); participants in two meetings of study leaders in the SD&R program; and James Dobbins, John E. Peters, and other RAND colleagues who offered helpful comments and suggestions on the study.

Glossary

GWOT	Global War on Terrorism
NATO	North Atlantic Treaty Organization
OEF	Operation Enduring Freedom
OIF	Operation Iraqi Freedom
PIPA	Program on International Policy Attitudes
PSRA	Princeton Survey Research Associates
UN	United Nations
UNITAF	Unified Task Force (Somalia)
UNSCR	United Nations Security Council Resolution
WMD	Weapons of Mass Destruction

CHAPTER ONE

Introduction

While anecdotal evidence suggests that public opinion is not a dominant factor in decisions on whether or not to undertake military operations, there is ample evidence that the public opinion environment shapes the way military operations are justified and even, in some cases, the way they are designed and conducted.[1] And, as shown in the Vietnam War, Lebanon, and Somalia, presidents ultimately can find that an unfavorable public opinion environment can impose constraints on the range of politically feasible policies.[2]

This report describes American public opinion toward the global war on terrorism (GWOT), and it identifies the key factors that are associated with—and can be used to predict—support for or opposition to military operations conducted under the umbrella of the GWOT. The study builds upon the insights of an earlier RAND analysis that identified the key factors associated with support or opposition—and the willingness to tolerate casualties—in a wide range of wars and military operations, including World War II, the Korean War, the Vietnam War, the first Gulf War, and the U.S. interventions in Panama and Somalia (Larson, 1996a).

---

[1] See Chapter Four, "Domestic Constraints on Coercion," in Byman, Waxman, and Larson (1999). Public opinion considerations also frequently lead the president to try nonmilitary means before military ones, not because of any belief that they will necessarily work, but in order to demonstrate that all other nonmilitary alternatives have been exhausted and that military action is "the last resort."

[2] To be clear, while public opinion can impose political costs for pursuing unpopular policies, it does not necessarily prevent presidents from pursuing them. Moreover, the willingness to remain on a politically costly path can vary by president, and by policy issue.

Background

Scholarly work on American public opinion during U.S. wars and military operations has generally tended to focus on four issues:

1. Efforts to understand the circumstances under which presidential uses of force lead to "rallies" in support for the president;[3]
2. Efforts to understand whether presidents use force in an effort to boost their approval ratings or otherwise divert attention from political woes;[4]
3. Analyses of the dynamics of American public opinion during past U.S. wars and military operations;[5] and
4. Efforts to understand the factors that influence public support or opposition to uses of military force more generally.[6]

The present work generally seeks to make a contribution to the third and fourth of these areas of research: analyzing the dynamics of public opinion during specific military operations, and better understanding the factors that influence support and opposition.

It also, however, seeks to break new ground on the fourth area. In addition to analyzing ecological (aggregate) public opinion data, it relies on bivariate and multivariate analyses of respondent-level data for each case, including multivariate statistical modeling of the factors that influence individual-level decisions to support or oppose specific military operations. This combined approach offers a better chance of

---

[3] See, for example, Mueller (1973), Edwards (1990), especially pp. 143–152, and Brody (1991).

[4] Some scholars have noted that presidents often see a "rally" in their presidential approval ratings when they use military force, and others have contended that U.S. presidents engage in "political" or "diversionary" uses of force, i.e., they seek to divert attention from domestic woes and increase their public standing by undertaking military action abroad. For various views in this debate, see Ostrom and Job (1986), Gelpi (1997), Levy (1993), Meernik (1994), Meernik and Waterman (1996), and Leeds and Davis (1997).

[5] Examples of this genre include Mueller (1973, 1994), Larson (1996a), Sobel (1989, 1998), and Klarevas (2000).

[6] See, for example, Jentleson (1992), Oneal, Lian, and Joyner (1996), Jentleson and Britton (1998), Klarevas and O'Connor (1994).

understanding, in a robust way, which factors have been most influential in individuals' support for and opposition to past military operations, and it avoids the problems associated with regression analyses of ecological data that do not adequately control for important influences on support and opposition that are to be found in cues in the wording of public opinion poll questions.[7]

Approach

The study used a four-step approach for the analysis of the public opinion data.

First, we conducted searches of The Roper Center's POLL database, Gallup's database of questionnaires,[8] and other relevant websites[9] for relevant data on each war or military operation. We typically used a keyword connoting the location of the operation (e.g., "Somalia," "Haiti"), sometimes in combination with other keywords to find specific polling questions of interest (e.g., "Haiti and casualties," "Iraq and approve").

Second, because responses can be so sensitive to question wording and other factors,[10] we sought to develop multiple indicators for each of the attitudes of interest by using a variety of questions and building trend data wherever that was possible. To heighten comparability and transparency, we emphasized data from questions that

---

[7] Jentleson (1992), Klarevas and O'Connor (1994), and Jentleson and Britton (1998), for example, regressed the percentages approving of a wide number of military operations on judgments the authors made about the nature of the policy objectives or other characteristics of the situation, but did not control for all of the potential sources of variation that can influence approval or disapproval.

[8] Gallup has a keyword-searchable database of all of the questionnaires that have been used in its surveys.

[9] For example, The Los Angeles Times, Washington Post, and New York Times, ABC News, CBS News, Cable News Network, and NBC News publish their survey results, often including full questionnaires and graphics, and PollingReport.com provides useful compilations of data.

[10] See Kagay (1992).

were worded in a straightforward fashion and asked about support and opposition of various kinds,[11] or about beliefs that have been shown to be closely associated with support in past wars and military operations.[12]

In most cases, to ensure that we were reaching robust conclusions, we also compared these results with other questions that contained cues that would be expected to raise or lower support. In this, we tried to take a page from Franklin Roosevelt, who, it is said, would not accept a polling result regarding a policy issue as a firm statement of the public's opinion on the issue unless it could be shown that it reflected fully crystallized public opinion. His test was whether polling questions whose wording was favorable toward the policy and those whose wording was critical of the policy returned essentially the same percentages supporting and opposing; results that fell short of this standard reflected public opinion that was not fully crystallized, which might firm up in response to events on the ground, presidential leadership, or public deliberation of the underlying issues and tradeoffs.[13]

Third and finally, to refine our understanding of the factors that were at work in individuals' decisions to support or oppose past military operations, we acquired a number of datasets that contain respondent-level data from polls conducted during each operation.

---

[11] For example, to assess support, we searched for questions that asked about approval or disapproval for going to war or taking military action, the presence of U.S. troops, and presidential handling of the situation, and questions that asked respondents whether they thought the intervention had been a mistake, whether the United States had made the right decision, and whether it had done the right thing in using force.

[12] The most important of these beliefs have to do with the importance of the perceived stakes, whether in traditional national security or moral or humanitarian interests; the perceived prospects for success, i.e., the extent to which the public believes that the United States will secure its objectives, whatever they may be; the likely and actual costs of the operation; and party orientation, which will condition which leaders members of the public are most likely to respond to. For a discussion of these factors, see Larson (1996a, 1996b, and, especially, 2000).

[13] Daniel Yankelovich has explored the question of crystallization in public attitudes. See Yankelovich (1991). Kagay (1992) provides a nice discussion of uncrystallized public opinion and the various factors that can affect responses, and he advocates "looking at the preponderance" of evidence, as we do.

We performed bivariate tests of association between support and our various independent variables—the importance of the stakes, prospects for success, casualties and other costs, party, information consumption, and so on—and estimated one or more multivariate models that predicted individuals' support for or opposition to each operation.[14]

As just described, the research presented here actually illuminates the beliefs, individual-level characteristics, and basic logic that individuals have used in deciding whether or not to support a wide range of military operations. Throughout, it emphasizes robust findings—within and across cases—rather than odd results that may have arisen from tendentiously worded questions, so-called "house effects," or other idiosyncrasies.[15]

A Note on the Importance of Question Wording

To illuminate the influence of question wording on responses, we now present two examples involving public opinion on a U.S. intervention in Bosnia from 1993 to 1995; our analysis of support for the U.S. intervention in Bosnia in the next chapter provides an even more systematic and compelling illustration of the importance of question wording.

Example One

Table 1.1 presents the results of two questions from polling on May 6, 1993, that asked respondents if they favored or opposed air strikes in Bosnia. As shown, although the questions were asked the same day, the results varied dramatically, with anywhere from 35 to 65 percent favoring and 32 to 55 percent opposing air strikes, depending on question wording.[16]

---

[14] In the case of Somalia, our model predicted escalation or withdrawal sentiment.

[15] For example, Sobel (1996) and Larson (2000) document apparent biases in polling done by the University of Maryland's Program on International Policy Attitudes (PIPA).

[16] The margin of error for polls with this sample size is plus or minus five percentage points.

Table 1.1
Support and Opposition for Air Strikes in Bosnia, May 6, 1993

As you may know, the Bosnian Serbs rejected the United Nations peace plan and Serbian forces are continuing to attack Muslim towns. Some people are suggesting the United States conduct air strikes against Serbian military forces, while others say we should not get militarily involved. Do you favor or oppose U.S. air strikes? (Gallup/CNN/USA Today, May 6, 1993, N=603)

Favor	36%
Oppose	56
No opinion	6
Depends	3

Specifically, would you support or oppose the United States, along with its allies in Europe, carrying out air strikes against Bosnian Serb artillery positions and supply lines? (ABC News, May 6, 1993, N=516).

Favor	65%
Oppose	32
No opinion	3

The higher level of approval in the second question *could* be attributable to the fact that the question mentioned the participation of European allies (such cues typically can boost support), or that the first question might imply to some that air strikes would be unlikely to influence the rejectionist Serbs, or that the first question explicitly mentions that some oppose military involvement. It also could be that questions asked before one of these two questions included cues that colored responses to subsequent questions as well; we simply cannot know for certain.

If these were the only data available on the question, however, it would be impossible to say whether most Americans favored or opposed air strikes, as the two results suggest that opinion on the matter was highly sensitive to differences in question wording and therefore probably not very well crystallized.[17] In such a case, it would be critical both to avoid the use of single-poll results and to compare the re-

---

[17] By comparison, if both results had found comparable majorities approving or disapproving, that would suggest that attitudes on the matter had crystallized.

sults from various polling efforts to understand the extent to which responses were sensitive to question wording and other factors.

Example Two

As a second illustration, as shown in Table 1.2, three different polling organizations asked about support or opposition for U.S. participation in a peacekeeping force in Bosnia immediately after President Clinton's November 27, 1995 speech on the matter.

As shown, we cannot say for certain what percentage of Americans actually supported or opposed the use of force in Bosnia (the former ranged between 33 and 46 percent, and the latter between 40 and 58 percent), but if the percentages in Table 1.2 were the only

Table 1.2
Support and Opposition to Troops in Bosnia, November 27, 1995

Now that a peace agreement has been reached by all the groups currently fighting in Bosnia, the Clinton administration plans to contribute U.S. troops to an international peacekeeping force. Do you favor or oppose that? (Gallup/CNN/USA Today, November 27, 1995, N=632)

Favor	46%
Oppose	40
No opinion	14

(President Bill) Clinton said now that a Bosnian peace treaty has been signed, he's sending 20,000 U.S. troops there as part of an international peacekeeping force. Do you support or oppose sending 20,000 U.S. troops to Bosnia as part of an international peacekeeping force? (ABC News/Washington Post, November 27, 1995, N=519)

Support	39%
Oppose	57
Don't know	4

Do you favor or oppose sending up to 20,000 U.S. troops to Bosnia, as part of a NATO (North Atlantic Treaty Organization) peacekeeping force, to enforce this peace agreement between Bosnia, Serbia and Croatia? (CBS News, November 27, 1995, N=504)

Favor	33%
Oppose	58
Don't know/No answer	9

available data (as seems to be the case), we would be able to draw one reasonably robust conclusion: a majority of Americans at the time of the president's speech failed to support U.S. participation in the peacekeeping operation in Bosnia, even when cues that would have been expected to increase support were present in the questions.[18]

Although we can only speculate on the reasons for the observed differences because other influences also could have been at work,[19] they are probably largely attributable to question wording.[20] For example, we note that: the questions that mentioned the contribution of 20,000 U.S. troops received lower levels of support than the one that didn't (the implication of the potentially high costs accompanying such a large force would be expected to reduce support); the questions that mentioned President Clinton received higher support than the one that didn't (mentioning the president can increase support); and the question that mentioned U.S. participation in a NATO peacekeeping force that would "enforce" the peace agreement got lower support than the questions that simply mentioned U.S. participation in an "international peacekeeping force" (for many, "enforcement" seems to imply a higher possibility of combat, and casualties).

Robust Analyses, Robust Support

We use the concept of robustness in two distinct ways.

First, we use the term in the sense of robust results, i.e., results that emerge from analyses that have considered responses to questions

---

[18] Additional evidence can be found in the fact that only about four in ten approved of President Clinton's handling of the Bosnia situation in the ABC News/Washington Post and CBS News polls.

[19] These other influences can include differences that arise from such factors as differences in polling organizations' sampling frames, sampling error, question order effects, response option order effects, and other sources.

[20] To resolve the matter of whether question wording was at work, and assuming a large enough sample size, one could have used a split sample, where respondents were asked the same set of questions in the earlier part of the survey, but all three versions of the question were then asked of a third of the sample. This would have removed other potential causes of the difference. Of course, neither polling organizations nor scholars have shown a great deal of interest in understanding the degree to which support and opposition for a military operation in fact hinges on question wording.

that may vary in their wording, timing, and other features, and contrast with results that emerge from a single poll or highly selective use of polling results. For example, we sought to characterize support not only in terms of the overall percentages supporting, but also how often a majority actually supported or opposed the operation, and the structure of support (discussed next).[21]

Second, we use the term in the sense of robust support, i.e., support that appears to be relatively insensitive to increasing costs, setbacks on the battlefield, or other factors. This contrasts with conditional support, wherein support is contingent on a narrow set of conditions such as low casualties, coalition participation, or other factors. Operationally, the most robust support would be indicated by support that remained high even in questions that mention the distinct possibility of substantial casualties, a long and drawn-out campaign, or other undesirable characteristics.

The robustness of support can also be inferred from the distribution of responses in questions that asked respondents about the strength of their support for or opposition to a military operation (see Figure 1.1).

As suggested by the figure, robust support can be inferred in cases where a large majority of respondents strongly support the operation, and declining percentages offer weak support, weak opposition, and strong opposition (the dark columns); in a similar way, robust opposition could be inferred in cases where a large percentage strongly oppose the operation, with smaller percentages weakly opposing, unsure, or supporting.[22]

---

[21] For example, we report the average, the number of times questions of this kind were asked, and the number of occasions in which a majority supported.

[22] We assume something of a graceful failure mode in public support in response to marginal changes on the ground, i.e., that those who strongly supported an operation at the beginning but became disillusioned would first shift to weak support, then to weak opposition, and finally to strong opposition. Of course, major events could well yield far more dramatic shifts, but absent any data on the matter, the assumption certainly is a plausible and testable one.

Figure 1.1
Robust Support and Opposition

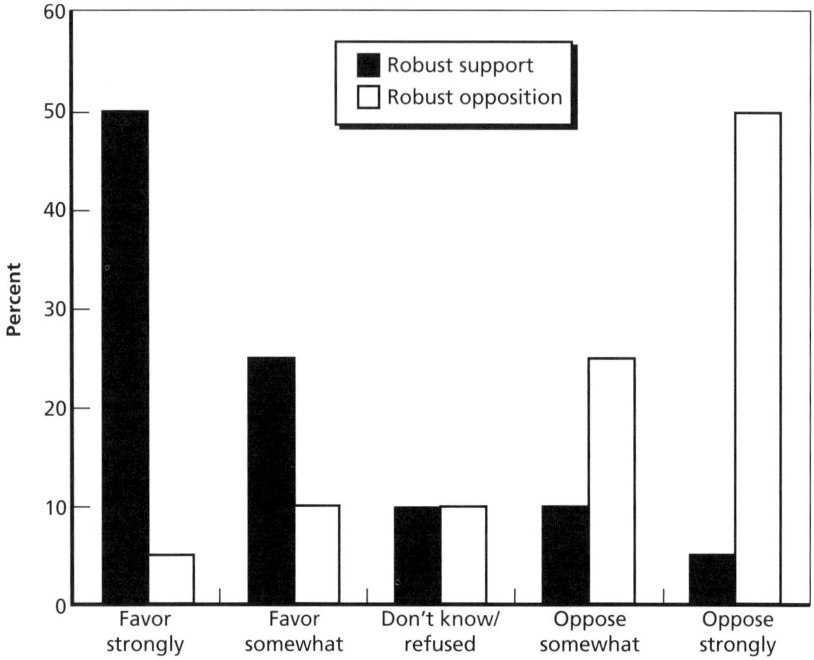

RAND *MG231-A-1.1*

In cases where subgroups (e.g., party) divide, and where the attitudes of one subgroup (e.g., members of the president's party) are characterized by robust support and another subgroup (e.g., members of the opposition party) by robust opposition, the result can be said to be "highly polarized by party," which is typically not a very robust structure for support, since it diminishes the prospects that a majority of Americans support the operation.

Organization of This Report

This report is organized as follows:

- Chapter Two presents an overview of two models that in combination can be used to diagnose public opinion toward past military operations, and which provide the logic and theory for the multivariate statistical modeling that predicts individual-level support or opposition to past military operations based upon a very small number of predictors.
- To better understand the foundations and dynamics of public support and opposition for recent past U.S. military operations, Chapter Three applies the model developed in Chapter Two to diagnose the key beliefs and individual-level factors affecting American public opinion on a number of military operations conducted over the last decade. These include withdrawal and escalation sentiment in the final stages of the U.S. intervention in Somalia, and support for and opposition to the U.S. interventions in Haiti, Bosnia, and Kosovo.
- In Chapter Four, we assess the beliefs and individual-level characteristics related to support and opposition to U.S. military action conducted under the umbrella of the GWOT, including Operation Enduring Freedom (OEF) in Afghanistan, and military action in other locales such as Yemen, the Philippines, the Sudan, and Somalia. Most of the analysis was completed in September 2003, although modest efforts were made to update key data series in May 2004.
- In Chapter Five, we assess the beliefs and individual-level factors related to support for and opposition to Operation Iraqi Freedom (OIF), the U.S. military action in Iraq. As with Afghanistan, most of the analytic work was concluded in September 2003, with modest efforts to update key data series in May 2004. We conclude the chapter with a few words on changes in Americans' attitudes toward Iraq as of August 2004.
- In Chapter Six, we provide conclusions and discuss the implications of our analysis for the U.S. Army and national political and military leaders.

We also include an appendix that reexamines some of the conclusions from RAND's 1996 study, *Casualties and Consensus*, in light of these new cases.

Finally, in a separate volume we provide more detailed technical information on our statistical analyses: see Eric V. Larson and Bogdan Savych, *American Public Support for U.S. Military Operations from Mogadishu to Baghdad, Statistical Appendixes,* Santa Monica, CA: RAND Corporation, TR-167-A, 2004.

CHAPTER TWO

Understanding Support for Military Operations

The factors that lead to changes in support and opposition to military operations can be understood using two simple models that have strong theoretical and empirical foundations: a simple model of the public's calculus of ends and means that captures the essential logic of how the public decides whether or not to support the operation, and a simple social process model that explains the diffusion of beliefs and attitudes about the operation.

A Simple Model of the Public's Ends-Means Calculus

We first consider the main predictors of support—the specific beliefs members of the public hold about the importance of the stakes that are involved, the prospects for the operation's success, and the expected or actual casualties—in a simple calculus that weighs ends against means.

While much of the research on public opinion about military operations has focused on "rally effects" or average levels of support for various military operations, there has been less work on general models that can explain the observed patterns in support for a particular military operation over time.[1] A few scholars have in fact recognized the policy-relevance of two core phenomena: declines in sup-

Note: An earlier version of this material appeared in Larson (2000).

[1] On the "rally effect," see Mueller (1973), Brody (1991), and Burbach (1994).

port over the course of an operation, and diverging preferences regarding the level of commitment.[2] Beyond these authors, however, little additional research has been undertaken to place these recurring phenomena into a broader theoretical framework.

The model, described below, is a deductive model that provides a cogent explanation for two distinct aspects of support for military operations: (1) the factors associated with increasing and decreasing support for military operations and (2) the factors associated with diverging preferences regarding strategy and the level of commitment.

The Deductive Model

At the most fundamental level, members of the public attempt to weigh ends, ways, and means in deciding whether to support a military operation. A simple model has been shown to assist in thinking about support for military operations by characterizing support as the result of a series of tests or questions that need to be answered collectively by political leaders and the public:[3]

- Do the interests that are at stake or the likely benefits of the operation seem to be important enough to justify the use of force?
- Are the prospects for success high enough?
- Are the expected or actual costs low enough?
- Taken together, does the probable outcome seem (or seem still) to be worth the costs?

The nature of the relationships can be encapsulated in a simple mathematical expression. Let each individual i's utility be defined by the following function, which relates the three variables in an intuitively logical way:[4]

$$EU_i = (p_i \cdot s_i)/c_i,$$

[2] See Converse and Schuman (1970), Modigliani (1972), and Mueller (1973).

[3] See Larson (1996a, 1996b, 2000).

[4] A comparable formulation of this pseudocardinal utility measure can be found in Churchman and Ackoff (1954). Other, more elaborate formulations are also possible. This is an area of future research for us.

where

EU_i = the utility that individual i has for the military operation.

p_i = the individual's subjective estimate of the operation's probability of success.

s_i = individual i's judgment about the perceived stakes that are involved in the operation, or the benefits of undertaking the operation.

c_i = the anticipated or actual costs in blood and treasure.

This expression tells us that an individual's utility from a military operation will depend on the ratio between the expected benefits and the costs. Now, let

$Umin_i$ = the minimal acceptable utility for individual i to remain a supporter of the operation.[5]

Put another way, the individual will be a supporter of the operation so long as the following inequality is true:

$$U_i \geq Umin_i,$$

where each of the three parameters (p_i, s_i, and c_i) and $Umin_i$ are greatly influenced by the positions of political leaders and experts, to the extent that individuals are aware of them (discussed below). If an individual's utility falls below this threshold, he will oppose the operation, and if the utility climbs above this threshold, he will support it.

Key Beliefs and Opinion Mediators

Figure 2.1 portrays the theorized relationship between support for military operations and the key beliefs and opinion mediators that are predictors of support or opposition.

---

[5] In the vernacular of microeconomics, this can be thought of as the level of utility at which an individual is just indifferent between support and opposition.

Figure 2.1
Relationship Between Support and Key Beliefs and Opinion Mediators

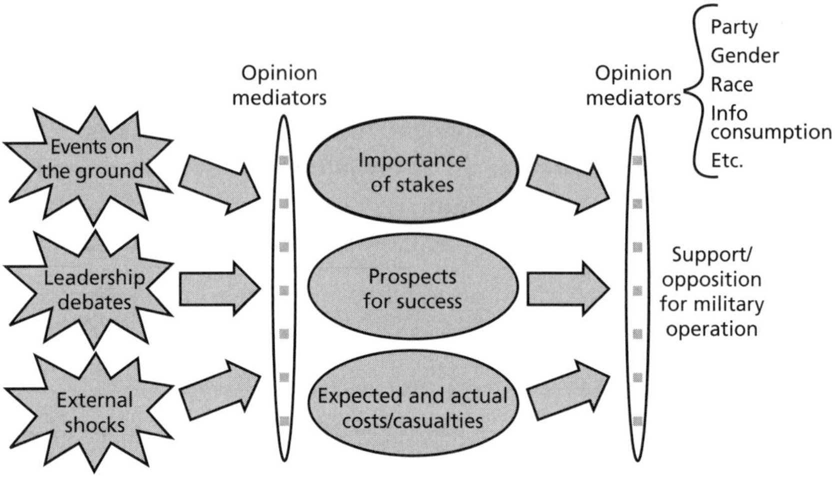

RAND *MG231-A-2.1*

As shown in the figure, beliefs about the importance of the stakes, the prospects for success, and the expected and actual costs (especially in terms of U.S. casualties) are influenced by actual events and conditions, and are filtered through individual-level opinion mediators such as party identification, gender, race, and other individual-level characteristics that affect the individual's willingness to support what is essentially a gamble on whether or not the U.S. military venture is likely to be successful at a cost that is acceptable to the individual.[6]

Importance of the stakes (s). A number of different approaches have been used to characterize the importance of the stakes that are involved in military operations.[7] To simplify analysis, we can evaluate

---

[6] As a practical matter, for purposes of statistical modeling, the variables for stakes, prospects, costs, party, gender, race, and information consumption simultaneously enter into a probit or ordered probit model. Future work will explore the predictive power of alternative specifications.

[7] Some of this work has identified differences in support based upon the objectives being pursued. For example, Mueller (1977), Russett (1990–91), and Jentleson (1992) report that U.S. military responses to external aggressions typically received higher levels of support than

the stakes of a military operation in terms of two dimensions:[8] the first is the importance of the security interests that are directly engaged in a situation (the litmus test for the Realist), and the second is the importance of the normative or moral interests, values, or goals being promoted (the litmus test for the Idealist).[9] All else equal, the greater the importance of the security and moral interests that are believed to be engaged, the higher the level of utility, and the greater the likelihood the individual will support the operation;[10] conversely, military operations that lack a compelling rationale are also less likely to yield a sufficiently high utility to justify their support.

On the basis of simple microeconomic theory, one would expect that individuals will be willing to trade off across the two dimensions at a nondecreasing marginal rate, i.e., the absence of important security interests in a situation may not be critical if important moral in-

---

strictly internal conflicts; Jentleson and Britton (1998) believe that humanitarian objectives typically receive more support than internal change objectives, but less than external restraint objectives. Richman (1994, 1995) provided a broader list of factors that could be used to impute importance. Finally, Wittkopf (1990) associated willingness to use force with the extent it comports with broader value structures. What has been lacking is a broader structure for integrating these empirical findings with the other factors that are associated with support. See the appendix in Larson (1996b) for a complete discussion in simple microeconomic terms, animated by public opinion data.

[8] By virtue of semantics, efforts by individuals to achieve cognitive consistency, and other factors, these two dimensions are most likely not entirely independent for most individuals, nor necessarily all-inclusive. For example, the promotion of an important principle could easily be viewed by some individuals as an important interest. The benefits dimension is not very well understood at present, and it is deserving of more serious empirical research. See Wittkopf (1990) for a related discussion.

[9] The two dimensions described here aim to tap the impulses that animate two competing normative views of foreign policy—Idealism and Realism. For the Idealist, the aim of foreign policy is world order through promotion of important principles as embodied in international law, multilateral organizations, and democracy and human rights. For the Realist, the aim is world order through a strong defense, the preservation of vital interests, and responses to changing power calculations. For a recent effort to classify U.S. interests in terms of their importance, see Commission on America's National Interests (1996). This work also provides a framework for mapping political or policy objectives. For example, humanitarian operations promote humanitarian goals.

[10] Departures from strict rationality may lead to inconsistent evaluations of utility that occur under certain circumstances (e.g., prospect theory). See Kahneman, Slovic, and Tversky (1982) and Nincic (1997).

terests are engaged, and vice versa.[11] The benefits will be highest for military operations that are seen to engage U.S. vital interests, and operations whose political objectives promote foreign policy goals or principles that are viewed as quite important.[12]

The probability of success (p). In addition to being animated by principles and interests, public attitudes toward the use of force are suffused with a strong component of pragmatism that tempers unquestioning support for pursuit of these abstractions.[13] Therefore, the second parameter of the simple model of ends and means has to do with the prospects for a successful outcome. Because the deductive model of ends and means incorporates the probability of success in the numerator, the probability of success operates in the same fashion as the level of benefits: as the probability of a successful outcome declines, the expected benefits to be achieved by the operation also decline. Put another way, operations that are clearly failing to achieve their objectives will tend to lose support.[14]

Costs (c). The third parameter of the simple model has to do with the expected or actual costs of the military operation, including blood and treasure, and any opportunity costs. The deductive model

---

[11] The rate at which individuals are willing to trade off security and moral interests may vary, however. For example, those who place the greatest importance on principles in the use of force may support a use of force only when absolutely vital (e.g., existential) interests are at stake.

[12] In fact, there is strong evidence that the aggregate public displays a somewhat differentiated but consistent view about where U.S. interests lie abroad and what foreign policy goals are most important, and as will be seen in the case study, this hierarchy can be used to assist in the diagnosis of the perceived benefits in actual military operations. The quadrennial surveys by the Chicago Council on Foreign Relations (CCFR) show a high degree of year-to-year consistency in the ranking of nations on the basis of whether the United States has a vital interest there, as well as in the ranking of various foreign policy goals. See the appendix of Larson (1996b).

[13] For example, Schuman (1972) found that opponents of the Vietnam War opposed the war for at least two distinct reasons. One group opposed the war for moral reasons, the belief that Vietnam was not a just war. The second group opposed the war for pragmatic reasons, the belief that the costs being incurred were in vain and that there was no relationship between inputs and outputs.

[14] There are numerous examples where declining belief in success has led to declining support for a policy option. For example, in the fall of 1990, as belief in the efficacy of sanctions against Iraq declined, so too did support for reliance upon that policy.

predicts that as the costs increase, any individual's estimate of utility will decline, and these declines in individuals' utilities will result in lower aggregate levels of public support for the military operation, as the weakest supporters pass their minimal utilities for supporting the operation.

The role of casualties in support for a military operation is far more complex and sensible than most realize.[15] The record reveals two important lessons: (1) support generally declines as casualties increase, but (2) the sensitivity to casualties (i.e., the rate at which support declines as a simple function of casualties) varies greatly across past wars and military operations.

The simple algebraic model explains why this should be so: there is an interaction between casualties and other factors such that sensitivity to casualties is regulated by beliefs about the importance of the benefits and evaluations of the prospects for success.[16]

To illustrate, in World War II, the stakes were judged to be vitally important and there was generally continued optimism about the outcome of the war; the result was continued high support for the war in the face of horrific casualties and changing fortunes on the battlefield. In the limited wars in Korea and Vietnam, both the perceived stakes and the prospects for success came into question even as casualties mounted, resulting in much greater sensitivity to casualties than in World War II. In the Gulf War, important stakes and high prospects for success led to relatively high *prospective* tolerance for casualties, but not quite the tolerance for casualties as in Korea or Vietnam. And following the change of U.S. objectives in Somalia in May 1993 (from providing a secure environment for humanitarian relief operations to engaging in nation building) and the subsequent deterioration in the situation, the importance of the objectives and the prospects for success declined for most, even as the costs increased. The result was very high sensitivity to costs in Somalia, and a general de-

---

[15] Larson (1996a, 1996b).

[16] Put another way, when the expected benefits are low, an individual's utility from an operation will be low, and when casualties are increasing, an individual's utility will fall at a much faster rate when the numerator (the expected benefits) is declining.

sire to abandon the mission even before the October 3–4, 1993 firefight in Mogadishu.[17]

The minimal acceptable utility ($Umin_i$). Finally, there is the parameter $Umin_i$: the individual's minimum utility for supporting the military operation. This parameter suggests that at some level of utility—whether as a result of changed benefits, prospects for success, or costs—every individual will be indifferent between supporting and opposing the military operation; any additional costs or decline in benefits or prospects will push the individual into opposition.[18]

Several additional individual-level characteristics also serve as opinion mediators that influence the risk-acceptance or risk-aversion of individuals: these include partisan leadership and followership, and characteristics such as race and gender.

The key role of partisan leadership and followership. Individuals are greatly influenced by and tend to accept the positions held by political leaders they most trust. For any individual, interpretations of objective events and conditions and beliefs about the value of the parameters just described will be influenced by the positions taken by trusted political leaders and experts as reported in the media, as well as those taken by friends, co-workers, or other opinion leaders that are known personally to the individual.[19] Partisan ties play in a straightforward way: members of the president's party are more likely to support military operations than are Independents or members of the opposing party.[20]

Other individual-level characteristics. Past research has shown that other individual-level characteristics such as race and gender also

---

[17] Few are aware, however, that support for Somalia in fact had declined to about four in ten even *before* the deaths in Mogadishu.

[18] This parameter is included simply to be complete—the model is entirely agnostic as to whether an individual establishes *a priori* a threshold below which he will withdraw his support, or simply represents the observed level at which the individual withdraws his support.

[19] Zaller (1992), for example, is somewhat agnostic as to whether the media or personal networks are in fact more important in the diffusion of mass attitudes.

[20] See "International Conflict, the Presidency, and Party ID," in *Public Perspective,* August/September 1999, p. 55, and Eric V. Larson, "The Use of Force and the Persistence of the Partisan Divide," *Yale Politic*, May 2004.

are systematically associated with the probability of supporting military operations.[21]

We can now explore the implications of this model in more detail.

Predictions of the Model

The simple model of ends and means makes predictions about two distinct phenomena:[22] (1) the level of support or opposition for a military operation and (2) the changing level of commitment to a military operation, i.e., preferences regarding an increased or decreased level of commitment.[23]

Predictions regarding the level of support or opposition. When individuals are aggregated, the *ceteris paribus* predictions of this model are as follows:

- Because the political objectives of a war or military operation provide the basis for assessing the possible stakes or benefits of the operation, a change in objective or mission ("mission change" or "mission creep") can entail a change in the perceived benefits of the operation for any individual. In response to a change in objectives, the benefits may either increase or decrease, depending on the individual's value structure and the particular configuration of variables in the case at hand. When there is a net increase in the number of individuals who believe the stakes or benefits have declined, this will result in a decline in the percentage supporting the operation; net increases in the number of individuals believing that the stakes or benefits have

---

[21] For example, Nincic and Nincic (2002) found statistically significant gender-based differences in support for a number of past military operations (Korea in 1952, Vietnam in 1966, Vietnam in 1972, Operation Desert Shield in 1990, Operation Desert Storm in 1991); statistically significant race-based differences also were found in many (but not all) cases.

[22] The point of view taken here is consistent with Milton Friedman's (1953) "as if" argument—that people behave *as if* the model underlies their behavior.

[23] See Converse and Schuman (1970) and Mueller (1973) for the seminal discussions of the differences between the two.

increased will result in sustained—or increased—levels of support.

- Net increases in the number of individuals believing that the probability of success has declined will also occasion a loss of support, while net increases in the percentage believing the probability of success has increased will lead to gains in support. Similarly, quicker-than-expected success will lead to higher support, while uneven or slower-than-expected success will lead to lower support.
- Higher (or higher-than-expected) costs will lead to lower support, while lower (or lower-than-expected) costs may lead to higher support.
- Finally, the sensitivity to costs will increase when *either* the stakes/benefits or prospects for success are declining, and sensitivity to casualties will be highest when both are declining.

Predictions regarding the level of commitment. The individual's support or opposition is not the end of the story, nor does it adequately address what is perhaps the key dimension in understanding public attitudes toward military operations: the individual's diagnosis and preferred prescription for successful conclusion of a military operation.

As seen in Korea and Vietnam, domestic support for limited wars can be difficult to sustain, and presidents almost certainly understand that either outright defeat or high war costs can erode their political standing. Although a cheap victory is rationally preferred to a costly defeat, leaders—and members of the public—may disagree about whether a costly victory is preferred to a cheap defeat.[24] And when political leaders and members of the public come to oppose a limited war or military operation, they can arrive at opposition via two very different diagnoses.

As the costs increase—and especially as judgments about the benefits of continuing and prospects for success diverge—leaders have

---

[24] See Bueno de Mesquita and Siverson (1995). And the absence of a total victory may be viewed by many as defeat.

tended to become polarized as some advocate escalation or an increased commitment, while others advocate withdrawing or otherwise reducing the level of commitment. As presidents Truman and Johnson found, presidents can thus come to be criticized both by those who would increase the level of commitment and by those who would decrease or terminate it.[25] Importantly, there is a logic to each position, keyed to the set of beliefs about the operation that influence diagnosis and prescription.

- **The logic of an increased commitment.** Support for an increased commitment arises from beliefs that extremely important (or vital) interests and/or principles are engaged, including crucial matters of credibility or national pride, and that the losses already incurred must be redeemed through a successful outcome. In this analysis, not enough effort is being made to assure a successful outcome:[26] forces are fighting "with one hand tied behind their backs," and victory is not only possible but could perhaps even come cheaply (e.g., through strategic bombing).[27] The prescription is escalation and elimination of restrictions on combat operations.
- **The logic of a decreased commitment.** The second diagnosis is that the hoped-for outcome of the military operation is simply not worth the costs in blood and treasure, that there is little relationship between losses and actual progress on the battlefield, and that in any case the operation is unlikely to yield success at an acceptable cost. The prescription that emerges from this analysis is that the best course of action is to reduce the level of commitment and withdraw once U.S. prisoners of war are returned.

---

25 See Hamilton (1968), Converse and Schuman (1970), and Mueller (1973) for what appear to be the first analyses of this phenomenon.

26 This was basically the analysis of those who wanted to escalate in the Korean and Vietnam wars.

27 Advocates of this position either would tend to discount the possibility of a widened war and the costs attendant with such an outcome, or would never be deterred by that prospect.

When the stakes are important enough (e.g., in Korea and Vietnam), there may be a plurality or majority supporting a third, or middle course: simply concluding the war on acceptable terms (e.g., a "peace with honor"). This course of action is politically costly to presidents, as Truman and Johnson discovered, because in pursuing a middle course, a president is subject to criticism from both those who would escalate and those who would reduce the level of commitment and withdraw. By way of contrast, in cases where most view the stakes as not very important (e.g., in Lebanon or Somalia), an orderly withdrawal following recovery of U.S. servicemen held hostage is typically preferred—the stakes are simply not important enough to most members of the public to justify any greater commitment than ensuring the safe recovery of U.S. servicemen.[28]

This divergence between a president's sustained level of commitment to war or military operation and the lower level of commitment evidenced by political opponents and many members of the public has found expression in a small body of scholarly work. Milstein (1974) described the phenomenon in terms of differences in the willingness of policymakers and members of the public to trade off costs and benefits. Since most of the benefits (e.g., a reputation for successfully wielding the military instrument) would accrue to policymakers, they were posited to be more willing to accept higher costs to achieve political objectives than are members of the public. Perhaps a better metaphor is the one provided by Nincic and Nincic (1995): policymakers (and by extension, one might conclude, their key supporters) tend to treat incurred costs as part of an investment function, which costs need to be recovered through victory, while members of the public treat it as a demand function, where they are asked to pay an increasingly high price, and fewer are willing to do

---

[28] Contrary to the conventional wisdom, support for *immediate* withdrawal from military operations has typically not been supported by a majority of the public—even in low-stakes cases such as Somalia. See Larson (1996a, 1996b).

so.[29] Both views offer promise in that they are fully extensible to include differences among partisan or ideologically based subpopulations.[30]

We next describe a social process model that connects attitudes toward military operations to events on the battlefield and leadership.

A Simple Social Process Model

Consider the following simple social process model of the president's decision to use force, and the broader political and social environment:[31]

- Based upon an assessment of the particular crisis situation, the president decides whether to use force, what political objectives are to be achieved, and what (if any) constraints are to be imposed on the military operation to better ensure support.[32]
- The president makes his case to his audiences (other political leaders, experts, and the public) that the nation's interests— including both security interests and whatever moral principles

[29] This can lead to distortions in decisionmaking as leaders become increasingly willing to accept risks in a "bargain for resurrection" that might yield a successful outcome. See Downs and Rocke (1994).

[30] That is, some members of the public may most closely identify themselves with the president's position and view casualties as an investment to be redeemed, some might identify themselves with those leaders and experts who would increase the level of commitment, and still others with leaders and experts who would decrease or terminate the commitment. See Modigliani's (1972, p. 972) discussion of how some groups may be more oriented toward costs, while others are more oriented toward achievement of the objectives.

[31] Lasswell (1971, pp. 15–26) posited the "social process model" as describing the context in which and with which the policymaker interacts. In the context of a military operation, the president (and Executive branch) interacts with external actors, including allies, neutrals, adversaries, and international organizations, and with such internal actors as Congress, the media, and the public.

[32] The literature on presidential leadership strategies is somewhat limited. The best works include Neustadt (1990), Skowronek (1993), Zaller (1994), Kernell (1993), and Pfiffner (1996). A great deal of scholarly research on presidential decisionmaking regarding the use of force is, to this author's mind, somewhat problematic from a policy perspective. However, a well-balanced analysis can be found in Meernik (1994 and 1996).

may be engaged—are important enough to justify the risks of a military operation, and that the operation is likely to achieve its objectives at an acceptable cost in lives and treasure.[33]

- Other political and opinion leaders decide whether or not they agree that the operation is worthwhile and "doable" and, if not, make their case that the intervention is not worth doing or that it is unlikely to achieve its objectives at an acceptable cost.[34]
- Editorial decisions about newsworthiness determine the level of media reporting given to the military operation, while the tone of media reporting—the balance of pro and con positions presented—is roughly "indexed" to the tone of the debate among political leaders.[35] The initial deployment and any subsequent combat—whether military action on the ground or political debate in Washington—will cue higher levels of media reporting because they are inherently newsworthy (i.e., members of the public are interested in, and concerned about, combat and political dissension). The probability that members of the public will be aware of events or exposed to political messages, and that the issue will be considered more salient or important at the time of polling, is associated with media reporting levels.[36]
- Members of the public, who vary in their level of attention to political issues, develop opinions on the military operation based upon selective attention to pro and con arguments in elite de-

---

[33] See Kernell (1993) for a discussion of the strategy of "going public" and how it differs from Neustadt's (1990) classic conception of presidential strategies that rely upon bargaining with Congress.

[34] See Brody (1991) and Zaller (1984, 1992) for discussions of the role of debates among political leaders in establishing frames of reference on policy issues.

[35] A classic in this area is Cohen (1963). For recent scholarly work on the media, see Iyengar (1991), and Bennett (1996). A number of perspectives on media reporting on the Gulf War can be found in Bennett and Paletz (1994) and Jeffords and Rabinovitz (1994). Neuman (1996) places current ruminations on the media and foreign policy in historical perspective. Bennett (1990) showed that the media tended to "index" the slant of their coverage to the range of opinions prevailing in the elite discourse.

[36] MacKuen and Coombs (1981), MacKuen (1984a, 1984b), and Behr and Iyengar (1985). Zaller (1994, p. 201 and ff. 15 and 16) provides a cogent discussion of the difficulties of determining the relative importance of political leadership and media effects.

bates reported by the media or as a result of conversations with associates.[37] As Zaller (1992) has suggested, the rate at which members of the public *receive* these messages is a function of media reporting levels as just described, as well as individual-level news gathering habits, political interest, and sophistication (the extent to which a respondent pays attention to politics and understands what has been encountered).

- Members of the public judge both the credibility of political leaders' and experts' interpretation of objective events and conditions and their normative judgments about the operation.[38] The rate at which messages in the media-reported elite discourse are *accepted or rejected* is determined by political predispositions (more stable, individual-level traits like partisan or ideological orientation that regulate the acceptance or rejection of the persuasive communications that are received).[39]

Chapter Conclusions

The conceptual model presented in this chapter provides a systematic framework for understanding much of what follows in this report. In the next chapter, we diagnose public attitudes toward the final stage of the Somalia mission, as well as support for the U.S. interventions in Haiti, Bosnia, and Kosovo. This analysis demonstrates the utility of the model in diagnosing public opinion and provides evidence of its ability to predict support or opposition across a wide range of mili-

---

[37] Zaller's (1992) three-stage Reception-Acceptance-Sampling (RAS) model provides a recent discussion of the process by which mass attitudes become diffused that seems likely to become the standard analysis. Downs (1957), Converse (1964), McCloskey (1964), Gamson and Modigliani (1966), Hastie (1986), Newman (1986), Ferejohn and Kuklinski (1990), and Popkin (1994) offer views that share much with Zaller's, while Downs and Popkin also offer credible discussions of the political reasoning processes used by members of the public.

[38] Zaller (1992, pp. 16–28).

[39] This observation seems to be amply supported by psychological research on persuasion. See, for example, Petty and Cacioppo (1981, 1986). Ajzen and Fishbein (1980, pp. 219–221) provide a good review of the relevant literature.

tary operations. In Chapter Four, we use the model to diagnose attitudes toward the war in Afghanistan and the larger global war on terrorism (GWOT), and in Chapter Five we examine attitudes during the recent war in Iraq.

CHAPTER THREE

Past as Prologue: Mogadishu to Kosovo

In this chapter we review the nature and sources of support in a number of U.S. military operations in the 1990s. In turn, we assess sentiment toward withdrawal and escalation in the U.S. operation in Somalia, and toward support and opposition to the peace operations in Haiti, Bosnia, and Kosovo.

Endgame in Somalia

Background

In response to a growing famine and increasing attacks on humanitarian relief operations in Somalia, and following a UN vote authorizing a U.S.-led Unified Task Force (UNITAF) there,[1] on December 4, 1992, President George H.W. Bush announced that U.S. troops would intervene in Somalia with the objective of establishing a secure environment for humanitarian relief operations.[2]

By March 1993, with the Clinton administration then in office and the humanitarian objectives effectively achieved, the operation was redirected from its ostensible humanitarian focus to a much more ambitious (and, as it turned out, risky) effort to turn Somalia from a

---

[1] United Nations Security Council Resolution 794 of December 3, 1992.

[2] George H.W. Bush, "Address to the Nation on the Situation in Somalia," December 4, 1992.

failed state into a stable nation-state.[3] The situation deteriorated over the summer and early fall until, on October 3–4, 1993, a firefight took place in Mogadishu in which 18 U.S. servicemen died. A political firestorm erupted in Washington over how best to conclude the operation. With the administration under heavy pressure from both Republicans and Democrats in Congress and members of the public,[4] a basic agreement was reached on October 7 between the White House and congressional leaders that U.S. forces would be withdrawn by the end of March 1994, after U.S. servicemen held hostage had been recovered and a smooth transition to a UN operation could be accomplished.[5]

Overview of Support for the Operation

Although the initial justification for the military intervention in Somalia was a purely humanitarian one, the compelling nature of the humanitarian case, the widespread belief that the mission was likely to succeed with few or no casualties,[6] and bipartisan congressional

---

[3] On March 26, 1993, the United Nations Security Council voted in favor of UNSCR 814, which authorized the largest, most expensive, and ambitious peacekeeping operation in its history, described by then–United Nations ambassador Madeline K. Albright as "an unprecedented enterprise aimed at nothing less than the restoration of an entire country as a proud, functioning and viable member of the community of nations." By this time, the initial aims of securing humanitarian relief operations had been accomplished. See Paul Lewis, "U.N. Will Increase Troops in Somalia," *The New York Times*, March 27, 1993, p. 3.

[4] According to data from the White House Correspondence Office, nearly one-third (13,007) of the 39,416 pieces of personal mail (i.e., mail not part of a write-in campaign) received by the White House during the seven-day period ending October 14, 1993 dealt with the U.S. presence in Somalia. Of these, 10,761 letters (82.7 percent) opposed the U.S. presence in Somalia and only 788 (6 percent) supported the U.S. presence there. An additional 1,458 (11.2 percent) were neutral on the matter.

[5] The morning of October 7, 1993, President Clinton met with over 30 leaders from the House and Senate, and announced his new strategy for Somalia that evening. See White House, "List of Members of Congress Attending Meeting With The President on Somalia," October 7, 1993, and William J. Clinton, "Address to the Nation on Somalia," October 7, 1993.

[6] Gallup found 64 percent who said they were very or somewhat confident that the United States would accomplish its goals in Somalia with very few or no casualties. Gallup/Newsweek, December 4–6, 1992, N=1,005.

support for the mission led to nearly three out of four Americans initially supporting the U.S. intervention in Somalia.[7]

RAND's earlier analysis of public opinion on the U.S. intervention in Somalia[8] suggested that the principal cause of the decline in support was not the losses in the October firefight, nor even the accumulation of U.S. casualties (especially battle deaths) more generally, as U.S. deaths in Somalia before the firefight were quite modest. Rather, the decline in support seems to have been attributable to three factors. Although it is exceedingly difficult to apportion the decline in support among various causes, the shift from a focus on humanitarian relief to stabilizing the political situation in May 1993 seems to have eroded support, from about 75 percent to the 50–60 percent range.[9] The combination of increasing pessimism about the likelihood that the new mission would result in success and growing bipartisan congressional opposition to the operation[10]—both resulting from the deteriorating political and security situation over the summer and early fall of 1993—in combination seem to have accounted for a further loss of support, leaving support at about four in ten in September 1993.[11] And the October 3–4 firefight in Mogadishu and the criticism that followed it accounted for perhaps another 5–10 points' loss, taking support below four in ten.

---

[7] See Lydia Saad, "'Operation Restore Hope' Gets Public's Blessing," *The Gallup Poll Monthly*, December 1992, pp. 18–20.

[8] For additional data and details of the analysis, see Larson (1996a, 1996b).

[9] CBS News reported 51 percent supporting Somalia in June 1993, while ABC News reported 62 percent in June 1993. CBS News/New York Times, June 21–24, 1993, N=1,363, and ABC News, June 28, 1993.

[10] For a good discussion of the erosion of congressional support, see Congressional Quarterly, "Hill Demands Early 94 Somalia Withdrawal," *1993 CQ Almanac*, Washington, D.C.: CQ Press, 1994, pp. 486–493.

[11] Times Mirror found 41 percent approving of the president's handling of Somalia on September 9–15, 1993, and Time/CNN found only 43 percent approving the presence of U.S. troops in Somalia on September 23–24, 1993. Fifty-two percent of those polled by NBC News/Wall Street Journal on September 10–13, 1993, felt that the United States was too deeply involved in Somalia. Times Mirror/PSRA, September 9–15, 1993, N = 2,000; Time/CNN/Yankelovich, September 23–24, 1993, N = 800; and NBC News/Wall Street Journal/Hart & Teeter, September 10–13, 1993, N=1,006.

Preferences Regarding Withdrawal and Escalation

It is critically important to understand Americans' policy preferences on Somalia in the September–October 1993 period because Somalia is the only case in all of the peace operations of the 1990s in which withdrawal and escalation became a highly salient issue. Understanding whether most Americans reacted to the deterioration of the situation in Somalia by preferring withdrawal or continuing—or even escalating—lies at the heart of the willingness of Americans to shed blood, and stay the course, in peace operations that don't involve core security interests.

Past work has shown that those who oppose wars and military operations may differ on the reasons for their opposition: some believe that the best course of action would be cutting losses by withdrawing, while others believe that the best course of action would be escalating to ensure a successful outcome.[12] There are, moreover, conceptually distinct sets of beliefs associated with each position, having to do with estimates of the likely benefits and costs of escalating or withdrawing.[13]

Earlier analyses of escalation and withdrawal sentiment in Somalia prior to the firefight were hobbled by the unavailability of conclusive data on the matter before the firefight. New data from polling done by ABC News just before the firefight recently has come to light, however, that illuminates this question (see Table 3.1).[14]

As shown, those polled before the firefight preferred pulling troops out of Somalia by a nearly two-to-one margin, and there was an increase in this sentiment between this poll and another conducted

---

[12] The seminal treatment of this issue, in the context of the Korean and Vietnam Wars, is Mueller (1973). See also Schuman (1972).

[13] See Larson (1996a, 1996b, 2000) and the discussion in Chapter Two.

[14] Data provided by Gary Langer of ABC News. It is not clear why these polling results were never incorporated into Roper's poll database.

Table 3.1
Somalia Withdrawal Sentiment Before and After Firefight

Do you think the United States should keep troops in Somalia until there's a functioning civil government there that can run things, OR do you think the U.S. should pull its troops out of Somalia very soon, even if there is no functioning civil government in place there?

(Of those answering "pull out") How soon do you think U.S. troops should be removed from Somalia—immediately, before the end of the year, or what?

	September 27–October 3, 1993	October 5, 1993
Keep troops in Somalia	31	28
Pull troops out of Somalia:	58	64
Immediately	28	37
Before the end of the year	26	25
Longer than year's end	2	1
No opinion	1	1
No opinion	11	8

SOURCE: ABC News, "Americans Want Troops Out of Somalia," October 6, 1993, and cross-tabs from September 27–October 3, 1993 poll provided by ABC News Polling Unit.

by ABC News several days later, on October 5, two days before the president's speech announcing a withdrawal by March 31, 1994.

The principal change between the two polls was a six-point increase in the percentage that wanted to pull troops out of Somalia, which grew from 58 to 64 percent, and a nine-point increase in the percentage that wanted an immediate withdrawal, which grew from 28 to 37 percent. Those desiring an immediate withdrawal did not constitute a majority, however. This is a robust finding, replicated by most of the other polling of the time.[15]

[15] Of the three questions that were asked between September 27 and October 7, 1993 that gave respondents a full range of options for Somalia, including escalation, the status quo, and withdrawal, the average support for withdrawal was 63.3 percent, the average support for maintaining the troop levels was 6.5 percent, and the average support for an increased commitment was 26 percent. See the questions asked in Gallup, October 5, 1993, CBS News, October 6–7, 1993, and Time/CNN, October 7, 1993. The average support for withdrawal for 16 questions asked between September 27 and December 31 was 66.9 percent, while 24.7 percent favored the status quo, and 30.3 percent favored an increased commitment.

And as shown in Table 3.2, this sentiment was widely shared across partisan lines in the public, just as it was in the Congress;[16] between 55 and 60 percent of Democrats, Independents, and Republicans polled before the firefight favored pulling troops out of Somalia, even before the firefight.

Put another way, not only had support fallen below a majority before the firefight, but these newly available data show that a majority of Americans wanted the United States to withdraw from Somalia *even before the firefight*, and this sentiment hardened in its immediate

Table 3.2
Withdrawal Sentiment Before the Firefight, by Party

Do you think the United States should keep troops in Somalia until there's a functioning civil government there that can run things, OR do you think the U.S. should pull its troops out of Somalia very soon, even if there is no functioning civil government in place there?

(Of those answering "pull out") How soon do you think U.S. troops should be removed from Somalia—immediately, before the end of the year, or what?

	Dem	Ind	Rep
Keep troops in Somalia	34	30	33
Pull troops out of Somalia:	55	60	59
Immediately	28	28	28
Before the end of the year	23	28	29
Longer than year's end	3	2	1
No opinion	2	2	1
No opinion	11	10	8

SOURCE: ABC News Polling Unit, cross-tabs from September 27–October 3, 1993 poll.
NOTE: Due to rounding, calculations for preferences of those wanting to pull troops out may not sum to totals.

[16] See Michael Ross and Art Pine, "Angry Lawmakers Threaten to Push for Somalia Pullout; Africa: After Meeting with Aspin and Christopher, Members of Both Parties Warn They May Cut Funds. Clinton Confers with His Top Security Advisors," *Los Angeles Times*, October 6, 1993, p. A1; Doyle McManus and John M. Broder, "Festering Problem Leaves Clinton No Good Choices," *Los Angeles Times*, October 7, 1993, p. A1; and Michael Ross, "Policy Appears to Quell Revolt in Congress," *Los Angeles Times*, October 8, 1993, p. A12.

aftermath. This is an important finding, and one that resolves an important ambiguity in the public opinion record. This preference for withdrawal also is a very robust finding.[17]

The reason that there was such strong support for withdrawal was that few believed the United States had particularly important stakes in Somalia beyond recovering U.S. servicemen held hostage,[18] there was a widespread belief that the United States was more likely to get bogged down than accomplish its ambitious goals,[19] and most believed that nothing the United States could accomplish in Somalia

---

[17] Altogether, we identified a total of 19 questions that allowed respondents to choose between an increased commitment or withdrawal from Somalia in polls conducted between September 27 and December 31, 1993. The average level of support for withdrawal for these questions was 67 percent, whereas the average support for an increased commitment was only 31 percent. Put another way, when actually given a choice between an increased commitment or withdrawal, respondents generally preferred withdrawal by a greater than 2-to-1 margin. Support for an orderly withdrawal—withdrawal only after the recovery of captured U.S. servicemen—typically was preferred over an immediate withdrawal by a wide margin. Other analyses that have reached the same conclusion include See ABC News, "Americans Want Troops Out of Somalia," ABC News Poll, October 5, 1993, and David W. Moore, "Public: 'Get Out of Somalia,'" *The Gallup Poll Monthly*, October 1993, pp. 23–24; Louis J. Klarevas, "The Polls—Trends: The United States Peace Operation in Somalia," *Public Opinion Quarterly*, Vol. 64, 2000, pp. 523–540; and John E. Mueller, "Public Support for Military Ventures Abroad: Evidence From the Polls," in John Norton Moore and Robert F. Turner (eds.), *The Real Lessons of the Vietnam War: Reflections Twenty-Five Years After the Fall of Saigo*n, Durham, NC: Carolina Academic Press, 2002, pp. 173–219, but especially pp. 181, 185, 189, and 191.

We also identified a number of other questions that asked whether respondents supported an increased commitment in Somalia, for example, sending additional forces to Somalia, or capturing the warlord Aidid. On average, a majority of Americans failed to support sending additional forces to Somalia—the average level of support was 49.5 percent for the six questions that were asked. Moreover, all three of the questions that received majority support—ranging from 55 to 61 percent—included cues in the question that suggested that the purpose of sending the additional forces was to assist in recovering U.S. servicemen held captive, or to protect U.S. forces in place until they could be withdrawn; the three questions where these cues were missing showed support between 38 and 44 percent.

[18] Only 21 percent of those polled by ABC News on October 5 and 23 percent of those polled on October 12 said the United States had vital interests in Somalia.

[19] Nearly half (48 percent) of those polled by ABC News on October 5 said that they thought the United States would get bogged down, while 44 percent said they thought that U.S. involvement would end quickly.

was worth incurring additional costs;[20] all of these arguments were made by congressional leaders at one time or another after the firefight. A detailed reanalysis of questions on withdrawal and escalation confirms the conclusion that most Americans preferred withdrawal from Somalia, both before and after the firefight, and that the favored form of withdrawal was an orderly one, coming only after U.S. servicemen held hostage were recovered.[21]

As will be seen in Chapter Five, the shoot down of a Chinook helicopter in Iraq in November 2003 was met by a far more steadfast response from the American public.

Sources and Fault Lines in Support for Escalation and Withdrawal

As described above, the newly available polling results provide additional support for earlier analyses that suggested that support for Somalia had collapsed and that most preferred withdrawal, even before the firefight.[22]

We would hypothesize that support for escalating or otherwise increasing the U.S. commitment in Somalia would be higher for those who believed that the United States had important interests in Somalia and those who believed the United States had good prospects for a successful outcome there; we would hypothesize that support for withdrawal would be higher for those who have less optimistic views on these matters.[23]

---

[20] Sixty percent of those polled by Time/CNN on October 7, 1993 agreed with the statement "Nothing the U.S. could accomplish in Somalia is worth the death of even one more U.S. soldier." Time/CNN/Yankelovich, October 7, 1993, N=500.

[21] Burk (1999) confirmed our earlier findings on support having collapsed before the firefight, but disagreed that most Americans desired withdrawal; he instead believes that Americans would have continued to support a humanitarian operation even after the firefight. It is not clear that his analysis takes into consideration the role of leadership, however. Klarevas (2000) confirmed both our finding on the collapse of support and our finding that most Americans preferred withdrawal over escalation in Somalia. Our findings on the myth of a CNN effect in Somalia were confirmed by Mermin (1997) and Strobel (1997).

[22] See Larson (1996) and Klarevas (2000).

[23] For a discussion of the logic of escalation and withdrawal, see Appendix B of the technical appendix, published separately.

In fact, our modeling of respondent-level data from the October 5, 1993 ABC News poll provides evidence that supports this view: it suggests that a model that includes beliefs about the importance of U.S. interests and the prospects for success correctly predicts the withdrawal preferences of more than 60 percent of the respondents (Tables 3.3 through 3.5).[24]

As shown, the model correctly predicts 63 percent of the respondents and also shows, as predicted, that a willingness to stay hinged on the belief that the United States had vital interests involved and good prospects for a successful outcome, whereas a preference for withdrawal was associated with a failure to see vital interests or good prospects in Somalia. Given that fewer than one in three actually believed that the United States had vital interests in Somalia, and a plurality of 47 percent thought the United States was going to get

Table 3.3
Somalia: Marginal Probability from Probit Estimates of Withdrawal (Q3)

Variables	Change in Probability at Mean Values
Vital interests (Q6)†	0.229 (0.063)***
Prospects (Q10)†	0.167 (0.047)***
Party 1 if Republican†	0.023 (0.060)
Party 1 if Independent†	–0.056 (0.060)
Gender 1 if female†	–0.169 (0.048)***
Wald Chi-square (Prod > Chi2)	40.69 (0.000)
Log likelihood	–227.656
Observations	401
Correctly specified	63%

† dF/dx is for discrete change of dummy variable from 0 to 1.
* Significant at 10%.
** Significant at 5%.
*** Significant at 1%.
Robust standard error in parentheses.
SOURCE: ABC News, October 5, 1993. The withdrawal question was coded as 0 if the respondent wanted to pull out, and 1 if he/she wanted to keep troops in Somalia.

[24] The results are summarized later in this section and presented in more detail in Appendix B of the technical appendix, published separately.

Table 3.4
Somalia: Marginal Probability from Probit Estimates of Escalation (Q7)

Variables	Change in Probability at Mean Values
Vital interests (Q6)†	0.135 (0.058)**
Prospects (Q10)†	0.231 (0.048)***
Party 1 if Republican†	0.042 (0.065)
Party 1 if Independent†	–0.053 (0.067)
Gender 1 if female†	–0.129 (0.052)**
Wald Chi-square (Prod > Chi2)	35.90 (0.000)
Log likelihood	–263.25612
Observations	413
Correctly specified	64%

† dF/dx is for discrete change of dummy variable from 0 to 1.
* Significant at 10%.
** Significant at 5%.
*** Significant at 1%.
Robust standard error in parentheses.
SOURCE: ABC News, October 5, 1993. The escalation question was coded as 0 if the respondent did not support sending additional troops to Somalia, and 1 if he/she supported additional troops.

bogged down there, the net result was lukewarm support for staying. The bipartisan support for withdrawal meant that membership in the president's party made little difference—differences between Democrats and Republicans, and between Democrats and Independents, were not statistically significant.

Our modeling of escalation sentiment had roughly the same level of success in predicting outcomes. Despite the missing costs parameter, the first model correctly predicts 64 percent of the respondents' positions on sending more troops, and the second correctly predicts 60 percent of the cases.

Both models for escalation sentiment suggest that the desire to escalate was associated with a belief in the importance of the stakes, and a belief that the U.S. effort would be successful; membership in the president's party did not make a statistically significant contribution. The diagnostics for both models also are quite good.

Table 3.5
Somalia: Marginal Probability from Probit Estimates of Escalation (Q8)

Variables	Change in Probability at Mean Values
Vital interests (Q6)†	0.128 (0.060)**
Prospects (Q10)†	0.180 (0.050)***
Party 1 if Republican†	–0.039 (0.066)
Party 1 if Independent†	–0.081 (0.067)
Gender 1 if female†	–0.099 (0.052)*
Wald Chi-square (Prod > Chi2)	22.41 (0.000)
Log likelihood	–267.06
Observations	404
Correctly specified	60%

† dF/dx is for discrete change of dummy variable from 0 to 1.
* Significant at 10%.
** Significant at 5%.
*** Significant at 1%.
Robust standard error in parentheses.
SOURCE: ABC News, October 5, 1993. The escalation question was coded as 0 if the respondent did not support additional efforts to capture Aidid, and 1 if he/she supported such efforts.

A comment on history's revisionists. One conclusion of RAND's 1996 report was that following the firefight in Mogadishu, most Americans preferred withdrawal from Somalia, although not until U.S. servicemen held hostage could be recovered. Most Americans also were willing to use force to secure the hostages' release, if necessary, and to punish the warlord Aidid as long as it didn't delay a U.S. withdrawal.

Since the publication of the earlier RAND report, some have argued—somewhat remarkably—that Americans didn't prefer withdrawal from Somalia after the firefight at all, but in fact preferred an *increased* commitment there;[25] others have argued that there was a deep well of latent support that President Clinton could have drawn upon to continue or expand the operation.[26]

In light of these very different conclusions, we decided to revisit our earlier findings on the matter and reanalyzed all of the available

[25] See Kull and Destler (1999).

[26] See Feaver and Gelpi (1999).

questions on escalation and withdrawal—several dozen in all. As described earlier, this analysis confirmed that most Americans preferred a withdrawal both before and after the firefight, and that majority support for increasing the U.S. commitment in Somalia typically was evident only in questions whose wording suggested that it would facilitate the withdrawal of U.S. forces there and wouldn't delay a withdrawal.

This result suggests that those who have argued that Americans actually preferred escalation over withdrawal in Somalia,[27] or that most Americans would have supported President Clinton if he had fought congressional and other critics and pursued a more assertive strategy on Somalia,[28] are on exceedingly dubious empirical ground—as demonstrated in Somalia, Haiti, and Bosnia, *deus ex machina* arguments that a president can change preexisting opposition to a military operation simply by taking his case to the public are not credible:

- As demonstrated here, a preference for withdrawal had crystallized even before the firefight and strengthened in reaction to it: the ABC News' September 27–October 3, 1993 poll found that nearly six in ten Americans preferred withdrawal before the firefight, and this sentiment grew modestly to nearly two in three favoring withdrawal in polling on October 5, two days before the president's speech announcing a withdrawal at the end of March 1994.
- Regarding the claim that the president could have generated support for a more assertive course in Somalia, as was described in Table 3.2, the president would have needed to mobilize nearly 20 percent from each party to build a majority in support of such a course of action, this at a time when he was facing bipartisan opposition within Congress,[29] when the public's confi-

[27] See Kull and Destler (1999), especially pp. 106–109.

[28] See Feaver and Gelpi (1999).

[29] Some research has shown that rallies in support of the president are larger when a president has bipartisan support from congressional and other party leaders for his response to a

dence levels in his handling of Somalia, foreign affairs, and defense issues were all at a nadir,[30] and when the basic predisposition was in favor of withdrawal. ABC News' poll just prior to the firefight found only one in three who approved of President Clinton's handling of Somalia, for example, and on October 5 it was essentially unchanged:[31] not a particularly good indicator of a deep well of support that might have been tapped through a defiant presidential speech.

- Recalling from footnote 4 above the nature of the correspondence received in early October 1993 by the White House about the U.S. presence in Somalia, opposition to a U.S. presence in Somalia was quite strong even after the president announced a withdrawal by the end of the following March. It is difficult to imagine that the reaction would have been more favorable had he refused to withdraw U.S. troops.

Haiti

The Clinton administration's fall 1994 "regime change" in Haiti is a case of a peace operation in which practical concern about refugee flows, and altruistic concern about the plight of Haitians, were tempered by a reluctance to put U.S. soldiers in harm's way for what most saw as less than compelling reasons. In spite of an explicit United Nations authorization and the widely touted participation of a multinational coalition of other nations, the tepid support for the operation reflected the public's basic ambivalence about the venture.

---

crisis, and when critics are silent; in the case of Somalia, most Republican, and many Democratic, leaders opposed the President's Somalia policy. For a good analysis of rallies in presidential approval (not support for military operations), see Brody (1991), especially pp. 45–78.

[30] See Wheeler and Moore (1993) and Newport (1993).

[31] Gallup found that slightly less than a majority—49 percent—approved of President Clinton's overall job handling in their October 1–20, 1993 polling, down from the 56 percent who approved in Gallup's September 24–26 poll. Gallup, September 24–26, 1993, N=1,003 and October 1–20, 1993, N=1,002.

Background

In September 1991, Jean-Bertrand Aristide, the democratically elected president of Haiti, was overthrown in a coup led by Haitian Lieutenant-General Raoul Cedras. In early 1992, about 11,000 asylum-seeking refugees fled Haiti and were admitted to the United States, which led to growing fears that large numbers of Haitian refugees would continue to try to escape oppression by coming to the United States in private boats, improvised rafts, and other, often non-seaworthy, craft. These fears were rekindled in 1994, when another wave of refugees fled Haiti.

This situation led to a number of United Nations Security Council Resolutions and other actions, including the Governor Islands Agreement, signed on July 3, 1993, in which Cedras agreed to give up power, and which sought, without much success, to provide for the restoration of democracy in Haiti. The most important of the resolutions, UNSCR 940, authorized members under Chapter 7 of the UN Charter to use "all necessary means"—including military force—to remove the Haitian dictatorship. While this resolution provided the administration with welcome political cover for intervening in Haiti, members of Congress argued that it was not a substitute for congressional authorization, and, as will be seen, it never persuaded a majority of Americans to actually support the intervention.

On September 15, 1994, President Clinton gave Haiti's rulers an ultimatum: "The message of the United States to the Haitian dictators is clear: Your time is up. Leave now, or we will force you from power."[32] At the 11th hour, a delegation made up of former President Jimmy Carter, former Chairman of the Joint Chiefs of Staff Colin Powell, and Senate Armed Services Committee Chairman Sam Nunn convinced Cedras to step down by October 15 or risk being forcibly removed from power by U.S. military forces.[33] U.S. forces entering

[32] William J. Clinton, "Remarks by the President in Television Address to the Nation," September 15, 1994.

[33] William J. Clinton, "Remarks by the President in Television Address to the Nation," September 18, 1994.

Haiti on September 19 faced no organized opposition, and Cedras and his partners stepped down on October 15, as promised.

Following the withdrawal of most U.S. troops from Somalia in March 1994, the administration had, in May 1994, "reformed" its policy for multinational peace operations;[34] this seems to have done little to increase enthusiasm in Congress for another peace operation, however.[35] In fact, there was nearly bipartisan congressional opposition to a U.S. intervention in Haiti. Republicans—joined by many centrist Democrats—nearly unanimously opposed any invasion of Haiti, and they pressed the administration to seek congressional authorization before taking military action but did little to block it, ultimately deferring to the president on the matter.[36] Only a small but vocal group of liberal lawmakers, members of the Congressional Black Caucus—joined by Florida lawmakers concerned about additional Haitian refugees—advocated tougher measures on Haiti, including military intervention.[37] This congressional sentiment also

[34] See the unclassified summary of PDD-25 in White House, "Administration Policy on Reforming Multilateral Peace Operations (PDD-25)," May 5, 1994, and White House, "Press Briefing by National Security Advisor Tony Lake and Director for Strategic Plans and Policy General Wesley Clark," May 5, 1994.

[35] See Congressional Quarterly, "U.N. Peacekeeping Proves Risky; Congress, Clinton Administration Grow Cautious About Providing Troops for Multinational Efforts," *1993 CQ Almanac*, Washington, D.C.: CQ Press, 1994, pp. 483–486, and "Clinton, Congress Struggle to Define U.S. Interests; With Framework Imposed by the Cold War Gone, Focus Shifts from One Crisis to the Next," *1993 CQ Almanac*, Washington, D.C.: CQ Press, 1994, pp. 445–446. Moreover, there is some evidence that as early as September 1993 the administration was backing away from the "assertive multilateralism" that had been the hallmark of its foreign policy in the early months of the administration. For example, in his speech to the United Nations General Assembly on September 27, 1993, President Clinton said: "The United Nations simply cannot become engaged in every one of the world's conflicts. If the American people are to say yes to U.N. peacekeeping, the United Nations must know when to say no." William J. Clinton, "Remarks to the 48th Session of the United Nations General Assembly in New York City," September 27, 1993. See also Menkhaus (1995), Devroy and Preston (1993), and Sloyan (1993b). I am grateful to Nora Bensahel for bringing some of this literature to my attention.

[36] See Congressional Quarterly, "Clinton's Haiti Gamble Pays Off," *1994 CQ Almanac*, Washington, D.C.: Congressional Quarterly Press, 1995, pp. 449–451, and Hendrickson (2002), pp. 51–56 and 65–67.

[37] Hendrickson (2002), p. 445.

seems to have colored the public opinion on the matter of a U.S. intervention in Haiti.

Overview of Support for the Operation[38]

Although it is possible that there was a fleeting rally in support for the U.S. intervention in Haiti,[39] support for an invasion generally remained below a majority: on average, 47 percent favored putting U.S. troops in Haiti before September 19, 1994, when U.S. troops began arriving,[40] and 46 percent approved of the action after.[41] The average approval for the president's handling of Haiti before the September 19 intervention was 34 percent, while the postintervention average was 48 percent.[42] Perhaps more tellingly, 64 percent of those polled in November 1994 took the position that the next Congress should give a high priority to pulling American troops out of Haiti.[43]

As can be seen in Figure 3.1, the structure of support was also polarized, with the general tendency toward disapproval: about half

---

[38] Additional detail is provided in Appendix C of the technical appendix, published separately.

[39] See Moore and Saad (1994) and Newport and McAneny (1994). According to Gallup, 46 percent approved of the presence of U.S. troops in Haiti on September 19, 1994, and this rose to 54 percent on September 23–25, only to fall again, to 36 percent October 7–9, and 48 percent October 18–19.

[40] There were some differences based on question wording: the average approval for seven questions that asked if the respondent approved of sending troops to Haiti, and that for seven other questions that asked if sending troops was a mistake or if it was the right thing to do, was 42 percent; and the average approval in five questions that asked whether the respondent approved of the president's *decision* to send U.S. forces to Haiti was 48 percent.

[41] Thirty-one polling questions asked respondents if they approved of U.S. troops in Haiti between October 1993 and April 1995, 12 before the intervention, and 19 after. The average level of approval for all 31 questions was 46 percent, the average pre-intervention level of approval was 50 percent, and the average post-intervention approval was 44 percent.

[42] The average level of approval in the 50 polling questions that asked about the president's handling of Haiti from October 1993 to March 1995 was 39 percent. Gallup's presidential approval rating just before the president announced the intervention was 39 percent. Gallup, September 6–7, 1994, N=1,023.

[43] Time/CNN/Yankelovich, November 9–10, 1994, N=800.

Figure 3.1
Structure of Support for Haiti

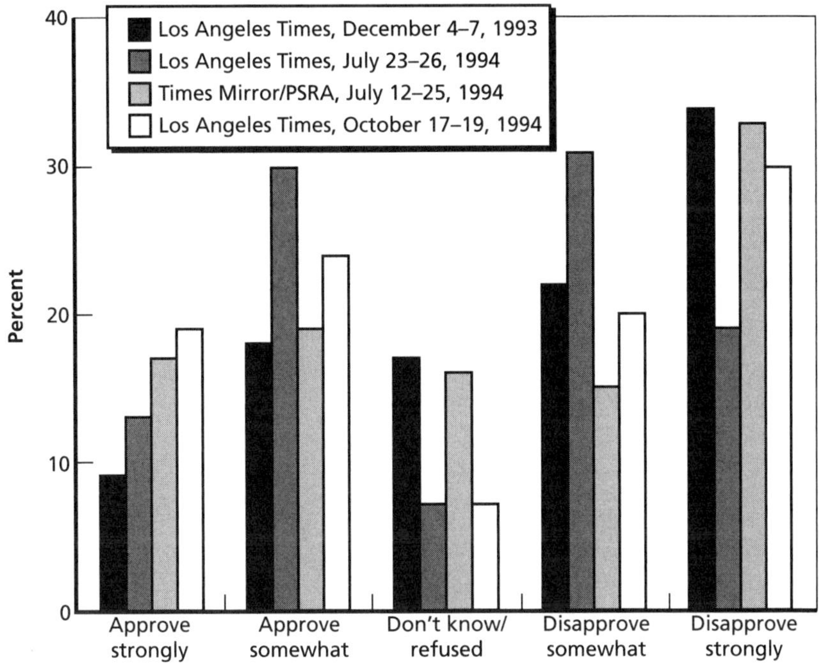

RAND *MG231-A-3.1*

NOTE: Question wordings were as follows. Los Angeles Times, December 4–7, 1993, N = 1,612: "Would you favor or oppose the use of U.S. troops to restore and support the democratically elected government of Haiti? (If favor/oppose) Would you (favor/oppose) that strongly or (favor/oppose) that somewhat?" Times Mirror/PSRA, July 12–25, 1994, N = 3,800: "Please tell me if you strongly favor, favor, oppose, or strongly oppose each one . . . Using American military force, if necessary, to restore democratic government to Haiti." Los Angeles Times, July 23–26, 1994, N = 1,515: "On another subject, would you favor or oppose the use of U.S. (United States) troops, as part of a United Nations sponsored multinational invasion force, to help restore and support the democratically elected government of Haiti. (If favor or oppose, ask:) Would you (favor/oppose) that strongly or (favor/oppose) that somewhat?" Los Angeles Times, October 17–19, 1994, N = 1,272: "Do you approve or disapprove of President (Bill) Clinton's decision to occupy Haiti with more than 20,000 U.S. (United States) troops? (If approve/disapprove, ask) Do you (approve/disapprove) strongly or (approve/disapprove) somewhat?"

disapproved—30 percent strongly—while about four in ten approved—fewer than 20 percent strongly.

The structure of support for the president's decision to intervene at the time of the intervention showed majorities of Democrats barely approving and even larger percentages of Independents and Republicans disapproving—and most of these strongly disapproving—of the decision (Figure 3.2).

Figure 3.2
Structure of Support for U.S. Intervention in Haiti, October 1994

Do you approve or disapprove of President Clinton's decision to occupy Haiti with more than 20,000 U.S. troops? (If approve/disapprove, ask) Do you (approve/disapprove) strongly or (approve/disapprove) somewhat? (Los Angeles Times, October 17–19, 1994, N=1,272)

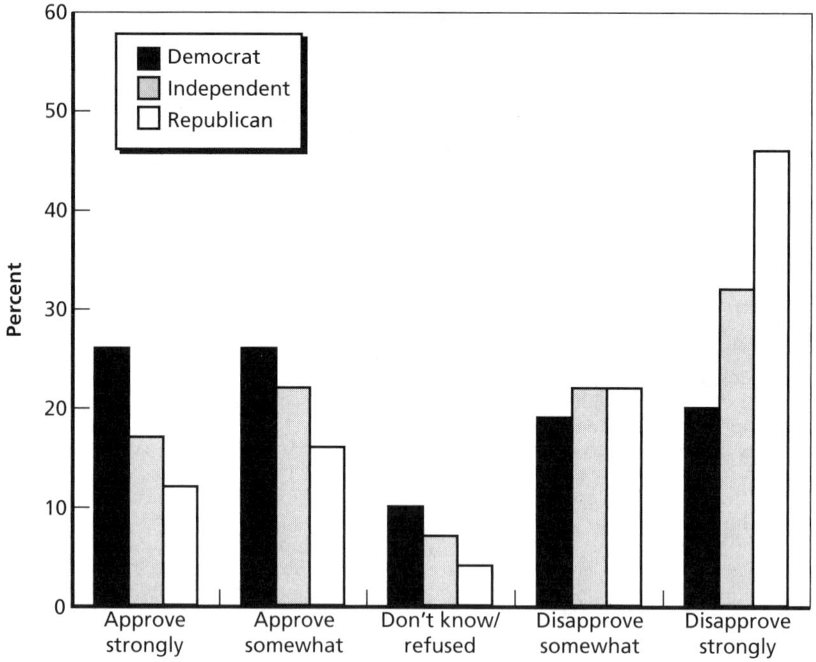

RAND *MG231-A-3.2*

This suggests that support for Haiti—such as it was—was highly polarized on the basis of party: only about one-quarter of the Democrats polled strongly approved, and nearly half of the Republicans strongly disapproved. Had the situation in Haiti deteriorated, the public opinion data suggest that the president would have had few supporters in the public for continuation of the intervention. Fortunately, the situation turned out to be casualty-free, and the public, viewing the intervention as being of small consequence, were willing to tolerate it in such a case.

Thus, the distinct impression one gets from the data is ambivalence: while one can find polling questions that showed a majority favoring the U.S. intervention in Haiti, most such questions didn't.

Sources and Fault Lines in Support

Our bivariate analyses of respondent-level data suggested that support for and opposition to the U.S. intervention in Haiti were associated in a statistically significant way with beliefs about the stakes that were involved, the prospects for a successful outcome, the expected casualties, and respondents' party orientation. Statistical modeling using probit regression correctly classified 75 percent of the respondents in terms of whether they supported or opposed U.S. forces in Haiti, based upon respondents' beliefs about the importance of the stakes, the prospects for success, the likely costs, and their party orientation (Table 3.6).

The coefficients (the probability of support given an increase in the independent variable) suggest that a belief that the United States had moral or security interests in Haiti, and whether the respondent was a member of the president's party (i.e., Democrat), were the most important factors that conditioned whether or not the respondent approved of the presence of U.S. troops in Haiti. Next most important were beliefs that the casualties would be low, and finally, that the prospects for success were good.[44]

---

[44] The president's Gallup approval rating at the time of the poll was 44 percent. Gallup, September 23–25, 1994, N=1,008.

Table 3.6
Haiti: Marginal Probability from Probit Estimates of Approval (Q15)

Variables	Change in Probability at Mean Values
Moral interests (Q22)	0.238 (0.036)***
Security interests (Q19b)†	0.173 (0.040)***
Prospects (Q18b)	0.084 (0.026)***
Casualties (Q18a)	–0.124 (0.026)***
Party 1 if Republican†	–0.167 (0.053)***
Party 1 if Independent†	–0.173 (0.050)***
Info (Q14)	0.035 (0.026)
Race 1 if black†	0.113 (0.075)
Gender 1 if female†	–0.059 (0.040)
Wald Chi-square (Prod > Chi2)	207.02 (0.000)
Log likelihood	–501.30
Observations	964
Correctly specified	75%

† dF/dx is for discrete change of dummy variable from 0 to 1.
* Significant at 10%.
** Significant at 5%.
*** Significant at 1%.
Robust standard error in parentheses.
SOURCE: Gallup, September 23–25, 1994.

This work led us to focus on the following key predictor variables:

- **Partisan leadership and followership.** Support for and opposition to the intervention in Haiti and beliefs about the merits of the operation (i.e., perceived stakes, prospects for success, and likely costs) were partisan-coded; membership in the president's Democratic party generally was associated with more favorable beliefs toward the intervention, while membership in the loyal opposition (Republican) party generally was associated with less favorable beliefs.
- **Nature of the perceived stakes.** Most Americans didn't see very compelling interests in Haiti: only one in four or fewer said that what happened in Haiti was very important to the interests of the United States;[45] on average, only 31 percent felt that the

[45] Between June and September 1994, CBS/New York Times asked the following question four times: "How important to the interests of the United States is what happens in

United States had vital interests in Haiti;[46] about one in four of those polled just before the intervention felt that the national interest of the United States was at stake in Haiti;[47] only about 1 percent ever mentioned Haiti when asked to identify the most important problems facing the country; and only 47 percent felt that the reasons the president gave were good enough to justify an invasion.[48] Although majorities agreed that there were a number of good reasons for intervening with U.S. troops—preventing human rights abuses, and restoring democratic rule, for example—as described above, these beliefs showed important partisan differences, with the president's natural constituency of Democrats more inclined to subscribe to these beliefs. As a result, they never actually translated into reliable majority support for the intervention.

- **Prospects for success.** Expectations regarding the outcome of the intervention were also somewhat mixed. On the one hand, about 56 percent were very (19 percent) or somewhat confident (37 percent) that the United States would be able to accomplish its goals with very few or no American casualties, and slightly fewer—51 percent—were very (13 percent) or somewhat confident (38 percent) that most U.S. troops would be able to withdraw within a few months, as planned.[49] On the other hand, only 44 percent or fewer thought that democracy actually would be restored in Haiti,[50] and a mere 36 percent thought that human rights abuses would stop as a result of U.S. involvement in

Haiti—very important, somewhat important, or not very important?" The highest percentage saying "very important" was 25 percent, and the lowest percentage was 19 percent.

[46] Between October 1993 and October 1998, there were eight polling questions that asked about vital interests in Haiti.

[47] Time/CNN/Yankelovich, September 16, 1994, N=600.

[48] ABC News, September 15, 1994, N=638.

[49] Gallup, September 23–25, 1994, N=1,008.

[50] Gallup found 44 percent who thought that democracy would be restored in Haiti as a result of U.S. involvement. Gallup, September 23–25, 1994, N = 1,009. The Los Angeles Times found 36 percent who were confident that a stable democracy could be established in Haiti. Los Angeles Times, October 17–19, 1994, N=1,272.

Haiti.[51] Moreover, 54 percent found very (29 percent) or somewhat convincing (25 percent) the argument that the United States should not get bogged down in a quagmire like Haiti.[52] By early October—prior to the October 15 deadline for the Haitian military leaders to step down—only 43 percent of those polled by Gallup said that U.S. efforts to restore democracy in Haiti had been mostly successful.[53] Beliefs about the United States' prospects for achieving its aims in Haiti also were highly partisan, with the president's natural constituency of fellow Democrats expressing the most optimism.

- **Expected costs.** Expectations were that casualties were likely to be relatively low—a little over half expected 50 or fewer U.S. casualties in Haiti,[54] and 64 percent expected light or no casualties.[55]
- **Balancing costs and benefits.** Despite the basic optimism about casualties, most of those polled expressed the view that the U.S. intervention in Haiti was not worth the possible loss of American lives and other costs involved: 61 percent felt this way, while only 32 percent did not,[56] and 50 percent agreed with the statement that nothing the United States could accomplish in Haiti was worth the death of even one soldier.[57] These beliefs also exhibited partisan differences, although pluralities or majorities of Democrats, Independents, and Republicans typically expressed an unwillingness to accept the risks of casualties.[58]

---

[51] Gallup, September 23–25, 1994, N=1,008.

[52] Program on International Policy Attitudes, June 23–July 13, 1994, N=1,339.

[53] Gallup, October 7–19, 1994, N=1,013.

[54] According to Gallup's September 23–24, 1994 polling, about 52 percent of those polled expected 50 or fewer casualties.

[55] Los Angeles Times, September 20–21, 1994, N=1,340.

[56] CBS News/New York Times, September 19, 1994, N=504.

[57] An average of only 39 percent disagreed with the statement. Time/CNN/Yankelovich, July 13–14, 1994, N=600.

[58] The Los Angeles Times question cited above showed 52 percent of Democrats, 57 percent of Independents, and 71 percent of Republicans stating that sending U.S. troops to Haiti

Déjà Vu All Over Again: The 2004 U.S. Intervention in Haiti

When compared to support for the 1994 intervention, the public opinion data on the February 2004 intervention in Haiti by U.S. Marines provides some of the best evidence that partisanship plays a critical role in support and opposition for military operations.

Although the location of the intervention was identical and the nature of the stakes comparable, and in both cases the missions were relatively similar—facilitating a transition from a corrupt, undemocratic, and violent Haitian regime to, it was hoped, a more democratic, honest, and humane one—the partisan composition of support and opposition for each operation was strikingly different, yet entirely predictable.

Nearly ten years after Haiti's September 1994 regime change, on February 29, 2004, the U.S. military, in response to a rebel uprising against the Aristide government in February 2004, once again intervened to depose a Haitian regime. Haitian president Aristide took flight from his country as sizable numbers of U.S. Marines were introduced into Port-au-Prince as the leading element of an interim international force, the mission of which was to help bring order and stability to Haiti.[59] By late April 2004, the Multinational Interim Force comprised approximately 3,800 troops, including about 2,000 U.S. military personnel (mostly Marines), as well as more than 900 French troops, more than 500 Canadian troops, and more than 300 Chilean troops,[60] and the UN Security Council had approved a new UN peacekeeping operation to replace the interim, U.S.-led force.[61]

---

was not worth the possible loss of American lives and other costs involved. The Time/CNN/Yankelovich result showed 49 percent who agreed with the statement that nothing the United States could accomplish in Haiti was worth the death of even one soldier (43 percent disagreed), while 49 percent of Independents agreed (40 percent disagreed) and 55 percent of Republicans agreed (35 percent disagreed).

[59] See White House, "President Bush Urges Haitians to Reject Violence," February 29, 2004, and DoD, "Department of Defense Statement on Haiti," News Release No. 137-04, February 29, 2004.

[60] See http://www.globalsecurity.org/military/ops/haiti04.htm, accessed May 2004.

[61] Maggie Farley, "U.N. to Send Troops to Haiti," *The Los Angeles Times,* May 1, 2004.

It should come as little surprise, given the relatively modest U.S. stakes in Haiti, that the small amount of polling done on the issue found that support for the U.S. military intervention in Haiti was not terribly robust, ranging between 43 and 67 percent depending on timing, question wording, and other particulars.[62]

Although there are differences in question wording, polling organization, and other features of the questions, Table 3.7 demonstrates in a striking way the critical importance of partisan leadership

Table 3.7
Support for U.S. Interventions in Haiti by Party and Other Characteristics, March 2004 and September 1994

Do you strongly favor, favor, oppose, or strongly oppose using American military force to maintain order in Haiti? (Pew Research Center, March 17–21, 2004, N=1,703)

The elected president of Haiti, Jean-Bertrand Aristide, was overthrown by the Haitian military in 1991. In order to remove the military and restore President Aristide to his position, do you favor or oppose the United States sending in ground troops? (CBS News/New York Times, September 19, 1994, N=504)

	March 2004	September 1994
Total	43%	40%
Republican	55%	29%
Independent	41	44
Democrat	36	49
Men	50%	46%
Women	36	34
White	43%	37%
Black	38	65
Hispanic	36	NA

NOTE: NA = Not available.

[62] For example: Fox News/Opinion Dynamics, March 3–4, 2004, N = 900, found that 52 percent said it was necessary for the United States to send peacekeeping troops to Haiti. NBC News/Wall Street Journal/Hart & Teeter, March 6–8, 2004, N = 1,018, found that 67 percent approved of President Bush deploying Marines in Haiti as part of an international force to help restore order following the resignation of Haiti's president. Pew Research Center, March 17–21, 2004, N = 1,703, found that 43 percent strongly favored (7 percent) or favored (36 percent) using American military force to maintain order in Haiti.

and followership in support for the two interventions, as well as the roles of gender and race.

As shown, although only about four in ten respondents in each poll supported the U.S. military intervention in Haiti, the partisan composition of support and opposition was entirely predictable: the president's natural supporters were far more likely to support the intervention in each case than his natural opponents. Thus, in September 1994, Democrats were more than 1.5 times more likely than Republicans to support President Bill Clinton's intervention in Haiti,[63] whereas in March 2004, Republicans were more than 1.5 times more likely than Democrats to support George W. Bush's intervention. Also as expected, in both cases women were less likely to support the operation than men. And whereas the 2004 result conforms to the general prediction that blacks are less likely than whites to support military operations, the 1994 case showed just the opposite result, although it is easy to imagine several reasons for that result.[64]

Bosnia

Bosnia is the third of four major peace operations undertaken in the 1990s that we examined, and another case that demonstrates the lim-

[63] This partisan gap in support for the 1994 U.S. intervention in Haiti is a robust finding, repeated in Time/CNN/Yankelovich, September 21–22, 1994, N = 800, Gallup/CNN/USA Today, September 23–25, 1993, N =1,009, Associated Press/I.C.R. Survey Research Group, September 23–27, 1994, N = 1,005, Gallup/CNN/USA Today, October 7–9, 1994, N = 1,013, Time/CNN/USA Today, October 11–12, 1994, N = 800, and Los Angeles Times, October 17–19, 1994, N = 1,272. It also turns up in questions about approval of President Clinton's handling of Haiti. It also has been observed in many, if not most, other military operations. See Eric V. Larson, "The Use of Force and the Persistence of the Partisan Divide," *The Yale Politic*, May 2004.

[64] Three plausible and not mutually exclusive reasons for the 1994 result occurred to us. First, blacks comprised a core constituency of support for Bill Clinton and were highly predisposed to provide their support for the president's intervention. Second, black respondents may have been more moved by the dire humanitarian plight in Haiti in 1994, a nation that was, after all, predominantly black. Third, the Clinton administration's widely criticized failure to intervene during the Rwandan genocide may have increased blacks' support for an intervention in Haiti.

its of support when clear national interests are elusive and national leaders are divided over the wisdom of the operation. It is also a case in which, on average, less than a majority supported the operation in spite of the fact that the United States had UN authorization for the operation[65] and contribution of troops from its major allies.

Background

In 1992, civil war erupted in Bosnia-Herzegovina after it declared its independence from the Serbian-run Yugoslav federation. The Bush administration generally struggled in vain to forge an effective policy toward Bosnia, and it sought to avoid U.S. military intervention in what it generally seems to have considered a "problem from hell"; it accordingly limited its military response to humanitarian relief operations. Although it supported firmer action in Bosnia in the form of multilateral air strikes,[66] the Clinton administration's own commitment to securing peace in Bosnia vacillated between assertiveness and restraint, and it also stopped short of risking ground troops in combat operations there.[67] As was shown in Table 1.1, the public also ap-

---

[65] The Bosnia operation was authorized by United Nations Security Council Resolution 1031 of December 15, 1995.

[66] For a good discussion of the Clinton administration's evolving Bosnia policy and the congressional reaction, see Congressional Quarterly, "Administration Struggles With Bosnia Policy," *1993 CQ Almanac*, Washington, D.C.: CQ Press, 1994, pp. 493–499; "Bosnian War Remains Intractable," *1994 CQ Almanac*, Washington, D.C.: CQ Press, 1995, pp. 446–449; and "Bosnian War Sparks Conflict at Home," *1995 CQ Almanac*, Washington, D.C.: CQ Press, 1996, pp. 10-10 to 10-15.

[67] For example, on May 23, 1995, President Clinton said "[F]rom the beginning of my campaign for president, I said that the one thing we should not do is to send American troops into combat into Bosnia." On June 7, 1995, Secretary of Defense Perry affirmed this view: "I do not believe—that while this war is in our interest, it is not in our vital interest. And therefore, it does not pose a sufficiently great risk to U.S. interest to warrant the risk of the lives of thousands of troops." And as the president put it in his November 27, 1995, address to the nation announcing the deployment of U.S. troops to implement the peace agreement in Bosnia-Herzegovina:

> When I took office, some were urging immediate intervention in the conflict. I decided that American ground troops should not fight a war in Bosnia because the United States could not force peace on Bosnia's warring ethnic groups, the Serbs, Croats, and Muslims. Instead, America has worked with our European allies in searching for peace, stopping the war from spreading, and easing the suf-

peared to be somewhat ambivalent about more forceful action: according to polling done on May 6, 1993, either one-third or two-thirds supported air strikes at the time, with the result highly sensitive to question wording or other factors.

In developing policies for Bosnia, President Clinton was caught between those who supported an intervention with ground troops to halt the fighting and those who opposed virtually any other form of U.S. involvement in Bosnia.[68] As a consequence, the Clinton administration pursued a presidential leadership strategy that navigated a turbulent course between these two camps, while seeking to retain a permissive public opinion environment for the eventuality of a peace agreement in Bosnia and the introduction of U.S. peacekeepers to underwrite that agreement. As in Haiti, part of the administration's strategy was to keep opposition to a dull roar by laying the groundwork for an unopposed intervention by ground troops in Bosnia. In this case, however, the administration relied upon a short air war designed to force the warring parties (but especially Serbs) into negotiations that ultimately would lead to the introduction of a multinational peacekeeping force.[69]

In his November 25 radio address and his November 27 address to the nation,[70] President Clinton sought to build support by emphasizing three main themes. First, he sought to appeal to those who would be moved by arguments that emphasized core American values. Second, he sought support from those who would be moved by references to national interests. Finally, he hoped to move those who would respond to claims that U.S. leadership was at stake in Bosnia.

The president's was not the only voice on Bosnia, however, and

fering of the Bosnian people . . . I refuse to send American troops to fight a war in Bosnia, but I believe we must help to secure the Bosnian peace.

[68] Air strikes and arming the Muslims was a policy preferred by many Republican congressional leaders, although some others opposed any sort of deeper involvement.

[69] Operation Deliberate Force, which was NATO's first-ever offensive military operation, conducted between August 29 and September 14, 1995.

[70] William J. Clinton, "Radio Address of the President to the Nation," November 25, 1995, and "Address to the Nation on Implementation of the Peace Agreement in Bosnia-Herzegovina," November 27, 1995.

members of Congress engaged in lively debate over a possible U.S. peacekeeping operation in Bosnia.[71] During the congressional debates leading up to December 13, 1995 votes on Bosnia, although support and opposition were present on both sides of the aisle, the Democrats generally seemed to see more important U.S. stakes in Bosnia than did Republicans; but each group used very different language to express the presence or absence of U.S. equities. Among the Democrats who supported the president's line, some argued that vital interests were in fact involved, some focused on the humanitarian dimension, and some expressed approval for the president's emphasis on the centrality of the rule of law. In contrast, Republican congressional leaders generally tended to diminish the importance of the U.S. moral and strategic interests in Bosnia as well as the potential consequences of the United States failing to send forces to Bosnia.[72]

In the final analysis, then, the peacekeeping mission to Bosnia sparked a highly partisan debate, and the congressional resolutions on Bosnia were far from fully supportive of the intervention, essentially supporting the troops while failing to endorse the president's policy. And the votes on the final resolutions exhibited both partisanship—most House Republicans and Senate Democrats approved their resolution—and intraparty divisions—House Democrats and Senate Republicans split on the matter.[73] As will be shown, the presi-

[71] See Congressional Quarterly, "Bosnian War Sparks Conflict at Home," *1995 CQ Almanac*, Washington, D.C.: CQ Press, 1996, pp. 10-10 to 10-15.

[72] According to Seelye (1995): "Those who supported the Hutchinson resolution [supporting the troops but opposing President Clinton's decision to send them] generally said that the United States had no vital strategic interest in Bosnia, that the mission was ill-defined, with no clear objective, and that Washington could not be the world's policeman." For example, Senator Phil Gramm (R-TX) stated that the United States had no vital national security interest in Bosnia, and Senator Arlen Spector (R-PA) argued that the Congress should support the troops without endorsing the president's policy because U.S. national security was not imminently threatened, and the United States was not "the world's policeman."

[73] On December 13, 1995, the House approved by a vote of 287 to 141 H.R. 302, which disowned the deployment decision but supported the troops and insisted that the United States remain neutral among Bosnia's warring parties; House Republicans voted 221 to 11 in favor of the resolution, while Democrats opposed the measure by a two-to-one margin, with 65 voting in favor and 130 opposing the measure.

dent was generally unable to translate the public's approval of his job handling just before the announcement into majority support for the operation.[74]

Overview of Support for the Operation

As was the case with Haiti, on average, prospective support for sending U.S. troops to Bosnia appears to have been somewhat higher than support for the actual intervention, but in neither case did a majority typically approve.[75]

The average level of support for putting troops into Bosnia from January 1993, when President Clinton entered office, until just before his November 27, 1995 speech announcing the deployment, was just shy of a majority: 49 percent.[76] As was shown in Table 1.2, polling done on November 27 consistently showed that fewer than half (33, 39, or 46 percent, depending on question wording) backed the introduction of U.S. ground troops as part of an international peacekeeping operation. In contrast, the average level of support for troops in Bosnia from November 27, 1995 forward was somewhat lower than before the speech: 43 percent.[77] On average, 42 percent ap-

---

The same day, the Senate rejected by a vote of 47 to 52 a resolution by Senator Hutchison (R-TX) that objected to President Clinton's policy but expressed support for the troops, and then adopted, by a vote of 69 to 30, SJRES44, which expressed support for U.S. troops in Bosnia but expressed reservations about the deployment of the troops. The measure also limited the deployment to "approximately" one year and required the president to limit the use of U.S. troops in Bosnia to the enforcement of the military provisions of the peace agreement and provide for an exit strategy from Bosnia that would include an international effort to achieve a military balance in Bosnia by arming the federation of Bosnia. Senate Democrats voted 45 to 1 in favor of the measure, while Republicans were divided, with 24 voting in favor and 29 opposing. See Congressional Quarterly, "Bosnian War Sparks Conflict at Home," *1995 CQ Almanac*, Washington, D.C.: CQ Press, 1996, p. 10-15.

[74] Fifty-three percent of those polled in Gallup's November 17–18, 1995 poll (N = 615) approved of the president's job handling.

[75] See Newport (1995).

[76] We found 45 questions that asked about the subject over that period.

[77] There were 13 questions that asked about the subject from November 27, 1995 until October–November 1999. Based on six questions asked between January 1996 and August 2001, the average level of approval for the president's decision to put troops in Bosnia was 48 percent.

proved of the president's handling of the Bosnia issue, although support was higher after the Dayton Accords were signed in December 1995.[78] Taken together, it appears that only about four in ten Americans supported the intervention once troops were on the ground.

Figure 3.3 portrays the structure of support and opposition for U.S. troops in Bosnia using 10 questions that were asked by the Program on International Policy Attitudes (PIPA) between May 1993 and May 1999.

If one relied on polling by PIPA alone, one would almost certainly conclude that the support for U.S. troops in Bosnia was quite robust: according to this polling, on average, 63 percent supported U.S. troops in Bosnia for a variety of purposes, and 31 percent opposed.

If one turns to other data, however, a somewhat different story emerges (see Figure 3.4). The figure presents data describing the structure of support for nine questions that were asked by other polling organizations, and it generally shows a heavier weighting toward opposition: on average, slightly less than a majority (49 percent) approved of U.S. troops in Bosnia, while 44 percent disapproved.

Moreover, the 45 percent who strongly supported the use of troops in the June 1995 polling by the Los Angeles Times (the tallest of the leftmost black columns) actually supported the use of troops to evacuate UN peacekeepers, not to establish or enforce a peace. If this observation is dropped, the average level of support for U.S. troops in Bosnia is 45 percent, and the average level of opposition is 47 percent.

Indeed, even among questions that, like PIPA's, asked about retrospective approval for the president's decision to send troops, PIPA's result stands out: its polling in June 1996 found 51 percent approv-

---

[78] Sixty-two questions asked between February 1993 and September 1997, the average approval of the president's handling of Bosnia before the Dayton Accords were signed was 41 percent, and the average after was 49.5 percent.

Figure 3.3
Structure of Support for Bosnia in Polling by PIPA

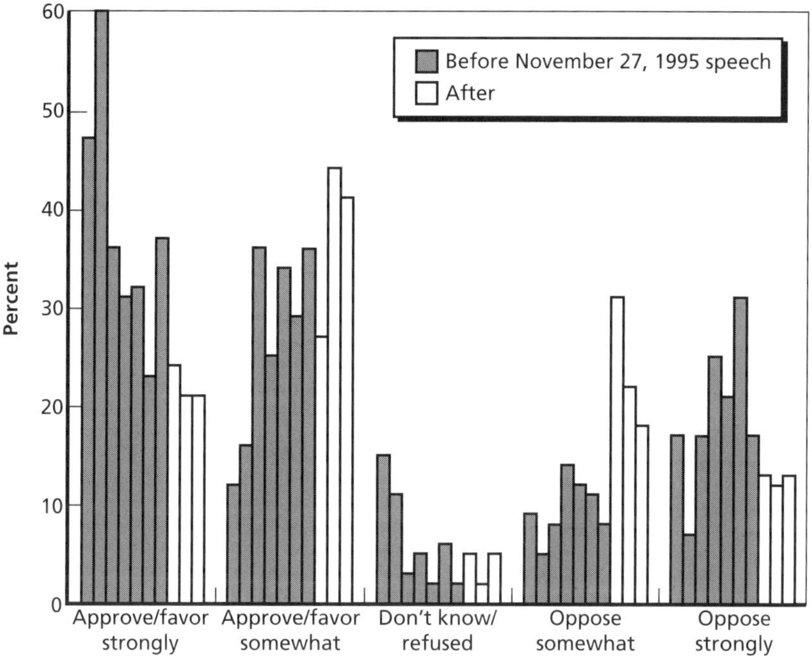

RAND *MG231-A-3.3*

ing of the decision,[79] whereas a similarly worded question asked by another polling organization just two weeks earlier showed only 43 percent supporting—an eight-point difference.[80] The evidence sug-

[79] The wording of PIPA's question was: "Do you approve or disapprove of President (Bill) Clinton's decision to send 20,000 U.S. (United States) troops to Bosnia as part of an international peacekeeping force? (If approve/disapprove, ask:) Do you feel that way strongly or somewhat?" PIPA, June 21–26, 1996, N=1,227.

[80] Pew/PSRA asked: "(I am going to read you a list of some programs and proposals that are being discussed in this country today. For each one, please tell me whether you strongly favor, favor, oppose, or strongly oppose it.) . . . . President (Bill) Clinton's decision to send 20,000 U.S. (United States) troops to Bosnia as part of an international peacekeeping force." Pew/PSRA, May 31–June 9, 1996, N=1,975.

Figure 3.4
Structure of Support for Bosnia in Polling by Others

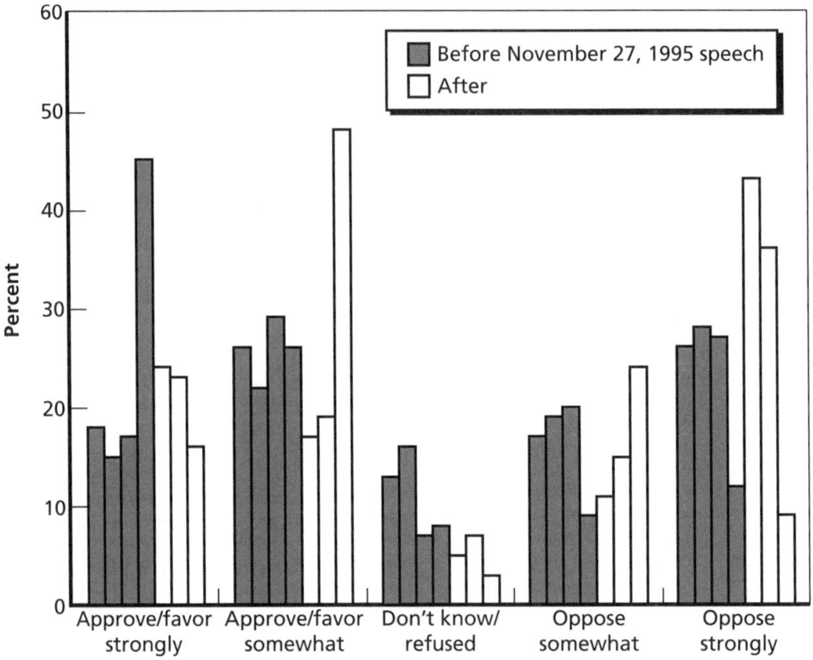

RAND *MG231-A-3.4*

gests potential bias in PIPA's polling: the tumescent level of support for U.S. troops in Bosnia that PIPA finds has rarely been replicated by other polling.

Support for the U.S. presence in Bosnia has changed little over the years: 43 percent approved of President Clinton's decision to extend the deadline for removing troops from Bosnia in polling in December 1997 and January 1998,[81] and in the most recent question on U.S. troops in Bosnia, 47 percent of those polled in August 2001 approved of President Bush's decision to keep U.S. troops in Kosovo

[81] Gallup, December 18–21, 1997, N = 1,005 and Pew/PSRA, January 14–18, 1998, N = 1,218. Forty-three percent also approved of the presence of U.S. troops in Bosnia in the Pew January 1998 poll.

and Bosnia;[82] the average approval of President Clinton's handling of the Bosnia issue from January 1996 to September 1997 (the last time such a question was asked) was 49.7 percent.[83] Put another way, despite the administration's success in achieving a virtually zero-casualty mission, it got little credit from the public for this, most likely because it simply was not viewed as a particularly important accomplishment.

Following the Bush administration's entry into office, as just mentioned, only 47 percent of those polled in August 2001 approved of President Bush's decision to keep U.S. troops in Kosovo and Bosnia.[84] In a departure from the general pattern of less-than-majority support for the U.S. presence in Bosnia, however, 64 percent of those polled in June 2002 approved of the continued participation of U.S. troops in the peacekeeping operation in Bosnia (Table 3.8).[85]

In this case, about six in ten Republicans actually supported the peacekeeping operation, which had by that time become accepted administration policy, while nearly three in four Democrats favored continued participation in an intervention that was, after all, begun under President Clinton.

Sources and Fault Lines in Support

We now turn to our analysis of the factors that lay behind support and opposition to U.S. military action in Bosnia, and the fault lines in support.

---

[82] Pew Research Center/PSRA, August 2–8, 2001, N=1,277.

[83] A total of 62 polls conducted over the period asked questions about approval for the president's handling of the Bosnia situation.

[84] Pew Research Center/PSRA, August 2–8, 2001, N = 1,277. President Bush noted his intention to continue working with NATO on Bosnia on June 13, 2001. See White House, "Press Availability with President Bush and NATO Secretary General Lord Robertson," June 13, 2001.

[85] Chicago Council on Foreign Relations/German Marshall Fund/Harris, June 1–30, 2002, N=3,262.

Table 3.8
Cross-Tabulation of Support of Peacekeeping Operation in Bosnia and Party, June 2002

As you probably know, our troops are participating in the peacekeeping operation in Bosnia. Are you strongly in favor, somewhat in favor, somewhat opposed or strongly opposed to this?

Generally speaking, do you usually think of yourself as a Republican, a Democrat, an Independent, or what?

	Favor	Oppose	N
Republican	61	39	215
Independent	64	36	185
Democrat	73	27	266
Other	77	23	26
Total	67	33	692

NOTE: $p < 0.05$ in a Chi-square test of independence.
SOURCE: CCFR, June 1–30, 2002, N=3,262.

Our statistical modeling was able to correctly predict support or opposition to U.S. action in Bosnia for 83 percent of the respondents in our dataset[86] using only key beliefs about the stakes, prospects for success, and costs in casualties; membership in the president's party was not a statistically significant predictor (Table 3.9).[87]

From the table we can see that the most important factor in determining support was the perception of security interests, the next most important factor was respondents' beliefs about whether the costs in casualties were likely to be high, the third most important

[86] Details are available in Appendix D of the technical appendix, published separately.

[87] Our full model also used some demographic characteristics but didn't greatly improve classification. In declining order of importance in determining support or opposition were the perception that the United States had security interests in Bosnia, respondents' beliefs about whether the costs in casualties were likely to be high, the perception that the United States had important moral interests in Bosnia, and the belief that a successful outcome was likely. Party was not a statistically significant predictor in the model, possibly due to the fact that we had to use a proxy variable for party. For details, see Appendix D of the technical appendix, published separately.

Table 3.9
Bosnia: Marginal Probability from Probit Estimates of Approval (Q2)

Variables	Change in Probability at Mean Values
Security interests (Q4)†	0.332 (0.064)***
Moral interests (Q7)†	0.273 (0.068)***
Prospects (Q5)	0.197 (0.044)***
Casualties (Q9)†	–0.274 (0.063)***
Party 1 if Republican†	–0.011 (0.079)
Race 1 if black†	0.032 (0.119)
Gender 1 if female†	0.054 (0.068)
Wald Chi-square (Prod > Chi2)	128.06 (0.000)
Log likelihood	–191.79
Observations	468
Correctly specified	83%

† dF/dx is for discrete change of dummy variable from 0 to 1.
* Significant at 10%.
** Significant at 5%.
*** Significant at 1%.
Robust standard error in parentheses.
SOURCE: Gallup, November 27, 1995.

factor was the perception of moral interests, and the fourth was the belief that a successful outcome was likely; although party was a statistically significant predictor on a bivariate basis, it proved not to be significant in this model.[88]

We accordingly focus on these factors:

- **Partisan leadership and followership.** As just described, partisanship figured prominently in key underlying beliefs about the U.S. military operation in Bosnia; they also figured prominently in support for the operation. In fact, public support or opposition to the intervention in Bosnia mirrored divisions in the leadership, with the fault lines running along essentially partisan lines; Figure 3.5 shows that the strength of support or opposition for intervening with U.S. troops also was highly polarized along partisan lines.

[88] Gallup did not ask about presidential approval in this poll.

Figure 3.5
Approval of Troop Presence in Bosnia, by Party, December 1995

Do you approve or disapprove of the presence of U.S. troops in Bosnia? (If approve/disapprove, ask:) Do you feel strongly about that, or not strongly? (Gallup, December 15–18, 1995, N=1,000)

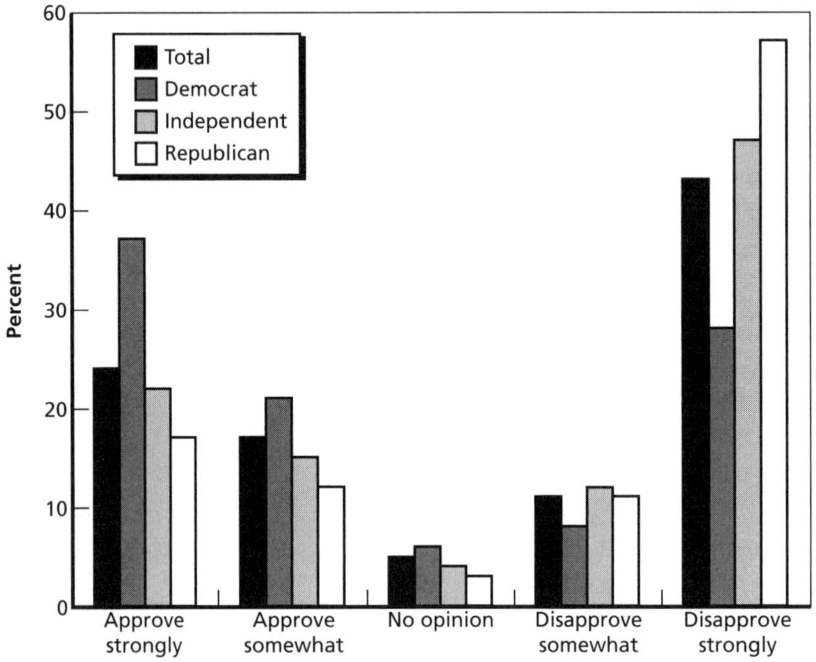

RAND *MG231-A-3.5*

- **Perceived stakes.** Few appear to have believed that the United States had particularly important security interests in Bosnia: the average percentage saying the United States had vital interests in Bosnia from June 1994 to December 1995 was 37 percent.[89]

[89] A total of seven polling questions asked about U.S. vital interests in Bosnia over this period. Interestingly, the Chicago Council on Foreign Relations polling shows a pattern similar to Haiti: its October 1994 poll found only 44 percent who thought the United States had a vital interest in Bosnia, but that rose to 51 percent at the time of its October 1998 poll, and fell again to 43 percent in its June 2002 poll. One conjecture, consistent with that for Haiti, is that the public thinks of vital interests in a somewhat different way than do national security experts, and that the simple presence of U.S. troops in Bosnia constituted, in the public's

Americans polled in May 1993 seemed to find as many good reasons for supporting as opposing air strikes against Serb forces, although more agreed with the arguments that opposed air strikes.[90] Although there were important partisan differences, 50 percent of those polled in June 1995 said that they thought the United States should be less involved in Bosnia because American lives should be put at risk only to protect U.S. national interests, and that was not the case in Bosnia; only 36 percent thought the United States should be more involved.[91] On average, only about three in ten respondents indicated that they felt the United States had a responsibility to do something about the fighting in Bosnia[92] or that the United States should do more to stop the war in Bosnia.[93]

---

mind at least, a vital interest. This interpretation also is consistent with the public's concerns about casualties in Haiti and Bosnia.

[90] For example, Gallup found that 71 percent thought the argument that air strikes could lead to the involvement of U.S. ground troops was a very good (30 percent) or good reason (41 percent) for opposing air strikes; 66 percent agreed that the argument that air strikes were unlikely to bring an end to the fighting was a very good (26 percent) or good reason (40 percent) for opposing air strikes; 62 percent said that the argument that the United States shouldn't get involved because of its economic problems was a very good (29 percent) or good reason (33 percent); and 55 percent thought the argument that Bosnia was more of a European problem than an American one was a very good (18 percent) or good reason (37 percent). On the other hand, 62 percent agreed that a moral obligation to stop atrocities was a very good (16 percent) or good reason (46 percent) for air strikes, and 57 percent saw containment of the conflict as a very good (17 percent) or good reason (40 percent), but only 49 percent of those polled said that the argument that the United States had national security interests at stake in Bosnia was a very good (12 percent) or good reason (37 percent) for air strikes against Serb forces in Bosnia. Gallup/CNN/USA Today, May 6, 1993, N=603.

[91] NBC News/Wall Street Journal, June 2–6, 1995, N=1,008. Republicans (at 56 percent) were most inclined to agree with this statement, while 48 percent of Independents and 45 percent of Democrats also agreed. Democrats (at 45 percent) were more inclined to agree with the alternative argument that "the U.S. should be more involved in Bosnia, because the U.S. cannot be a world leader and stand by while innocent Bosnian civilians are killed and other nations provide all the peacekeepers"; only 24 percent of Republicans and 41 percent of Independents agreed with this alternative statement.

[92] A typical result was the response to this CBS News/New York Times' question: "Do you think the United States has a responsibility to do something about the fighting between Serbs and Bosnians in what used to be Yugoslavia, or doesn't the United States have this responsibility?" The average result for the 13 polls that asked this question was 31 percent, never rose above four out of ten, and occasionally dipped as low as one in four. By compari-

- **Prospects for success.** The public opinion data suggest that few in fact believed that an increased U.S. commitment to Bosnia would yield a favorable outcome. According to polling by Gallup, 53 percent of those polled immediately after the president's November 27, 1995 speech thought that if the United States sent troops as part of a peacekeeping mission, it was likely to lead to a long-term commitment in Bosnia involving many casualties; only 35 percent thought this unlikely.[94] By mid-December, Gallup found only 44 percent who were very or somewhat confident that the U.S. effort to establish peace in Bosnia would succeed, and 46 percent were very or somewhat confident that U.S. troops would be able to withdraw within a year, as planned.[95] Important partisan differences were also evident in these beliefs.[96]
- **Expected costs.** As in the case of Haiti, part of the reason for the low levels of support observed for a U.S. intervention in Bosnia had to do with an unwillingness to put American servicemen at risk for what was at its heart a humanitarian cause. Regarding

---

son, more than half thought that the United Nations had a responsibility to do something about the fighting (Sobel, 1996).

[93] On 13 occasions, Yankelovich asked "Should the U.S. do more to stop the war in Sarajevo and Bosnia, or has the U.S. already done enough?" The average percentage favoring doing more was 31 percent; that figure never rose above 37 percent, and on five occasions it fell below 30 percent.

[94] The question asked by Gallup/CNN/USA Today on November 27, 1995, was: "If the United States sends troops as part of a peacekeeping mission, do you think that is likely to lead to a long-term commitment in Bosnia involving many casualties, or not?" Fifty-three percent expected a long-term commitment, while 35 percent thought that was not likely, and 12 percent had no opinion. A majority of both those who saw the speech and those who didn't expected a long-term commitment. *Gallup Poll Monthly*, November 1995, p. 47.

[95] Gallup/CNN/USA Today, December 15–18, 1995, N = 1,000. This represented an increase over the 31 percent who expressed confidence in Gallup's September polling and the 32 percent who expressed confidence in Gallup's October 1995 polling. Gallup, September 19–22, 1995, N=1,229, and October 19–22, 1995, N=1,229.

[96] For example, 61 percent of Democrats were very (20 percent) or somewhat confident (41 percent) that U.S. efforts to establish peace would succeed, while only 35 percent of Republicans were very (7 percent) or somewhat confident (28 percent), and 37 percent of Independents were very (11 percent) or somewhat confident (26 percent). Gallup, December 15–18, 1995, N=1,229.

the public's expectations for casualties, polling following the president's speech suggests that, depending on wording, an average of about 42 percent believed that the U.S. intervention in Bosnia would entail few or no American casualties, while an average of 52 percent expected somewhat or much higher casualties;[97] in comparison, the public were somewhat less optimistic about casualties in Bosnia than they had been in Haiti and Somalia; more than six in ten had expected few or no casualties in the latter operations.

- **Balancing costs and benefits.** As for the public's willingness to tolerate casualties in Bosnia, three questions asked in November 1995—just before U.S. troops were introduced—suggest that fewer than four in ten Americans were willing to risk lives in Bosnia,[98] and a question asked by Gallup in October 1995 suggested that a majority would oppose sending U.S. troops to Bosnia if it resulted in as few as 25 deaths.[99] Figure 3.6 presents

---

[97] Based on three polling results with different question wording, including Gallup/CNN/USA Today, November 27, 1995; Harris, November 30–December 3, 1995; and Gallup, December 15–18, 1995. Forty percent of those polled by Gallup in mid-December were very or somewhat confident that the United States would be able to accomplish its goals with very few or no American casualties when asked: "Regarding the situation in Bosnia, how confident are you that each of the following will happen? Are you very confident, somewhat confident, not too confident, or not at all confident that: . . . The U.S. will be able to accomplish its goals with very few or no American casualties?" The smaller percentage in the second question may be due to the fact that it asks the respondent if he feels the United States would be able to accomplish its goals with very few or no casualties, i.e., it asks about the joint probability of success and success at few or no casualties. *Gallup Poll Monthly,* December 1995, p. 32.

[98] The CBS News' November 2, 1995 poll found only 28 percent who thought that, given the possible loss of American lives and other costs involved, that sending U.S. troops to Bosnia was worth the likely cost; the ABC News' November 27, 1995 poll found only 30 percent who agreed that it would be worth the loss of some American lives if sending U.S. troops brought peace to Bosnia; and the Associated Press' November 29, 1995 poll found only 37 percent who thought that saving the lives of civilians in Bosnia was worth putting U.S. soldiers at risk. ABC News, November 27, 1995, N = 519; CBS News, November 2, 1995, N=504; and Associated Press, November 29, 1995, N=1,016.

[99] Gallup varied the hypothetical number of U.S. deaths and asked if the respondent would still favor sending U.S. troops. Sixty-eight percent said they would favor sending U.S. troops if there were no Americans killed, 31 percent said they would still favor if 25 soldiers were killed, 30 percent said they would still favor if 100 American soldiers were killed, and 21 percent said they would still favor sending U.S. troops if 400 American soldiers were killed. Gallup, October 19–22, 1995, N=1,229.

data from a poll by Gallup in October 1995 that asked respondents about willingness to support the use of U.S. troops in an operation for different casualty levels; as shown, two out of three said they would be willing to support the operation if there were no casualties, but support had fallen by more than a half (to 31 percent) if only 25 deaths resulted. Taken together, these data suggest that the public's tolerance for casualties in Bosnia was quite modest, and this could have been an important fault line in support.

Figure 3.6
Prospective Willingness to Tolerate Casualties in Bosnia, October 1995

Suppose that you knew that if the United States sent U.S. troops to Bosnia as part of an international peacekeeping force, that no American soldiers would be killed. With this in mind, would you favor or oppose sending U.S. troops to Bosnia? (Then asked if respondent would support with 25, 100, and 400 U.S. troops killed.)
(Gallup, October 22–24, 1995, N=1,229)

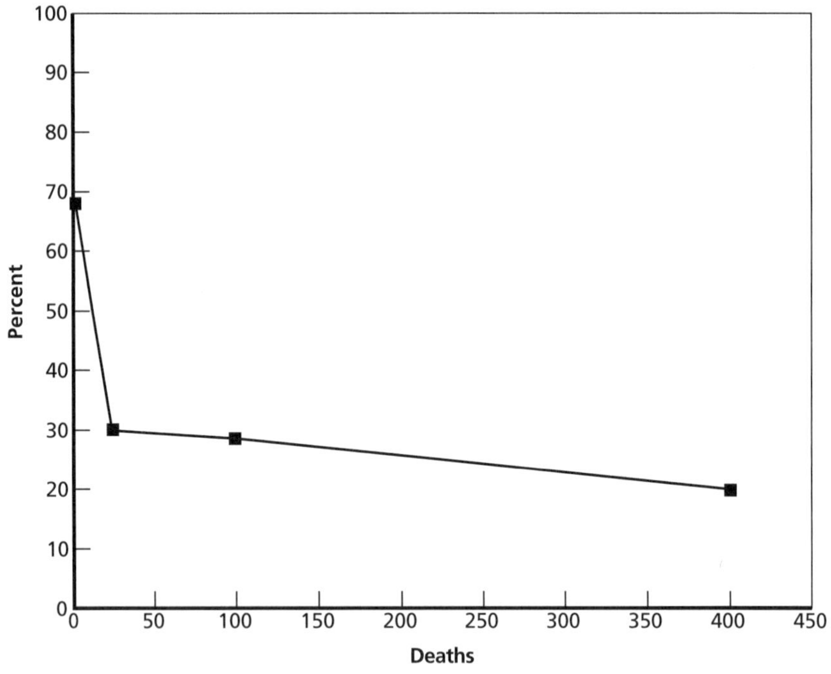

RAND *MG231-A-3.6*

A Note on Sensitivity of Support to Question Wording

To be sure, there are many factors that can color support or opposition to a military operation. For example, Table 3.10 illustrates this using the results from two questions asked in a poll done in April 1993, about the time that the no-fly zones in Bosnia were initiated.[100]

The data in the table show substantially higher support for the use of airpower than ground troops: 50 percent of those polled supported the use of air strikes in Bosnia, while only about four in ten supported the use of ground troops.[101] As will be described next, the difference in support is most easily explained by a reluctance to put U.S. troops at risk in Bosnia.[102]

Table 3.10
Support for Airpower and Ground Troops in Bosnia, April 1993

Thinking about the situation in Bosnia . . . would you support or oppose the United States using air strikes to stop the fighting in Bosnia? (If choice is made, ask:) Do you strongly or somewhat (support/oppose) that?

If air power alone did not stop the fighting would you support or oppose the use of American ground troops in Bosnia? (If choice is made, ask:) Do you strongly or somewhat (support/oppose) that?

	Air Strikes	Troops
Support strongly	28	19
Support somewhat	22	21
Unsure	13	9
Oppose somewhat	15	15
Oppose strongly	22	36

SOURCE: U.S. News & World Report, April 21–22, 1993, N=1,000.

---

[100] A Gallup poll done in February 1994 found an even more striking difference: 65 percent supported air strikes, but only 41 percent supported sending U.S. ground troops if the air strikes were ineffective. See Gallup/CNN/USA Today, April 16–18, 1994, N=1,002.

[101] Twenty-four polls between August 1992 and July 1995 asked questions about support for air strikes.

[102] Consistent with this interpretation is that there was higher support for the use of U.S. forces for humanitarian relief or to monitor a cease-fire than combat or peace enforcement, and that there was higher support for the use of ground troops to evacuate or withdraw UN peacekeepers under attack by Serbian forces than to simply protect them.

One of the great difficulties in interpreting public opinion data is not just that results can be highly sensitive to question wording, but that questions can contain a great many cues that can affect responses. In fact, a great many questions were asked about support for the use of force in Bosnia from 1992 to 1994 (and after), and the results appeared to vary greatly as a result of cues found in the wording of the questions.

To better understand the sensitivity of support and opposition for the use of force in Bosnia to these cues, we coded 48 questions that were asked between August 1992 and December 1994 in terms of the cues contained in each question, and we used a technique called dummy regression to isolate the effects that the presence or absence of these cues had on overall support or opposition.

After some experimentation, we found that we were able to account for 64 percent of the variance in the percentage favoring the use of force (Figure 3.7) and 72 percent of the variance in the percentage opposing the use of force (Figure 3.8) by simply knowing what cues were in the questions.

As shown in Figure 3.7, the regression model suggested that the base level of support for the use of force in Bosnia was 31 percent, with the following cues doing a fairly good job of predicting variations from that baseline:

- CLINTON = the mention of President Clinton in the question raised support by 15.8 points;
- USAIR = The mention of a reliance on air power raised support by 7.9 points;
- HUMAN = The mention of a humanitarian operation raised support by 14.1 points;
- USALONE = The suggestion that the United States was acting alone reduced support by 18 points;
- UNINTL = The suggestion that U.S. forces would be participating in a United Nations international peacekeeping operation raised support by 11.9 points; and
- ATROC = The suggestion that the purpose was to prevent atrocities raised support by 25.1 points.

Figure 3.7
Dummy Regression Results for Support for Force in Bosnia

Dependent variable is: **Favor**
R^2 = 68.9% R^2(adjusted) = 64.4%
s = 9.074 with 48 – 7 = 41 degrees of freedom

Source	Sum of squares	Degrees of freedom	Mean square	F-ratio
Regression	7481.37	6	1247	15.1
Residual	3375.61	41	82.3319	

Variable	Coefficient	Standard error of coeff	t-ratio
Constant	31.0406	2.408	12.9
CLINTON	15.8953	3.529	4.50
USAIR	7.89304	3.448	2.29
HUMAN	14.0533	3.424	4.10
USALONE	−18.0406	5.766	−3.13
UNINTL	11.8689	2.899	4.09
ATROC	25.0905	9.359	2.68

RAND *MG231-A-3.7*

In the case of opposition to the use of force in Bosnia, the model suggests that the base level of opposition was 49.4 percent, with the following cues being the best predictors of variation from that base level:

- CLINTON = The mention of President Clinton reduced opposition by 9.2 points;
- USGND = The suggestion that ground troops would be used raised opposition by 9.1 points;
- HUMAN = The suggestion that U.S. forces would be undertaking humanitarian operations lowered opposition by 13.3 points;
- PKAGREE = The suggestion that U.S. forces were being introduced into a peaceful environment following the establishment of a durable peace agreement reduced opposition by 10.2 points;
- USALONE = The suggestion that the United States was acting alone raised opposition by 35.6 points;

Figure 3.8
Dummy Regression Results for Opposition to Force in Bosnia

Dependent variable is: **Oppose**
R^2 = 75.7% R^2(adjusted) = 71.5%
s = 8.163 with 48 – 8 = 40 degrees of freedom

Source	Sum of squares	Degrees of freedom	Mean square	F-ratio
Regression	8315.79	7	1188	17.8
Residual	2665.19	40	66.6296	

Variable	Coefficient	Standard error of coeff	t-ratio
Constant	49.3720	2.153	22.9
CLINTON	–9.17366	3.405	–2.69
USGND	9.06528	2.765	3.28
HUMAN	–13.2720	3.013	–4.41
PKAGREE	–10.1865	3.226	–3.16
USALONE	35.6280	5.181	6.88
USDANG	19.3361	6.204	3.12
ATROC	–36.4372	8.562	–4.26

RAND *MG231-A-3.8*

- USDANG = The suggestion that U.S. forces were being introduced in an environment that might require combat raised opposition by 19.3 points;
- ATROC = The suggestion that U.S. forces would be used to halt atrocities lowered opposition by 36.4 points.

These models did a better job predicting majority support or opposition than accounting for variance: majority or nonmajority support was correctly predicted for 79 percent of the polling questions that asked about approval and for 81 percent of the questions that asked about disapproval.

The regression model correctly predicted majority support or opposition for about 80 percent of the questions using six or seven cues[103] and suggested that questions that mentioned the following

---

[103] Our dummy regression model correctly predicted a majority or nonmajority supporting 79 percent of the time for approval, and 81 percent of the time for opposition. For details, see Appendix D of the technical appendix, published separately.

cues tended to receive *higher* support (or lower opposition) for the use of force than those that didn't: Serb atrocities in Bosnia; acting with allies or as part of a United Nations or international force; President Clinton; a purpose that was humanitarian in nature or a peacekeeping mission (as opposed to combat or peace enforcement); and a reliance on airpower. Questions that mentioned the following cues tended to receive *lower* support (or higher opposition) for the use of force: the United States acting without allies; mention of possible threats to U.S. forces in Bosnia; and the use of ground troops, especially in peace enforcement or combat operations.

Based upon these results and those of the dummy regressions, it should be clear that polling organizations that found unusually high support for sending troops to Bosnia—i.e., well above the average for all polling on the matter—may have done so because their questions or questionnaires were larded with favorable cues that would be expected to enhance support. While still useful in understanding the sorts of factors that affect individuals' willingness to support military action, such results generally overstate support and turn out to be extremely poor predictors of the actual average level of support for a military operation.[104]

These results provide dramatic empirical evidence that cues in question wording can dramatically affect support and opposition, and that questions can easily be constructed to yield majorities that support (or oppose) military operations. It also helps to explain results like PIPA's, which showed much higher support than most other

---

[104] See, for example, the tumescent support for a U.S. military intervention in Bosnia found in polling by the Program on International Policy Attitudes, in which more than 70 percent supported the United States contributing troops to a peacekeeping operation that would enforce an agreement, 66 percent favored the United States contributing troops to a UN force or for the purpose of humanitarian aid and monitoring safe havens, 56 percent favored sending a very large force of ground troops including U.S. troops to occupy contested areas and forcibly stop ethnic cleansing, and 52 percent supported sending U.S. troops who volunteered for a peacekeeping operation. See Program on International Policy Attitudes, February 9–13, 1994, N = 700, April 5–8, 1994, N = 700, June 21–27, 1996, N = 1,227, and February 13–April 20, 1998, N = 2,747. For an assessment of the predictive accuracy of PIPA's results on Bosnia, see Larson (2000).

polling, probably because PIPA's questions typically included a great many cues that would have been expected to boost support.

The result also, somewhat incidentally, suggests that dummy regression analysis can be a very useful technique for systematically teasing out the impacts of question cues on support for and opposition to the use of force, and perhaps other issues, and better establishing the robustness of a result (or, as in the case of the PIPA result, its lack of robustness).

Kosovo

Kosovo is the fourth and last of the major peace operations conducted during the 1990s that we examined. As the president and other administration policymakers pointed out, the merits of Kosovo's case—the possibility of a new round of ethnic cleansing and genocide in the Balkans if the United States and its allies didn't intervene—provided the strongest possible moral argument for humanitarian intervention;[105] it thus provides a nearly ideal case for examining the limits of support for interventions whose justification is to be found in moral, humanitarian, or altruistic considerations, rather than traditional security reasons. This case explores how Americans wrestled with a central moral dilemma: how far the United States should go to halt what most saw as genocide even when a U.S. security interest remained somewhat questionable.

And although the United States did secure NATO approval for the campaign[106] and conducted its air war within a multilateral coalition consisting of other NATO members, as a result of Russian opposition to the war and the strong possibility of a Russian veto, the UN Security Council was never asked to authorize the use of force. It is

---

[105] William J. Clinton, "Statement by the President on Kosovo," March 24, 1999, and "Statement by the President to the Nation," March 24, 1999.

[106] This was only the second time that NATO had approved a military operation.

not clear how much this mattered to overall support,[107] which was, on average, relatively high for the air war and low for the use of ground troops in combat operations.

Background

After a year of effort to resolve the matter through diplomacy and coercion,[108] negotiations at Rambouillet, France, on the status of Kosovo broke down and Serbian President Slobodan Milosevic launched a brutal Serbian campaign of ethnic cleansing against Kosovo in January 1999.[109] Operation Allied Force, the NATO air war over Kosovo, was a response to this campaign.

As was the case with Bosnia, the president essentially forswore the use of U.S. ground troops in a combat role[110] and instead opted to use NATO (primarily U.S.) air power to bring Milosevic to heel so that a multinational peacekeeping force could be introduced once a peace agreement was in place. Unlike Bosnia, however, and quite contrary to expectations, Serbia did not capitulate after a short bombing campaign: the campaign dragged on for 78 days, raising the specter that ground troops in combat operations might be needed and that it might have been premature for the president to rule out their use.

Like Bosnia, although the Congress never took a consistent or clear position as a whole, critics of the administration's evolving strategy on Kosovo in Congress included those who thought the admini-

[107] Although mentioning UN approval tends to boost support in public opinion questions, the cases of Haiti and Bosnia, where UN authorization was present but a majority failed to support each operation, suggest that UN authorization is not a necessary or sufficient condition for majority approval.

[108] These efforts included a show of force by NATO air power in October 1998 dubbed Operation Determined Force, which appears to have temporarily stopped the fighting.

[109] The 1999 campaign was on a much larger scale than a February 1998 "reform" campaign against separatists, mostly the Kosovo Liberation Army, which killed hundreds and drove thousands from their homes.

[110] As the president put it: "NATO has agreed to help implement [the peace agreement] with a peacekeeping force. If NATO is invited to do so, our troops should take part in that mission to keep the peace. But I do not intend to put our troops in Kosovo to fight a war." William J. Clinton, "Statement by the President to the Nation," March 24, 1999.

stration should use military force to help resolve the crisis and those who thought it too willing to send troops,[111] but also those who thought the administration simply should have planned better for both the possibility of a long air war and the possibility that ground combat actually might be needed to ensure success. The result was a shifting set of criticisms of administration policy as the campaign played out on the battlefield,[112] with expressions of congressional sentiment that at one time or another seemed to take every side of the issue of using military force in Kosovo.[113] By comparison, the president may have benefited from the more than six in ten who approved of his job handling at the time.[114]

Overview of Support for the Operation

Support for the war in Kosovo was mixed and, although higher than for the U.S. interventions in Haiti and Bosnia, still much lower than the 1991 Gulf War.[115] There was substantial variability in support in

---

[111] Congressional Quarterly, "Lawmakers Conflicted Over U.S. Involvement in Kosovo Peacekeeping Effort," *1999 CQ Almanac*, Washington, D.C.: CQ Press, 2000, p. 14-20.

[112] For a detailed treatment of shifting legislative sentiment, see the following articles in Congressional Quarterly, *1999 CQ Almanac*, Washington, D.C., 2000: "Republicans Warn Clinton on Use of U.S. Peacekeepers in Kosovo," p. 14-19; "Kosovo Policy Gets Medley of Complaints," pp. 14-19 to 14-20; "House Votes in Support of U.S. Troops in Kosovo," pp. 14-20 to 14-22; "As Crisis Escalates, Lawmakers Reconsider Use of Ground Troops," pp. 14-22 to 14-24; "War Powers Act Forces House Vote; Senate Buys More Time," p. 14-24; and "Senate Kills 'All Necessary Force' Resolution," pp. 14-25 to 14-26.

[113] For example, the House voted to authorize peacekeepers in Kosovo (H Con Res 42, March 11) but later refused, on a tie vote, to back the air war even after it had begun, and prohibited the use of U.S. ground forces unless authorized by law (HR 1569, April 28). For its part, the Senate adopted a resolution in support of the NATO air strikes (S Con Res 21) and tabled (killed) one amendment that would have prohibited the use of ground forces in Kosovo, except for peacekeepers, unless Congress authorized them by a joint resolution or declared war, and another that would have authorized the president to use "all necessary force" to prevail in Kosovo.

[114] Gallup, March 12–14, 1999, N=1,024.

[115] See Frank Newport, "Public Support for U.S. Involvement in Yugoslavia Lower Than for Gulf War, Other Foreign Engagements," The Gallup Organization, March 30, 1999, which notes that public support for U.S. involvement in the Yugoslavian conflict was at the low end of the historical spectrum when compared to public opinion about other U.S. foreign interventions of the past two decades, but still higher than Haiti and Bosnia.

questions that asked about military action in Kosovo: the results were highly sensitive to cues about whether troops would be introduced in a peaceful or dangerous environment, what types of forces (e.g., air versus ground) would be used, and the specific ways the questions suggested they might be used; they were also sensitive to the timing of the poll.[116] For these reasons, rather than presenting global averages, we will focus on a comparison of support for various military options over time (Table 3.11).

Although support for the different options changed over time,[117] support for the air war and peacekeeping operations in Kosovo was substantially—and consistently—higher than support for peace enforcement or combat operations.[118]

---

[116] For a compilation of public opinion data, see The Gallup Organization, "Poll Topics & Trends: Kosovo," The Gallup Organization, available at http://www.gallup.com/poll/topics/kosovo.asp.

[117] A running record of Gallup's analyses of changing public attitudes on the U.S. intervention in Kosovo can be found in the following publications of The Gallup Organization: Lydia Saad, "Americans Hesitant, As Usual, About U.S. Military Action in the Balkans," March 24, 1999; Mark Gillespie, "Support Grows for Kosovo Mission, But Public Still Divided," March 26, 1999; Mark Gillespie, "Support for Mission Holds Steady, But Skepticism Grows," April 2, 1999; Frank Newport, "Despite Skepticism, Support Grows for U.S. Involvement in Kosovo Crisis," April 8, 1999; Frank Newport, "Gradual Increase in American Support for Kosovo Involvement Continues," April 16, 1999; Frank Newport, "Public Support for U.S. Involvement in Kosovo Diminishing," April 29, 1999; Mark Gillespie, "Support for NATO Air Strikes Hold Steady in Wake of Embassy Attack," May 11, 1999; Frank Newport, "Support for U.S. Kosovo Involvement Drops; Americans Strongly Favor Cease-Fire in Order to Negotiate Peace; Clinton Approval Drops to Lowest Level in Three Years," May 26, 1999; Frank Newport, "Americans Endorse Idea of Peace Plan, But Remain Skeptical of Serb Compliance," June 7, 1999; Frank Newport, "New Poll on Kosovo Finds an Underwhelmed Public," June 11, 1999; Frank Newport, "Americans Hesitant to Give Clinton Credit for Kosovo Peace," June 15, 1999.

[118] To construct the table, we calculated the average support in questions that asked about the air war, peacekeeping, peace enforcement, and ground combat in each month of the war. Questions were coded as being about the air war if they asked about approval for the air war or bombing; peacekeeping if they used the term "peacekeeping" or indicated that the question had in mind introducing U.S. troops following the establishment of a peace; peace enforcement if the question suggested that U.S. troops would be used to force the combatants to a peace agreement; and ground combat if the questions suggested that ground troops would be used in combat operations.

Table 3.11
Comparison of Support for Air War and Ground Options

	Average percent supporting each option:			
	Air War	Peace-Keeping	Peace Enforcement	Ground Combat
March 24–31	52.8%	54.8%	38.0%	NA
April 1–30	59.5	65.2	45.9	46.4%
May 1–31	51.4	NA	45.5	28.5
June 1–10	62.0[a]	54.5 [b]	NA	27.0 [c]
Overall average	56.4% [d]	59.5% [e]	43.1% [f]	34.1% [g]

NOTES: NA = Not available.
[a] One question only, by PSRA on June 9–13, 1999.
[b] Based upon six questions asked between June 1 and June 10, 1999.
[c] One question only, by Opinion Dynamics on June 2–3, 1999.
[d] Average based on a total of 30 questions that asked about support for the air war.
[e] Based on a total of 26 questions that asked about U.S. ground troops in a peace-keeping role.
[f] Based on a total of 15 questions that asked about U.S. ground troops in a peace enforcement role.
[g] Based on a total of nine questions that asked about U.S. ground troops in a combat role.

A paired comparison of 20 questions that asked about support for air and ground options in the same poll produced results comparable to those in the table: support for air options was anywhere from 7 to 16 percentage points higher than that for ground options.[119] As will be discussed, this generally reflected the public's aversion to placing U.S. troops in a situation involving interests that were only of secondary importance.

As shown in the table, support for the air war climbed in April and then fell back again in May, apparently as a result of increased criticism of the air campaign that followed a number of high-profile incidents of collateral damage and a growing fear that an air war alone might not force Milosevic's capitulation and that ground combat operations might therefore be needed. Support for the use of U.S.

[119] Three questions were from ABC News/Washington Post's polling on the matter, five were from Gallup, and two were from Princeton Survey Research Associates.

ground troops in peacekeeping and peace enforcement show the same basic pattern over time, although only the former was typically supported by a majority, while support for using U.S. troops in a ground combat role showed a steep decline from April to May and remained below three in ten in May and June.

Although initial support for the president's handling of the situation in Kosovo in March averaged only 49 percent, on average, a majority of Americans consistently supported the president's handling of Kosovo thereafter;[120] on average, 52 percent approved of the president's handling of the Kosovo situation over the March to June 1999 period,[121] and 55 percent approved of the president's decision to take military action against Serbia in polling done in March and April 1999;[122] by the time of Milosevic's capitulation in June, 68 percent said they thought taking military action in Kosovo had been the right decision.[123]

More recent polling on support for U.S. troops in Kosovo has hovered around 50 percent: 51 percent supported U.S. troops in Kosovo in March 2000,[124] and 53 percent supported a U.S. presence in April 2000.[125] However, as was mentioned earlier, in the most recent poll, in August 2001, only 47 percent of those polled approved of President Bush's decision to keep U.S. troops in Kosovo and Bosnia.[126]

---

[120] The average level of approval for 11 questions in March was 59 percent, the average of 14 questions in April was 54 percent, the average of four questions in May was 52 percent, and the average of six questions in June was 55 percent.

[121] A total of 35 polls asked questions about the president's handling of the Kosovo issue over the period March 19 to June 14, 1999.

[122] A total of five questions asked about approval of the president's decision to take military action in Kosovo between March 25, 1999 and April 8–9, 1999.

[123] Pew/PSRA, June 9–13, 1999, N=1,153.

[124] Pew Research Center/PSRA, March 15–19, 2000, N=1,184.

[125] Gallup/CNN/USA Today, April 7–9, 2000, N = 1,006. This represented a decline from the 66 percent who supported in two questions from Gallup in June 1999: Gallup, June 11–13, 1999, N=1,012, and June 25–27, 1999, N=1,016.

[126] Pew Research Center/PSRA, August 2–8, 2001, N=1,277.

Sources and Fault Lines in Support

Americans' beliefs about the nature of the United States' stakes, its prospects for success, and the likely costs of action in Kosovo also figured in their support or opposition to the operation: statistically significant results were observed in bivariate tests of association between support and these beliefs, and between support and membership in the president's party (Table 3.12).[127] The president may also have benefited from a relatively high approval rating.

Our reduced-form statistical models for Kosovo were able to correctly predict support or opposition for 66 percent of the respondents based upon these factors (the only difference between the two models was the inclusion of a variable for financial costs).

As shown in the table, according to our models the most important factor in predicting support or opposition was race; blacks were

Table 3.12
Kosovo: Marginal Probability from Probit Estimates of Approval (Q8)

Variables	Change in Probability at Mean Values	Change in Probability at Mean Values
Moral stakes (Q16b)	0.183 (0.037)***	0.191 (0.038)***
Prospects (Q17c)	0.107 (0.040)***	0.130 (0.038)***
Casualties (Q17a)	–0.040 (0.045)	–0.051 (0.044)
Financial costs (Q17b)	–0.068 (0.028)**	
Party 1 if Republican†	–0.062 (0.066)	–0.068 (0.065)
Party 1 if Independent†	–0.112 (0.065)*	–0.121 (0.064)*
Information consumption (Q4b)	0.093 (0.034)***	0.094 (0.034)***
Race 1 if black†	–0.199 (0.077)***	–0.207 (0.075)***
Gender 1 if female†	–0.032 (0.054)	–0.036 (0.054)
Wald Chi-square (Prod > Chi2)	63.69 (0.000)	58.88 (0.000)
Log likelihood	–278.57	–282.65
Observations	464	464
Correctly specified	66%	66%

† dF/dx is for discrete change of dummy variable from 0 to 1.
* Significant at 10%.
** Significant at 5%.
*** Significant at 1%.
Robust standard errors in parentheses.
SOURCE: Pew, April 15–18, 1999.

[127] Results are reported in Appendix E of the technical appendix, published separately.

nearly 20 percent more likely than whites to oppose military action in Kosovo. The belief that the United States had moral interests in Kosovo (there were no questions that asked about U.S. security interests in this poll) was the next most important predictor of support and opposition, and increased the probability of support by 20 percent. Next most important were membership in the president's party, beliefs about the prospects for success, information consumption, and the expected financial costs of the war.[128] Although expectations about casualties were associated with support on a bivariate basis, it washed out in the model, possibly because most reckoned that the air war would minimize U.S. casualties.[129]

The relationship between Americans' partisan orientations and their beliefs, and beliefs about the nature of the United States' stakes, its prospects for success, and the likely costs of action in Kosovo were as follows:

- **Partisan leadership and followership.** Support, and key beliefs about the nature of the stakes, the prospects for success, and concern about casualties all were partisan-coded, with Democrats generally holding more favorable beliefs and Republicans generally holding less favorable ones.[130]
- **Stakes in terms of security interests.** Although there were some exceptions,[131] majorities generally failed to perceive U.S. vital or

---

[128] The Pew Research Center/PSRA found 57 percent who approved of the president's job handling at the time of the poll we used in our statistical modeling. Pew/PSRA, April 15–18, 1999, N–751.

[129] To verify and cross-validate the model and ensure its robustness, we also used the coefficients estimated in this model to predict support or opposition for respondents in another poll: 68 percent of the respondents were correctly predicted.

[130] For cross-tabulations of support and key beliefs associated with Kosovo, see Appendix E of the technical appendix, published separately.

[131] Two exceptions were polling in April in which 55 percent said they thought that helping to stop Serb actions in Kosovo was in the nation's interest, and 56 percent said they found unconvincing the argument that Kosovo was far from the United States, that the United States had no real interests there, and that it therefore would be wrong to risk the lives of American soldiers in a NATO operation there. NPR/Kaiser/Harvard/ICR, April 23–28, 1999, N=1,022 and PIPA, May 13–17, 1999, N=1,206.

national security interests in Kosovo. For example, between 37 and 43 percent said that the United States needed to be involved to protect its own interests in February–March 1999,[132] 43 percent said stopping Serb actions in Kosovo was in the national interest in March,[133] 27 to 47 percent said the United States had vital interests in Kosovo over the March–April period,[134] and only 35 to 41 percent said that what happened in Kosovo was very important to the interests of the United States in March–May.[135]

- **Stakes in terms of moral interests.** Rather, U.S. stakes in Kosovo generally were viewed as moral and humanitarian, and this belief appears to have been the prime source of support for the operation even before it had begun:[136] the percentage who said the United States had a moral obligation to help keep the peace grew from 52 percent in February to 64 percent in March,[137] 66 to 71 percent of those polled in April 1999 said

[132] Three questions: Gallup, February 19–21, 1999, N = 1,000, March 19–21, 1999, N = 1,018, and March 25, 1999, N = 675. Comparable to the U.S. intervention in Bosnia in December 1995, when a tepid 36 percent held that belief, and the 44 percent in September 1994 who believed that the United States had interests in Haiti that were worth protecting by sending troops.

[133] Time/CNN/Yankelovich, March 25, 1999, N=1,049.

[134] Six questions: ABC News/Washington Post, March 11–14, 1999, N = 1,515, March 23, 1999, N = 534, March 26–28, 1999, N = 895, March 28–30, 1999, N = 939, April 5–6, 1999, N = 1,011, and April 8, 1999, N = 506.

[135] Four questions: CBS News, March 23–24, 1999, N = 527, April 1, 1999, N = 411, April 5–6, 1999, N = 811, and May 11, 1999, N = 578.

[136] In fact, those believing that the United States had a moral obligation in Kosovo rose by 10–15 points early in the operation, with some seven in ten subscribing to this view by early April (polling organizations thereafter stopped asking questions about this). Even at the end of the conflict in early June, 60 percent felt that the United States had a moral obligation to use military force to prevent genocide in the future.

[137] Three questions: Gallup, February 19–21, 1999, N = 1,000, March 19–21, 1999, N = 1,018, and March 25, 1999, N = 675. Compared to public opinion on past operations, the 64 percent who believed that the United States had a moral obligation at the beginning of the war was more than 10 points higher than the 53 percent who felt that way about Bosnia in late November 1995, and roughly comparable to the 67 percent in September 1994 who felt that it was worth sending U.S. troops to Haiti to stop the abuse of human rights that was occurring there.

the United States had a moral obligation to help establish peace in Kosovo,[138] and 58 percent of those polled in April 1999 said that they thought the United States had a moral obligation to try to help stop Serb actions in Kosovo;[139] 69 percent of those polled in early April said that the United States had a moral obligation to use U.S. ground troops to help the Kosovo refugees return to their homes and live in peace.[140]

- **Prospects for success.** As with the other peace operations we examined, the Kosovo operation was generally viewed as having somewhat uncertain prospects. Polling data suggest that the percentage who were optimistic about the success of the U.S. and NATO action declined by early- to mid-April as the air war failed to deliver the quick victory that some administration officials had suggested. According to polling by Gallup, only 46 percent in early April were confident that the United States would accomplish its goals without sending in U.S. ground troops,[141] while the percentage who were confident that the U.S. effort to establish peace would succeed ranged from 49 percent in February to 65 percent in June.[142] The perceived prospects for the Kosovo peacekeeping venture were roughly comparable to those in Haiti and Bosnia.[143]
- **Expected costs.** Most Americans did not anticipate particularly high casualties—the average (i.e., median) respondent antici-

[138] Two questions: ABC News/Washington Post, April 5–6, 1999, N = 1,011, and April 8, 1999, N = 506.

[139] Those who cited both a moral obligation and a national interest were asked which was more important: 68 percent cited the former and 26 percent cited the latter. NPR/Kaiser/Harvard/ICR, April 23–28, 1999, N=1,022.

[140] Gallup, April 6–7, 1999, N=1,055.

[141] Gallup, April 6–7, 1999, N=1,055.

[142] Three questions: Gallup, February 19–21, 1999, N = 1,000, June 11–13, 1999, N=1,022, and June 25–27, 1999, N=1,016.

[143] For Haiti, 50–52 percent were very or somewhat confident that the United States would achieve its goals, while 49–55 percent were very or somewhat confident that the operation would meet its timetable; the percentages for Bosnia were 44 and 46 percent, respectively.

pated fewer than 100 U.S. deaths in Kosovo[144]—but majorities worried about casualties during most of the war.[145] The expectation of relatively low casualties may in part have been due to the fact that at the beginning of the operation the president forswore ground combat operations, and the military effort relied upon the casualty-minimizing use of airpower. Other data from Gallup show that confidence that the United States would achieve its goals with very few or no American casualties declined from 54 percent in February to 49 percent in April, and then climbed again to the 56–62 percent range in June.[146] Nevertheless, 52 percent of those polled in June thought it at least somewhat likely that the peacekeeping mission in Kosovo would result in a significant number of casualties among U.S. ground troops.[147]

- **Balancing costs and benefits.** A second result of these beliefs, in addition to the level of support for the military action, was a fairly limited willingness to tolerate casualties in Kosovo. Nevertheless, the ultimate success of the operation, in terms of both the outcome and the absence of casualties, ultimately led most to judge the war as being, in some sense, "worth it." Because so

---

[144] Fifty-two percent of those polled by Gallup in March 1999 and 57 percent of those polled by Newsweek/PSRA in June 1999 expected 100 or fewer casualties. Gallup, March 25, 1999, N = 675, and Newsweek/PSRA, June 10–11, 1999, N = 756. A substantial 32 percent were unable or unwilling to render an opinion on Gallup's question. The median is the case at the 50th percentile, with an equal number or percentage of respondents having a lower value as a higher one.

[145] Three questions from March to May 1999 that asked how worried respondents were that U.S. troops might suffer casualties ranged from 55 to 66 percent; that percentage had declined by mid-June, when it was becoming clear that U.S. troops would be introduced into Kosovo as peacekeepers. Pew/PSRA, March 24–30, 1999, N = 1,786, April 15–18, 1999, N = 1,000, and May 12–16, 1999, N = 1,179.

[146] Four questions: Gallup, February 19–21, 1999, N = 1,000, April 6–7, 1999, N = 1,055, June 11–13, 1999, N = 1,022, and June 25–27, 1999, N = 1,016. Only 14–19 percent were "very confident" that the United States would be able to accomplish its goals with very few or no American casualties, a smaller percentage than observed in Somalia (27 percent) or Haiti (21–23 percent), but a larger percentage than observed in Bosnia (12 percent), an operation in which sensitivity to U.S. casualties appears to have been relatively high.

[147] Gallup/CNN/USA Today, June 10, 1999, N=521.

many different questions were asked about this, we will summarize the results chronologically:

- In late March, only 37–45 percent agreed that it would be worth the loss of some American soldiers' lives if the United States could help bring peace to Kosovo,[148] and only 33 percent agreed that if it could bring peace, U.S. involvement in a war in Kosovo would be worth the loss of a few American soldiers' lives,[149] but 54 percent said it was worth *risking* the lives of some American soldiers to demonstrate that Serbia should not get away with killing and forcing people from their homes in Kosovo.[150]
- In one poll in early April, 45 percent said that it would be worth the loss of some American lives if it would bring peace to Kosovo, and 32 percent said it would be worth the loss of 100 lives.[151] In another poll in early April, only 50 percent of those polled by Gallup judged the withdrawal of Serb forces and the return of refugees to be worth having a few American casualties in a limited military action, while only 12 percent said it would be worth many casualties in a lengthy military action.[152] At about the same time, however, 53 percent disagreed with the suggestion that it was not worth *risking* the lives of American soldiers to bring peace to Kosovo.
- By late April, 54 percent agreed with the statement that winning the war in Kosovo was not worth the loss of even a single life.[153]

---

[148] Two questions: ABC News, March 23, 1999, N=534, and March 26, 1999, N=518.

[149] Fox News/Opinion Dynamics, March 24–25, 1999, N = 900. Twenty-six percent said it would be worth the loss of a few American lives, and another 7 percent said it would be worth the loss of many lives, if necessary.

[150] Los Angeles Times, March 25, 1999, N=544.

[151] ABC News/Washington Post, April 5–6, 1999, N=1,011.

[152] Gallup/CNN/USA Today, April 6–7, 1999, N=1,055.

[153] Fox News/Opinion Dynamics, April 21–22, 1999, N=942.

– In early June, 47 percent said that the situation in Kosovo was worth going to war over, but that increased to 52 percent by late June;[154] 58 percent in late June, and 53 percent in late July, said that the U.S. involvement in the war in Kosovo ultimately was worth it.[155]

Figure 3.9 presents the results from seven polls done in the spring of 1999 in which respondents were asked about their prospective support for Kosovo given various hypothesized levels of U.S. casualties; the x-axis is the log of the hypothesized number of casualties, and the y-axis is the percentage who said that they would support a war in Kosovo if there were that many casualties.

As shown in the figure, with the exception of PIPA's predictably bullish results, which stand alone in showing majorities willing to accept casualties in Kosovo, a majority typically failed to support the operation when even a modest number of hypothesized casualties was suggested. Although the casualties variable washed out in our multivariate statistical modeling (probably because the operation was a low-casualty air war), the consistent bivariate association between support and casualties provides strong evidence that the willingness to support the U.S.-NATO operation in Kosovo was very closely related to beliefs about casualties, and that few expressed a willingness to support the operation if many casualties were incurred.

The implication is that if casualties had climbed—and particularly if growing casualties had occurred without accompanying evidence that the U.S.-NATO coalition was making progress on the ground—support could well have followed the sort of decline described by the curves in Figure 3.9. Since the air war and the subsequent peace operation were essentially casualty-free, Americans' basic view seems to have been one of tolerance rather than robust support.

---

[154] Two questions: Gallup/CNN/USA Today, June 10, 1999, N = 521, and June 25–27, 1999, N = 1,016.

[155] Two questions: NBC News/Wall Street Journal/Teeter, June 16–19, 1999, N = 2,011, and July 24–26, 1999, N = 1,007.

Figure 3.9
Prospective Willingness to Tolerate Casualties in Kosovo, April 1999

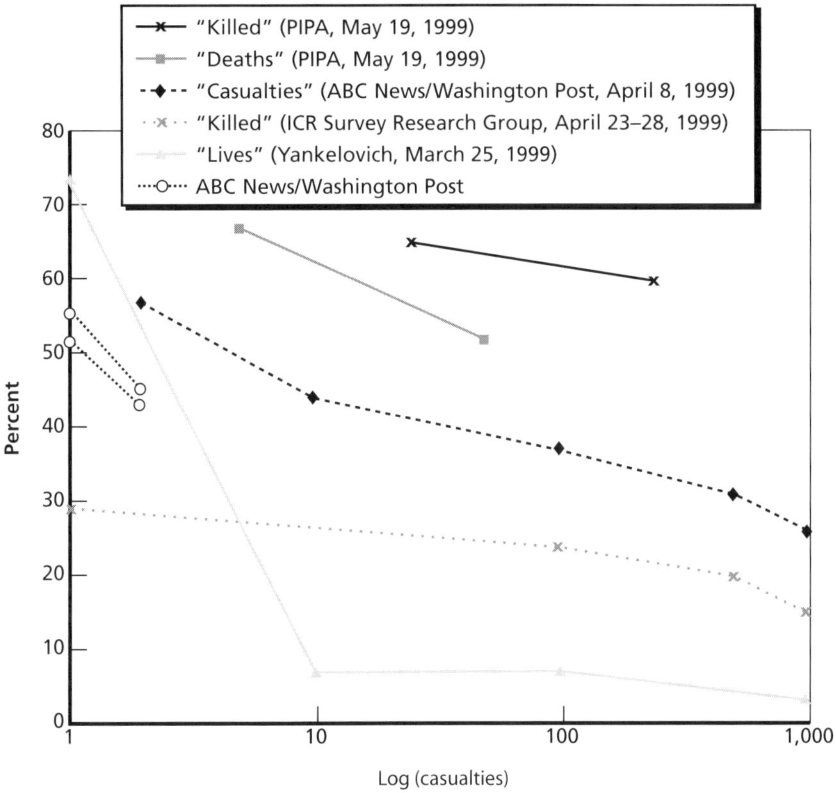

RAND *MG231-A-3-9*

NOTE: Question wordings are available from the lead author.

Key Lessons From the Peace Operations of the 1990s

We now offer some key lessons from our analyses of the public opinion on the peace operations of the 1990s:

- **Somalia.** The key lesson of Somalia is that preferences regarding withdrawal or escalation are tied to beliefs about the importance of the stakes and the prospects for success, and that a loss of faith in the importance of the campaign—for example, as a result of a change in objectives—or in the prospects for the campaign is likely to reduce support and the public's willingness to tolerate additional casualties. Moreover, when faced with a situation where few—including national leaders—believe any longer in the worth of the operation, even as casualties seem likely to grow, the most likely reaction of members of the public will be to prefer an orderly withdrawal, i.e., one that follows the recovery of servicemen held hostage and provides a "decent interval" for purposes of preserving national honor. Put simply, Americans are more inclined to be "casualty-phobic" than "defeat-phobic" when the stakes are widely viewed as modest. In such cases, exercises of presidential rhetoric seem unlikely to change public attitudes much.

- **Haiti.** The key lesson of Haiti is that even in cases where a peace operation has both United Nations authorization and multilateral participation, and where the operation goes well and avoids casualties, support may still be quite low if national leaders and the public don't believe that the stakes are particularly important or that it has particularly good prospects for succeeding. The avoidance of casualties in such cases may create a permissive public opinion environment, as few will care enough to expend the energy to actively express their opposition.
- **Bosnia.** This case also provides strong evidence that support—including support for using ground troops—is related to key beliefs about the stakes involved, the prospects for success, and expectations regarding likely casualties, and that these beliefs—and ultimately, support or opposition—flowed from partisan leadership and followership. The fact that only four in ten supported the operation in Bosnia in spite of United Nations authorization and NATO participation is largely attributable to underlying, generally unfavorable beliefs about the operation. Nevertheless, as in Haiti, the avoidance of casualties in Bosnia generally kept active public opposition to a minimum.

- **Kosovo.** This case demonstrates public ambivalence arising from a situation that engaged important U.S. moral and humanitarian interests but was otherwise judged to be of questionable importance to the nation's security interests and offered questionable prospects for a successful outcome. The result was both a moral dilemma—a desire for the United States to act to prevent further atrocities, but without incurring risks and costs that were incommensurate with the United States' modest stakes and prospects in the situation—and highly constrained support for an air war. In the end, the Clinton administration and NATO conducted the war in Kosovo in a way that generally met with most Americans' approval: it minimized the risks of U.S. casualties and prepared the way for the introduction of ground troops as peacekeepers in a permissive environment, while assiduously avoiding the commitment of U.S. troops to combat or peace enforcement operations. This appears to have resolved successfully the moral dilemma faced by most Americans: to do something in Kosovo, without making sacrifices that were disproportionately high given the secondary nature of the perceived stakes.

Chapter Conclusions

This chapter has presented data on four peace operations from the 1990s in which the absence of a favorable bipartisan consensus among national leaders in support of the operation led to partisan differences in beliefs about each operation's specific merits—the nature of the stakes involved, the prospects for success, and the likely costs—and, ultimately, to support that also was partisan, relatively low, and highly conditional.

In the next two chapters, we analyze the public opinion data on military operations conducted under the color of the global war on terrorism.

CHAPTER FOUR

9/11 and Operation Enduring Freedom in Afghanistan

In the most deadly terrorist attack in U.S. history, on the morning of September 11, 2001, 19 terrorists from Osama bin Laden's Al Qaeda group hijacked four U.S. airliners, flying two into the twin towers of the World Trade Center in New York City and another into the Pentagon in northern Virginia; the fourth airliner crashed in Pennsylvania after the passengers, apparently having learned of the other attacks, rebelled against the hijackers before their aircraft could be used against another target. All told, the attacks claimed nearly three thousand victims.

From the beginning, President Bush emphasized that the United States would hunt down and punish those responsible for the attacks[1] and that no distinction would be made between the terrorists who committed the acts and those who harbored them.[2] On September 15, the president promised "a comprehensive assault on terrorism," a "series of decisive actions against terrorist organizations and those who harbor or support them."[3] And he warned:

> I will not settle for a token act. Our response must be sweeping, sustained and effective. You will be asked for your patience; for

---

[1] George W. Bush, "Remarks by the President After Two Planes Crash Into World Trade Center" and "Remarks by the President Upon Arrival at Barksdale Air Force Base," September 11, 2001.

[2] George W. Bush, "Statement by the President in His Address to the Nation," September 11, 2001.

[3] George W. Bush, "Radio Address of the President to the Nation," September 15, 2001.

> the conflict will not be short. You will be asked for resolve; for the conflict will not be easy. You will be asked for your strength, because the course to victory may be long.[4]

In a departure from the typically partisan divisions that had accompanied most of the U.S. military operations over the preceding decade,[5] the president received strong and vocal bipartisan support in the wake of the 9/11 attacks and in support of his statements regarding his administration's planned response.[6] The president's job approval rating also skyrocketed, in part because of the nature of the crisis and in part because of the show of bipartisan support for his administration's efforts to meet the challenge of terrorism.[7] Thus, as a result of the 9/11 attacks, a "global war on terrorism" (GWOT) was launched that targeted not just Al Qaeda but also other terrorist groups with global reach.[8] This war would include military actions of varied scope and scale in Afghanistan, the Philippines, and Iraq, with the distinct possibility of military action elsewhere.

Support in the Aftermath of the Attacks

Public attitudes toward military action undertaken in support of the war on terrorism—including the use of ground troops—and the ad-

---

[4] Ibid.

[5] There was bipartisan congressional support for the initial intervention in Somalia, and, ultimately, a bipartisan expression of support for the first Gulf War in 1991. See Larson (1996a and 1996b). But as was seen in the last chapter, there were partisan divisions during the Bosnia, Haiti, and Kosovo interventions.

[6] As the president observed in his September 15 radio address, "In Washington, D.C., the political parties and both Houses of Congress have shown remarkable unity, and I'm deeply grateful. A terrorist attack designed to tear us apart has instead bound us together as a nation."

[7] President Bush's Gallup presidential approval rating rose from 51 to 86 percent. Gallup, September 7–11, 2001, N=1,004, and September 14–15, 2001, N=1,032.

[8] See George W. Bush, "Remarks by the President to the Warsaw Conference on Combating Terrorism," November 6, 2001.

ministration's handling of the terrorism issue were generally quite favorable. [9,10]

In fact, and in stark contrast to the tepid support for the use of ground troops in the peace operations of the 1990s that were described in the last chapter, even before 9/11, Americans showed a readiness to support the use of U.S. ground troops against terrorist groups: polling by Gallup/CNN/USA Today and the Chicago Council on Foreign Relations in the fall of 1998 showed anywhere from 57 to 65 percent supporting the use of ground troops for this purpose.[11]

Support for Military Action

Eight in ten or more of those polled after the 9/11 attacks approved of U.S. military action against the terrorists and their bases of support. For example, as shown in Table 4.1, more than four out of five of those polled on September 11 supported the use of force against those responsible for the attacks.

---

[9] An excellent compilation and analysis of a wide range of data on American attitudes toward terrorism and the U.S. response before and after 9/11 can be found in Huddy, Khatib, and Capelos (2002). Another excellent analysis of the American public's response to 9/11 can be found in Smith, Rasinski, and Toce (2001) and Rasinski, Berktold, Smith, and Albertson (2002).

[10] See the following publications of The Gallup Organization: David W. Moore, "Americans See Terrorist Attacks as 'Act of War'; But Want Culprits Clearly Identified Before United States Retaliates," September 12, 2001; Lydia Saad, "Americans Clearly Support a Military Response to Terrorist Assault," September 13, 2001; Frank Newport, "Retaliation; Americans Continue to Be Strongly Behind Retaliatory Military Actions," September 24, 2001; and Frank Newport, "Americans Remain Strongly in Favor of Military Retaliation; Nine Out of 10 Support Military Action Against Those Responsible for Terrorist Attacks," September 27, 2001.

[11] The Gallup question was: "Would you generally approve or disapprove of future attacks by the United States using . . . ground troops . . . to attack terrorist groups or their facilities?" The Gallup/CCFR question was: "In order to combat international terrorism, please say whether you favor or oppose each of the following measures. How about attacks by U.S. ground troops against terrorist training camps and other facilities?" Gallup/CNN/USA Today, August 21–23, 1998, N=1,317, and CCFR/Gallup, October 15–November 10, 1998, N=1,507. On August 20, 1998, the United States launched cruise missile strikes against terrorist targets in Sudan and Afghanistan; the above-cited polling suggests that majorities of Americans would have supported an even greater commitment of force that offered a greater risk of U.S. casualties.

Table 4.1
Support for U.S. Military Action, September 11, 2001

(As you have probably heard, apparent terrorist attacks today (September 11, 2001) destroyed the World Trade Towers in New York City, damaged the Pentagon in Washington D.C. and caused a plane crash in Pennsylvania. Apparently these attacks were carried out by terrorists who hijacked commercial airplanes.)...

If the United States can identify the groups or nations responsible for today's attacks, would you support or oppose taking military action against them?

Support	94%
Oppose	3
No opinion	3

What if that meant getting into a war: in that case would you support or oppose taking military action (against the groups or nations responsible for today's terrorist attacks)?*

Support	92% (~86% of total sample)
Oppose	4
No opinion	4

Apart from those responsible for today's attacks, would you support or oppose the U.S. (United States) taking military action against countries that assist or shelter terrorists?

Support	84%
Oppose	11
No opinion	5

*Asked of those who said if the United States can identify the groups or nations responsible for the attacks, they would support taking military action against them (94 percent).
SOURCE: ABC News/Washington Post, September 11, 2001, N=608.

Majorities or pluralities also consistently supported mounting a long-term war to defeat global terrorist networks over a more focused campaign that would only punish those groups responsible for the 9/11 attacks.[12] Equally important, most seemed undeterred by the

[12] See the following publications of The Gallup Organization: Frank Newport, "Overwhelming Support for War Continues; Americans Have Also Become More Likely to Support Long-Term War Against Global Terrorism," November 29, 2001; David W. Moore, "Public Optimistic on Progress of War on Terrorism; Willing to See War Expanded to Other Countries," January 25, 2002; Frank Newport, "Taking the War Beyond Afghanistan: Americans Generally Support Military Action in Iran, Iraq, and the Philippines," February 4, 2002; and Jeffrey M. Jones, "Support for Military Effort Remains High; Americans Less Positive in their Assessment of Progress in War on Terrorism," March 12, 2002.

prospect of a wider war, and they supported action against any other countries that might be assisting terrorist organizations.[13]

The campaign began military action against the Al Qaeda organization and the Taliban who harbored them in Afghanistan. U.S. military operations in Afghanistan, dubbed Operation Enduring Freedom,[14] began on October 7, 2001.

From the beginning, the operation exhibited what may have been the highest sustained levels of support for a military operation since World War II:[15] Newsweek's polling in the first months of the war found 86–90 percent approving the military action against terrorism,[16] for example, and others had similar findings.[17]

Moreover, Gallup's questions on approval for U.S. military action in Afghanistan averaged 87 percent,[18] the average level of approval for the use of ground troops in Afghanistan between Septem-

---

Between October 2001 and June 2002, Gallup asked the following question four times: "Which of the following comes closest to your view about the actions the United States should take to deal with terrorism: [ROTATED: the U.S. should mount a long-term war to defeat global terrorist networks, the U.S. should take military action ONLY to punish specific terrorist groups responsible for the attacks on the World Trade Center, or the U.S. should not take military action but should rely only on economic and diplomatic efforts to deal with terrorism]?" Those favoring a long-term war ranged between 49 and 62 percent, those favoring punishing the specific terrorist groups ranged between 31 and 43 percent, and those favoring reliance on only diplomatic and economic efforts ranged between 5 and 10 percent.

[13] We present data on this question at the end of this chapter.

[14] The operation earlier had been named "Infinite Justice," but some Muslims objected to the name, arguing that only Allah could dispense such justice; to accommodate these sensitivities, the name was changed to "Enduring Freedom."

[15] See David W. Moore, "Support for War on Terrorism Rivals Support for WWII; Vietnam War Received Least Support," The Gallup Organization, October 3, 2001.

[16] On nine occasions between October 11 and December 13, 2001, Newsweek asked "Do you approve or disapprove of the current U.S. military action against terrorism?" The percentage approving ranged from 86 to 90 percent, with an average level of 88 percent.

[17] David W. Moore, "Public Overwhelmingly Backs Bush in Attacks on Afghanistan; Expects New Terrorist Attacks," The Gallup Organization, October 8, 2001; and Frank Newport, "Support For Military Action Remains Strong; Eight Out of 10 Americans Also Support the Use of Ground Troops," The Gallup Organization, October 24, 2001.

[18] Gallup asked about approval for U.S. military action in Afghanistan 13 times between September 2001 and September 2002.

ber 2001 and June 2002 was 72 percent,[19] and 91 percent approved of the presence of U.S. troops in Afghanistan in a November poll;[20] in polling in November 2001 and January 2002, the percentages saying that sending military forces to Afghanistan had *not* been a mistake were 89 and 93 percent, respectively.[21] By May 2003, a slight majority supported committing additional troops for peacekeeping operations in Afghanistan.[22] Put simply, support for the use of U.S. forces, including ground troops, was consistently very high.[23]

The structure of support for U.S. military action in Afghanistan also appears to have been robust, with large majorities of respondents consistently strongly supporting military action (see Figure 4.1).

Somewhat remarkably, support for military action was not predicated upon a naïve or unduly optimistic view of the risks and challenges that lay ahead. Most Americans appear to have accepted the president's argument that the GWOT would be a long, difficult, and costly war (Table 4.2).

In fact, as shown in the table, the expectation of a long and difficult war was far more prevalent in the aftermath of 9/11 than it had been after Pearl Harbor in December 1941; as shown, whereas about nine out of ten expected a long and difficult war against terrorism, only about half to two-thirds actually had held such beliefs in December 1941.[24]

---

[19] A total of 17 polls asked questions on this between September 2001 and June 2002.

[20] Gallup/CNN/USA Today, November 26–27, 2001, N=1,025.

[21] Gallup, November 8–11, 2001, N=1,005, and January 7–9, 2002, N=1,015.

[22] Fox News/Opinion Dynamics, May 6–7, 2003, N=900. The question read: "Recently, Afghanistan's President Hamid Karzai asked the United States to commit more troops to help keep the peace in his country. Would you favor or oppose sending more U.S. (United States) troops to help keep the peace in Afghanistan? (If Favor or Oppose, ask:) Is that strongly or somewhat?" Twenty-six percent strongly favored and another 28 percent somewhat favored committing more troops.

[23] See Frank Newport, "Support For Military Action Remains Strong; Eight Out of 10 Americans Also Support the Use of Ground Troops," The Gallup Organization, October 24, 2001.

[24] Of course, the standard for what constitutes a "long and difficult war" could well have changed since 1941.

Figure 4.1
Structure of Support for Afghanistan

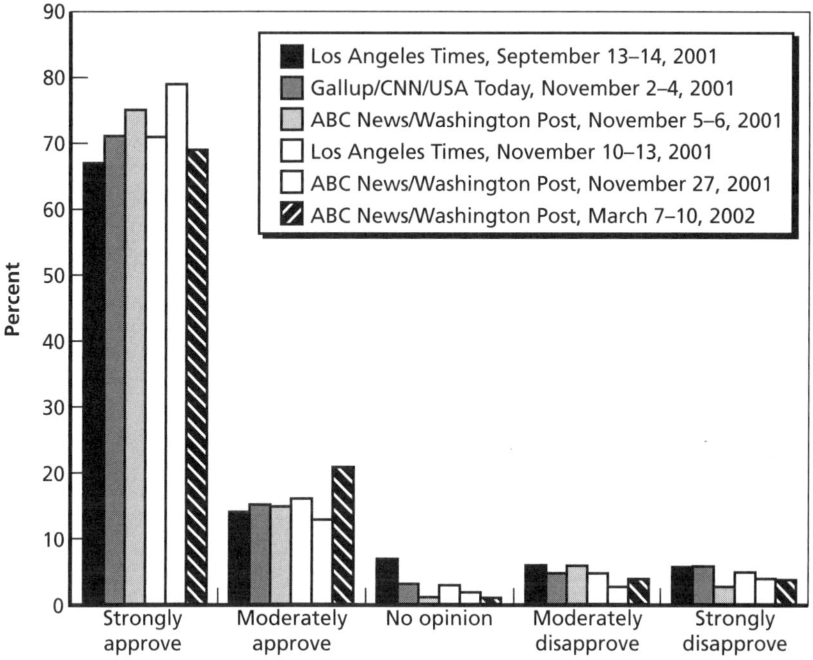

RAND *MG231-A-4.1*

Moreover, most Americans were undeterred by the prospect of potential military casualties—more than three out of four continued to support U.S. military action even if it was suggested that the U.S. military might suffer thousands of casualties, casualty levels not seen since the Vietnam War (see Table 4.3):[25] a much higher tolerance for casualties than had been observed in any of the peace operations of the 1990s that were described earlier.

---

[25] NBC News' polling on September 12, 2001 found 83 percent who supported "forceful military action" even if it meant risking further retaliation and the threat of war. NBC News/Hart & Teeter, September 12, 2001, N=618.

Table 4.2
Comparison of Attitudes on Duration and Difficulty of GWOT and Pearl Harbor

Do you think the war against terrorism will be a long war, or a short one?

Survey Date	Long War	Short War	No opinion
September 21–22, 2001	92	6	2
November 26–27, 2001	89%	11%	2

Do you think the war against Japan will be a long war, or a short one?

Survey Date	Long War	Short War	No opinion
December 12–17, 1941	51%	36%	9

Do you think the war against terrorism will be a difficult one, or a comparatively easy one?

Survey Date	Difficult War	Comparatively Easy War	No opinion
September 21–22, 2001	94%	5%	1%
November 26–27, 2001	95	4	1

Do you think the war against Japan will be a difficult one for us, or a comparatively easy one?

Survey Date	Difficult War	Comparatively Easy War	No opinion
December 12–17, 1941	65%	26%	9%

SOURCE: The Gallup Organization, "Poll Topics & Trends: War on Terrorism," available at http://www.gallup.com.

Table 4.3
Support for U.S. Military Action if "Thousands of Casualties," September 2001

Do you favor or oppose taking military action, including the use of ground troops, to retaliate against whoever is responsible for the terrorist attacks? [FORM 1 ONLY, N=416].

Favor	82%
Oppose	8
Don't know/refused	10

Do you favor or oppose taking military action, including the use of ground troops, to retaliate against whoever is responsible for the terrorist attacks, even if it means that the U.S. armed forces might suffer thousands of casualties? [FORM 2 ONLY, N=452].

Favor	77%
Oppose	9
Don't know/refused	14

SOURCE: Pew Research Center, September 13–17, 2001, N = 1,200, split sample.

Figure 4.2
Approval of the President's Handling of the War on Terrorism Abroad

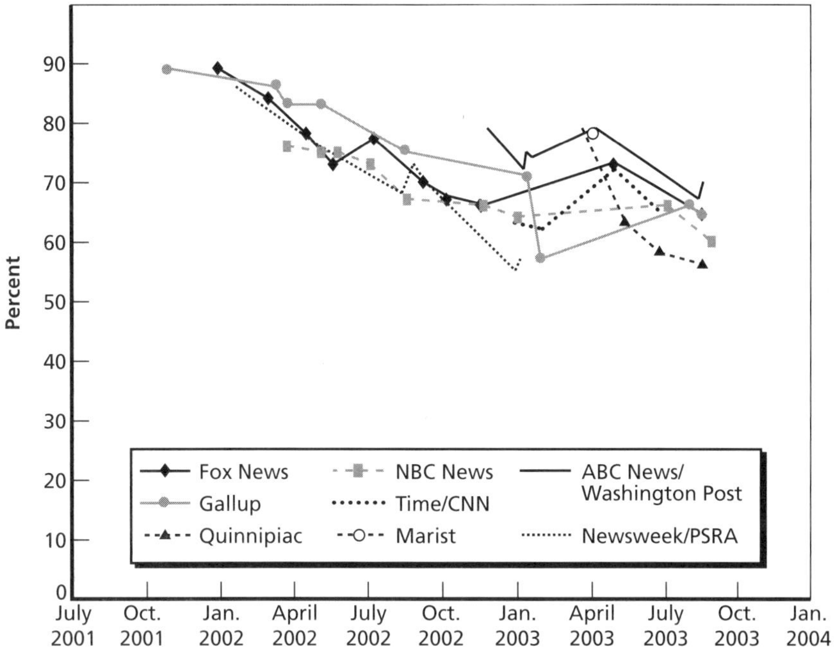

RAND *MG231-A-4.2*

Presidential Handling

As early as September 2001, nearly nine out of ten of those polled typically approved of the president's handling of the terrorism issue (see Figure 4.2),[26] and a strong majority of Americans expressed the

---

[26] Three questions were asked about the president's handling of the terrorism issue between September 2001 and late January 2002, with the number approving ranging from 86 to 89 percent. Question wording differed slightly, as follows. Gallup/Time/CNN, November 8–11, 2001: Do you approve or disapprove of the way George W. Bush is handling . . . terrorism?" (89 percent approved); Fox News/Opinion Dynamics, January 9–10, 2002: "Do you approve or disapprove of the job President (George W.) Bush is doing handling the issue of terrorism?" (89 percent approved); Newsweek/PSRA, January 31–February 1, 2002: "Please tell me whether you approve or disapprove of the way George W. Bush is handling

Figure 4.3
Approval of Presidential Handling of Terrorism, September 2003–April 2004

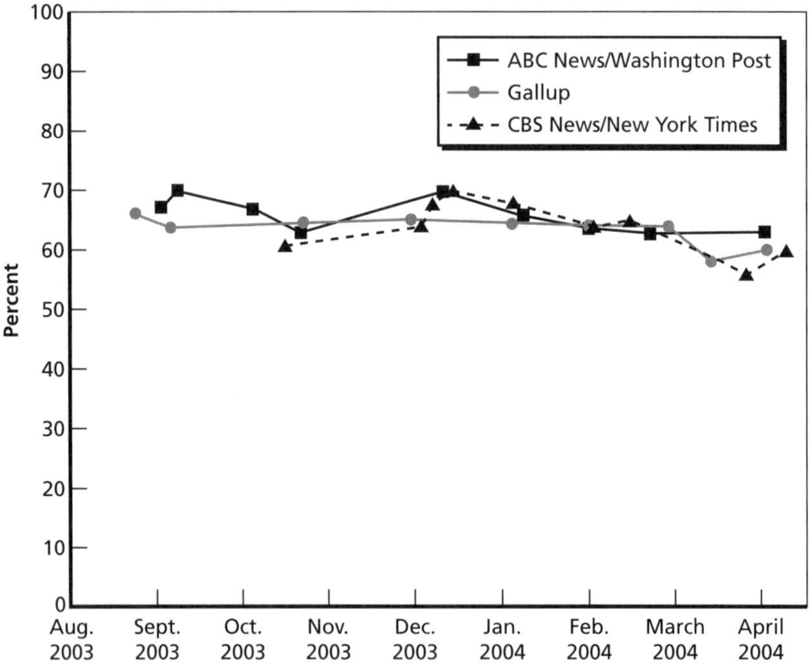

RAND *MG231-A-4.3*

belief that the administration had a clear and well-thought-out policy on terrorism.[27] By April 2004, six in ten still supported the president's handling of terrorism.

As shown in the figure, the percentage of Americans approving of the president's handling of the terrorism issue has eroded since the stratospheric levels of late 2001 and, by September 2003, was generally in the 55–70 percent range: still high by historical standards, but a substantial decline nonetheless. The trend for polling by ABC

---

each of the following specific aspects of his job. Do you approve or disapprove of the way he is handling . . . the war against terrorism overseas?" (86 percent approved).

[27] A late September poll by Time/CNN found 67 percent who thought that the administration had a clear and well-thought-out policy, and 27 percent who did not think so. Time/CNN/Harris Interactive, September 27–28, 2001, N=1,055.

News/Washington Post, Gallup, and CBS News/New York Times from September 2003 to April 2004, when we updated our data, showed that approval of the president's handling of the war on terrorism was generally in the 60–70 percent range during that period, although it was hovering closer to 60 percent by April 2004 (Figure 4.3).

The belief that the administration had a clear plan for its campaign on terrorism has also eroded (Figure 4.4); as of December 2003, when the question was last asked, a slight plurality of those polled thought that the administration's policy was reactive to events.

Figure 4.4
Does the Administration Have a Clear Plan on Terrorism Policy?

When it comes to the campaign against terrorism, do you think the Bush administration has a clear plan for its policy or do you think the Bush administration is just reacting to events as they occur? (CBS News/New York Times)

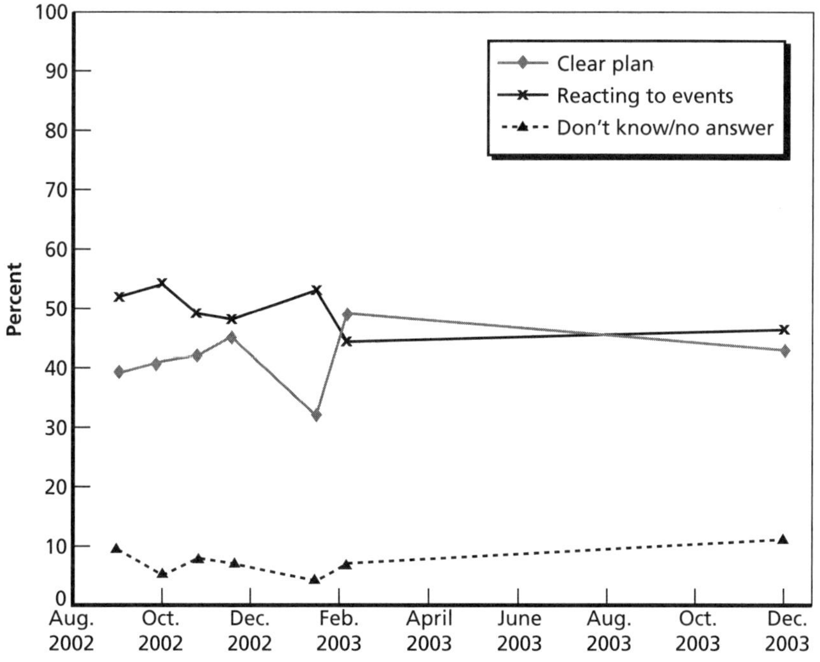

RAND *MG231-A-4.4*

Sources and Fault Lines in Support

Statistical Modeling Results

Our analyses of the bivariate association between support and membership in the president's party, beliefs about the stakes, prospects for success, and likely costs consistently showed a systematic, statistically significant relationship. And as described in Table 4.4, the model correctly classified about 85 percent of the respondents in terms of whether they approved or disapproved of the military action in Afghanistan.[28]

Table 4.4
Afghanistan: Marginal Probability from Probit Estimates of Approval (Q2)

Variables	Change in Probability at Mean Values
Stakes (Q8d)	0.012 (0.007)*
Prospects (Q5)	0.023 (0.007)***
Casualties (Q7)	–0.009 (0.005)*
Party 1 if Democrat†	–0.003 (0.012)
Party 1 if Independent†	–0.014 (0.012)
Ideology 1 if liberal†	
Ideology 1 if moderate†	
Race 1 if black†	–0.051 (0.034)
Gender 1 if female†	0.007 (0.008)
Education 1 if less than high school†	
Education 1 if some college†	
Education 1 if college graduate†	
Education 1 if postgraduate†	
Wald Chi-square (Prod > Chi2)	54.76 (0.000)
Log likelihood	–85.75
Observations	711
Correctly specified	84%

† dF/dx is for discrete change of dummy variable from 0 to 1.
* Significant at 10%.
** Significant at 5%.
*** Significant at 1%.
Robust standard error in parentheses.
SOURCE: ABC News/Washington Post, November 27, 2001.

[28] The president also may have benefited from his still-preternaturally high approval rating: ABC News/Washington Post found 80 percent approved of the president's job handling in the poll we used for our statistical modeling. ABC News/Washington Post, November 27, 2001, N=759.

Again, beliefs that are hypothesized to be the key predictors of support and opposition contributed the most: in declining order of importance, these were the prospects for success, the stakes, and U.S. casualties, although their generally small size raises questions about their substantive significance. It may be that because eight in ten or more had favorable beliefs and approved of the war, there was not much variation left to be accounted for. Although membership in the president's party was in the predicted direction, it was not statistically significant.[29]

Partisan Leadership and Followership

As was described above, there was significant bipartisan support from national leaders for a war in Afghanistan that would eliminate the terrorists. Although there were some partisan differences in support by party (see Figure 4.5), the basic tendency was the same whether respondents were Republican, Independent, or Democrat: strong support for the operation.[30] There were also partisan differences regarding the perceived stakes, prospects for success, and likely costs that were statistically, but not substantively, significant.

There appear to be two main reasons why initial support and the willingness to tolerate casualties were so high even in the face of widespread beliefs that the campaign would be a difficult and possibly costly one. The first is the view that nearly existential stakes were involved, and the second is that most believed that in the end the U.S. would succeed in eliminating this threat. Each will be discussed.

Beliefs About Stakes

On any number of measures, the 9/11 attacks and the war on terrorism were perceived by most to be among the most consequential and important developments in recent American history.

---

[29] We also estimated a number of other models using two other datasets that had differently worded questions; these correctly predicted approval or disapproval in 79–85 percent of the cases.

[30] These differences appear to have grown over time. See Heather Mason, "Public's Partisanship Evident on Terror Issue," The Gallup Organization, June 3, 2003.

Figure 4.5
Structure of Support for Military Action in Afghanistan, by Party

Do you support the military attacks in Afghanistan, or do you oppose them? (If support/oppose) Do you (support/oppose) them strongly, or only somewhat? (Los Angeles Times, November 10–13, 2001, N=1,995)

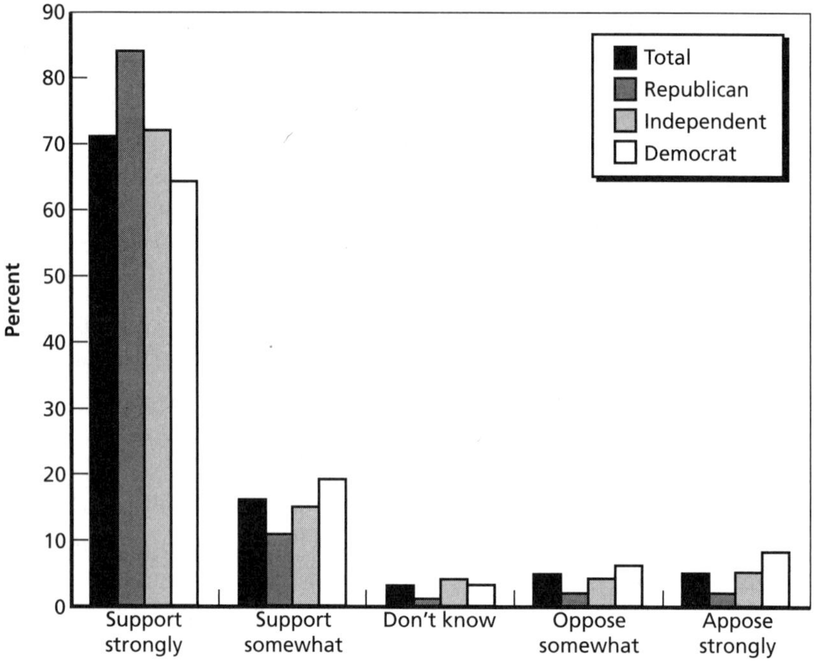

RAND *MG231-A-4.5*

Views on the importance of terrorism. One indicator of the importance of the war on terrorism is the importance that respondents attached to the terrorism problem itself.

Ninety-nine percent of respondents polled by the Los Angeles Times on September 13–14, 2001—including 99 percent of Republicans and 98 percent of Democrats and Independents—scored the problem of terrorism in the United States as "very serious," and two-thirds to three-quarters in each party said that they believed that the United States was in a state of war.[31]

Substantial percentages also have mentioned terrorism as the most important problem facing the country since 9/11. As shown in Figure 4.6, the percentage mentioning terrorism as the nation's most important problem peaked just after 9/11 at about 45 percent and has declined since; as of June 2003, fewer than one in five mentioned terrorism as the most important problem facing the country, still high by historical standards but nonetheless lower than the immediate post-9/11 period.[32] On average, about 18 percent have mentioned terrorism as the most important problem facing the country since 9/11, much higher than the average percentages mentioning Somalia (2 percent), Haiti (1 percent), Bosnia (4 percent), or Kosovo (8 percent) during those military actions.[33]

In a similar vein, polling by Gallup placed prevention of terrorism at the top of Americans' foreign policy concerns.[34]

Moral justification for military action. Another indicator of importance is the extent to which Americans believed military action was justified. Most Americans seemed to feel that military action against Afghanistan was morally justified: 90 percent of those polled by Time/CNN/Harris in October expressed this view,[35] and about six

---

[31] Los Angeles Times, September 13–14, 2001, N= 1,561. Seventy-four percent of Republicans, 70 percent of Democrats, and 66 percent of Independents felt that the United States was in a state of war.

[32] The terrorism issue generally has been eclipsed by concern about domestic economic problems.

[33] To provide a point of comparison, we collected data on those mentioning Somalia, Haiti, Bosnia, or Kosovo as the most important problem facing the country. The number of polls in which respondents mentioned each situation were as follows: Somalia (four polls), Haiti (two polls), Bosnia (ten polls), Kosovo (five polls).

[34] Lydia Saad, "Preventing Terrorism and Securing Energy Supplies Top Americans' Foreign Policy Concerns; Building Democracy Abroad Ranks Last Among Nine Possible Goals," The Gallup Organization, February 20, 2003.

[35] Time/CNN/Harris, October 12, 2001, N=1,044.

Figure 4.6
Percent Mentioning Terrorism as Most Important Problem

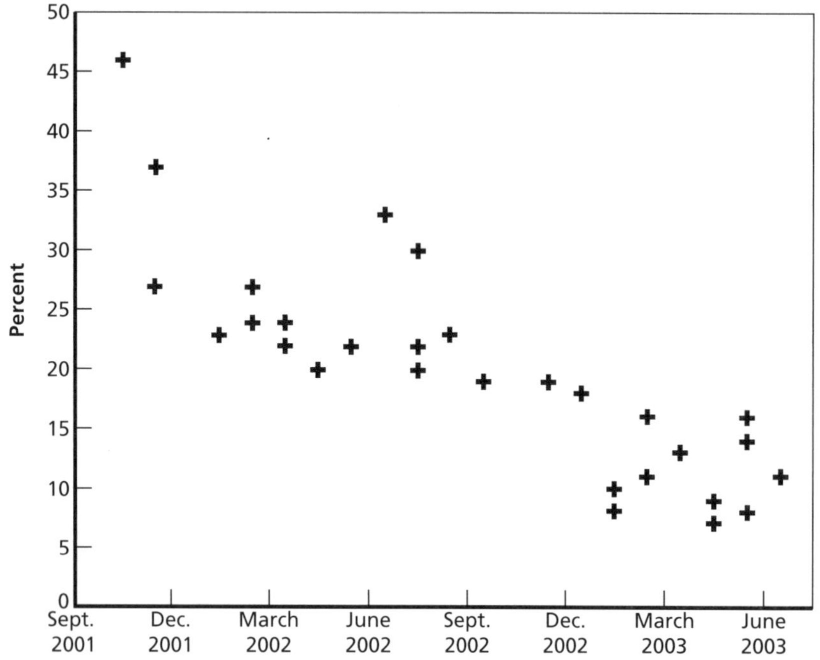

RAND *MG231-A-4.6*

in ten of those polled by Gallup in March 2003 who were asked to score the moral justification for military action in Afghanistan on a five-point scale ranging from 1 ("totally unjustifiable") to 5 ("totally justifiable") gave it a five, and another 14 percent gave it a four.[36]

Critical threats and priority foreign policy goals. Another indicator of importance is the extent to which the 9/11 attacks tracked with preexisting beliefs about critical threats and preferences regarding national security priorities.

The 9/11 attacks—and the prospect that terrorist organizations or others might acquire weapons of mass destruction that might be used against the United States—had long been precisely the sorts of

---

[36] Gallup, March 1–3, 2002, N=862.

critical threats that most Americans believed should be the highest priority of U.S. national security (see Table 4.5).

As shown, terrorism and weapons of mass destruction were identified by supermajorities as both the most critical threats to the vital interests of the United States and the highest-priority foreign policy

Table 4.5
Highest-Ranking Threats and Foreign Policy Goals, 1990–2002

I am going to read you a list of possible threats to the vital interest of the United States in the next 10 years. For each one, please tell me if you see this as a critical threat, an important but not critical threat, or not an important threat at all. (Percent saying "critical threat")

	1994	1998	2002
International terrorism	69	84	91
Chemical and biological weapons		76	86
Iraq developing weapons of mass destruction			86
The possibility of unfriendly countries becoming nuclear powers	72	75	85
Regional ethnic conflicts		34	
Civil wars in Africa			24

I am going to read a list of possible foreign policy goals that the United States might have. For each one please say whether you think that it should be a very important foreign policy goal of the United States, a somewhat important foreign policy goal, or not an important goal at all. (Percent saying goal "very important")

	1990	1994	1998	2002
Combating international terrorism			79	91
Preventing the spread of nuclear weapons	84	82	82	90
Helping bring democracy to other nations	28	25	29	34
Helping improve standard of living of less-developed nations	33	22	29	30
Promoting and defending human rights	40	34	39	47

SOURCE: Chicago Council on Foreign Relations quadrennial surveys.

goals for the nation in the Chicago Council on Foreign Relations' recent quadrennial surveys.[37]

By comparison, dealing with ethnic conflicts and civil wars, promoting democracy, improving the standard of living of less-developed nations, and promoting and defending human rights—the sorts of altruistic goals that appeared to serve as the principal rationales for the peace operations of the Clinton administration in the 1990s—were never really seen as very compelling by a majority of Americans (Tables 4.5 and 4.6).[38]

Historical comparisons with Pearl Harbor. Another indicator of importance is how the 9/11 attacks compared with past tragedies; for most Americans, 9/11 was the most tragic event in their lifetimes.[39] For many Americans, the closest historical analogy to the 9/11 attacks that came to mind was the December 1941 attack on Pearl Harbor, an attack that precipitated the United States' entry into a nearly four-year-long world war against German and Japanese fascism. In fact, to provide a gauge of the 9/11 attack's importance, some polling organizations asked respondents to compare the seriousness of the 9/11 attacks with the earlier Pearl Harbor attack.

---

[37] More recently, about eight in ten (79 percent) said that it was very important for the war on terrorism to prevent Iran, Iraq, and North Korea from developing weapons of mass destruction. Gallup/CNN/USA Today, February 8–10, 2002, N=1,001.

[38] Recent evidence that the public considers the promotion of democracy to be a relatively low priority can be found in Lydia Saad, "Preventing Terrorism and Securing Energy Supplies Top Americans' Foreign Policy Concerns; Building Democracy Abroad Ranks Last Among Nine Possible Goals," The Gallup Organization, February 20, 2003. The belief that ethnic conflicts and civil wars continue to be seen as being of secondary importance can be found in public attitudes toward a peacekeeping operation in Liberia. See ABC News/Washington Post Poll, "Bush Faces Rising Public Doubts on Credibility and Casualties Alike," news release, July 11, 2003, Darren K. Carlson, "Should the U.S. Keep the Peace in Liberia?" The Gallup Organization, August 5, 2003, and David W. Moore, "Americans Favor U.S. Peacekeeping Force in Liberia; Still Strong Support for U.S. Troops in Iraq," The Gallup Organization, July 11, 2003. Evidence also can be found in the public's views toward the 1999 peacekeeping operation in East Timor: see Frank Newport, "East Timor Has Yet to Register on Americans' Consciousness; But Majority Says a Peaceful Solution Is at Least Somewhat Important to U.S.," The Gallup Organization, October 4, 1999.

[39] Frank Newport, "Americans Still Consider Sept. 11 Most Tragic Event of Their Lives," The Gallup Organization, March 11, 2002.

Table 4.6
Importance of Foreign Policy Goals Associated with Various U.S. Interventions

As far as you are concerned, should [item] be a very important foreign policy goal of the United States, a somewhat important goal, not too important, or not an important goal at all?

	% Very Important
The removal of Saddam Hussein from power in Iraq	
March 2002	60.1%
April 2002	44.8
June 2002	47.2
The development of a peaceful solution to the conflict in East Timor (September 1999)	13.9
The development of a peaceful solution to the situation in Kosovo (August 1999)	41.3
The development of a peaceful solution to the situation in Bosnia	
September 1993	31.4
October 1995	30.2
The development of a peaceful solution to the situation in Somalia (September 1993)	27.8

NOTES: Iraq: Gallup, June 17–19, 2002, N =1,004, April 5–7, 2002, N = 1,009, and March 22–24, 2003, N = 1,011; East Timor: Gallup, September 23–26, 1999, N = 1,038; Kosovo: Gallup, July 23–25, 1999, N = 1,021; Bosnia: Gallup, September 10–12, 1993, N = 1,003, and October 19–25, 1995, N = 1,228; Somalia: Gallup, September 10–12, 1993, N = 1,003.

Although differences in question wording make comparisons somewhat problematic, immediately following the attacks, somewhere between six and nine out of ten of those polled said they thought the attacks were equal to or more serious than the attack on Pearl Harbor; by August 2002, four out of five felt this way.

For example, 67 percent of those polled by CBS News on September 11–12, 2001 said they thought the attacks on the World Trade Center were like another Pearl Harbor, or worse;[40] 91 percent of those polled by NBC News/Hart & Teeter on September 12 said

[40] CBS News, September 11–12, 2001, N=1,041.

that the attacks were equal to or more serious than Pearl Harbor;[41] and 72 percent of those polled by Gallup in November 2001 said they thought that 100 years from that date historians would say that the 9/11 attacks had had a greater impact on the United States than Pearl Harbor.[42] By August 2002, the Pew Research Center found 80 percent of Washingtonians and New Yorkers who said that the attacks were equal to or more serious than Pearl Harbor.[43]

The salience of terrorism. Another indicator of importance is the extent to which Americans have actually followed developments related to the war on terrorism.

The data suggest that relatively high percentages of Americans have closely followed developments in the GWOT since 9/11: the average percentage following the war on terrorism very closely was 66 percent,[44] the average percentage following developments in Afghanistan very closely was 47 percent, and the average percentage following the situation in Iraq very closely was 56 percent.[45]

As shown in Figure 4.7, which presents the percentages following Afghanistan very closely, and the number of New York Times stories on Afghanistan in the week preceding the poll,[46] the percentage following Afghanistan very closely peaked in November 2001 when military operations were peaking,[47] and attention to developments in Afghanistan persisted despite the drop-off in news reporting on Afghanistan, oscillating between 40 and 50 percent through July 2002, the last time the question was asked.

---

[41] NBC News, September 12, 2001, N=618.

[42] Gallup, November 26–27, 2001, N=1,025.

[43] Pew Research Center, August 14–25, 2002, N=1,001.

[44] A total of seven questions asked between October 2001 and February 2003.

[45] A total of 23 questions asked between August 2002 and June 2003.

[46] A total of 17 questions asked between October 2001 and July 2002; polling organizations evidently stopped asking about Afghanistan.

[47] See International Institute for Strategic Studies, "War in Afghanistan," *Strategic Survey 2001/2001*, Oxford: Oxford University Press, 2002, pp. 229–253.

Figure 4.7
Percent Following Afghanistan Very Closely

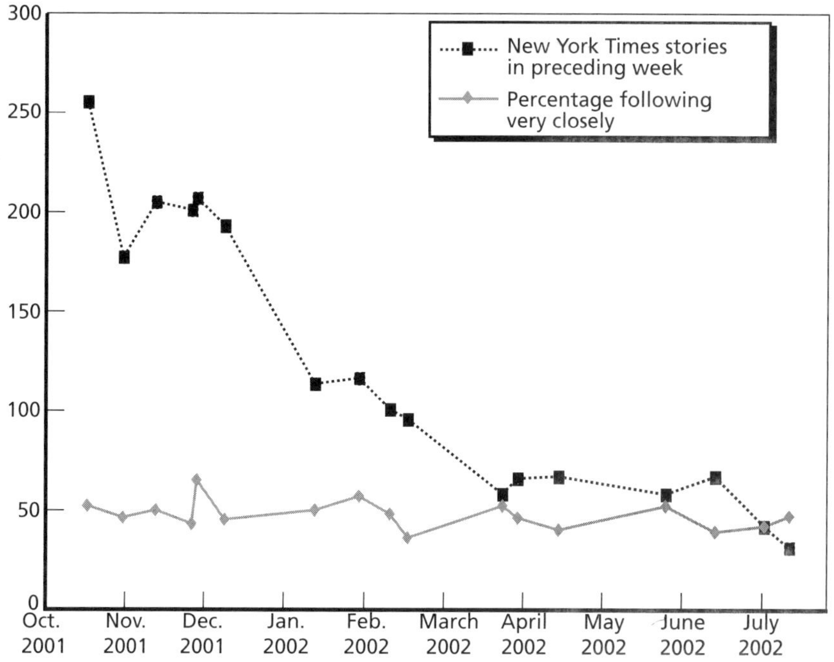

RAND *MG231-A-4.7*

By comparison, the peace operations of the 1990s never occasioned this much interest: the average percentage following Somalia very closely was 24 percent, Haiti was 22 percent, Bosnia was 17 percent, and Kosovo was 26 percent;[48] again, the data suggest that the war on terrorism engaged the American mind in ways that the peace operations of the 1990s never did.

---

[48] The number of questions used to calculate these averages were as follows: Somalia (7 questions), Haiti (11 questions), Bosnia (44 questions), Kosovo (19 questions).

Table 4.7
Expectations Regarding Outcomes of GWOT and World War II

In any war against terrorists, do you expect the United States will win or not?
(CBS News/New York Times, September 20–23, 2001, N=1,216)

Will win	84%
Will not win	8
Don't know/no answer	8

Do you think in the long run Germany will win the war, or lose it?
(Gallup, December 12–17, 1941, N=1,500)

Will win	2%
Will lose	92
Stalemate (volunteered)	2
No opinion	4

SOURCE: The Gallup Organization, "Poll Topics & Trends: War on Terrorism," available at http://www.gallup.com.

Prospects for Success

Beliefs about the likely outcome of the war. The second reason for the unusually high initial levels of support for military action is that in spite of the widespread belief that the campaign against terrorism would be anything but easy, optimism generally prevailed regarding its ultimate outcome: about eight in ten of those polled after the 9/11 attacks said they expected the United States to win the war against terrorism, a level of optimism nearly as high as that observed during World War II (see Table 4.7).

Although some partisan differences were evident, the general pattern was one of overwhelming optimism: six in ten or more Democrats, Independents, and Republicans all expressed high confidence that the U.S. military would succeed against the Taliban in Afghanistan (see Figure 4.8). And while still generally positive, confidence about the military's ability to capture or kill bin Laden was somewhat lower (see Figure 4.9).

Figure 4.8
Confidence in a Successful Mission in Afghanistan by Party, November 2001

How much confidence do you have in the military to carry out a successful mission in Afghanistan against the Taliban government? Do you have a lot of confidence, some confidence, not too much confidence, or no confidence at all? (Los Angeles Times, November 10–13, 2001, N=1,995)

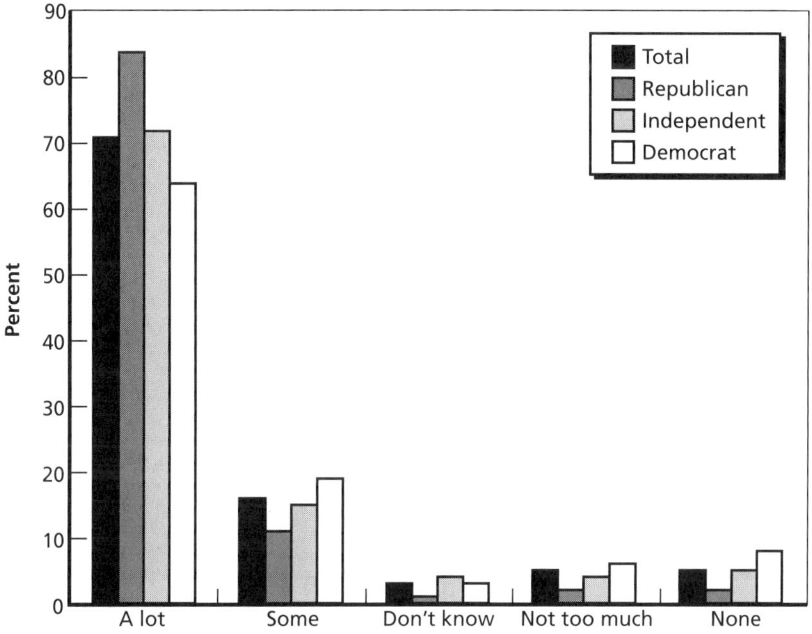

RAND *MG231-A-4.8*

Moreover, as shown in Figure 4.10, optimism about the war on terrorism has oscillated since October 2001, peaking when the United States concluded major combat operations in Afghanistan and Iraq[49] and declining thereafter.

---

[49] It is worth mentioning that Khalid Sheikh Mohammed, the alleged mastermind of the 9/11 attacks, was captured in the city of Rawalpindi, Pakistan on March 1, 2003; this also may have had some effect on optimism about the course of the war on terrorism in polling done between March and May 2003.

Figure 4.9
Confidence That U.S. Military Will Capture or Kill bin Laden by Party, November 2001

How much confidence do you have in the military to either capture or kill Osama bin Laden? (Los Angeles Times, November 10–13, 2001, N=1,995)

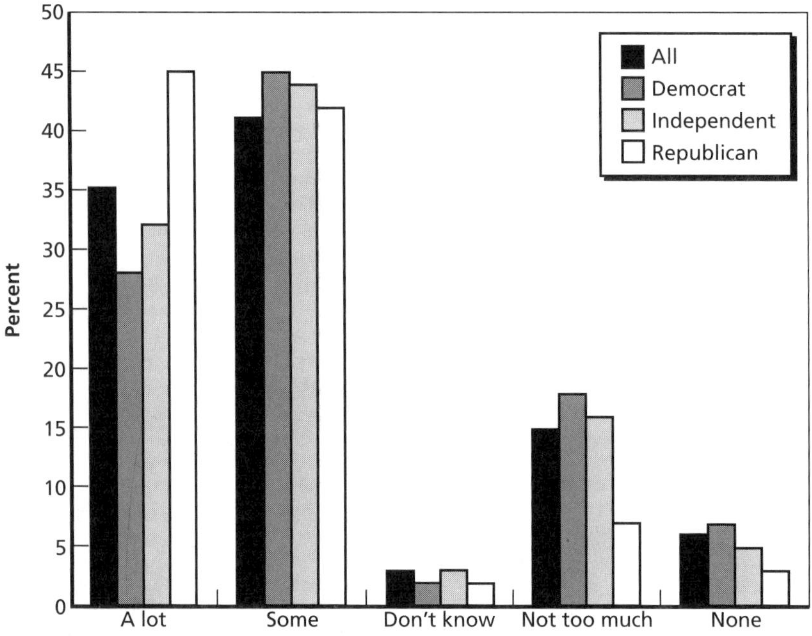

RAND *MG231-A-4.9*

The last polling on the matter, from June 2002, suggested that only about one in five remained absolutely confident that the United States would win, and another one in three were pretty confident (see Table 4.8).[50]

---

[50] Changing beliefs about the GWOT's progress and prospects for success are documented in the following publications from The Gallup Organization: David W. Moore, "Public Optimistic on Progress of War on Terrorism; Willing to See War Expanded to Other Countries," January 25, 2002; Jeffrey M. Jones, "Support for Military Effort Remains High; Americans Less Positive in their Assessment of Progress in War on Terrorism," March 12, 2002; Lydia Saad, "Fewer Americans Perceive Anti-Terror War as Successful; But Americans' Fear of Being a Victim Holds Steady," June 7, 2002; David W. Moore, "Americans Dubious

Figure 4.10
Who Is Winning the War on Terrorism?

Gallup: Who do you think is currently winning the war against terrorism: the U.S. and its allies, neither side, or the terrorists? Options were rotated [Percent saying "U.S. and its allies"]

Fox News: As of right now, do you think the U.S. and its allies are winning the war against terrorism? [% saying yes]

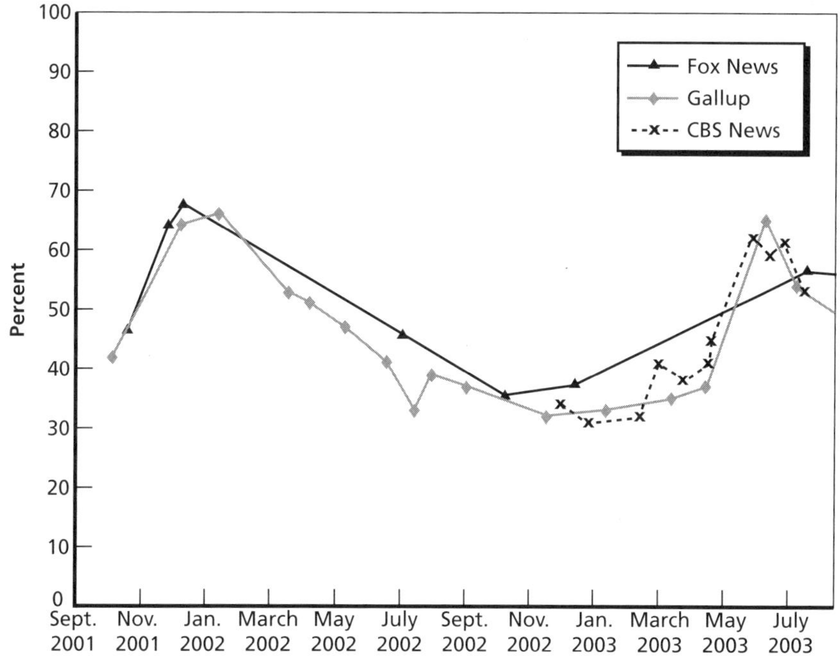

RAND *MG231-A-4.10*

About Progress in War on Terrorism; But Widespread Support for U.S. Troops in Afghanistan," June 27, 2002; and David W. Moore, "Public Uncertain About Success of War in Afghanistan; Half of All Americans Say Success Depends on Capturing Osama bin Laden," July 11, 2002.

Table 4.8
Confidence In U.S. Ability to Handle Terrorism, June 2002

How confident are you in the United States' ability to handle the problem of terrorism: absolutely confident—we will win, pretty confident, only somewhat confident, or not confident at all—there is no way to beat terrorism?

Absolutely confident—we will win	19%
Pretty confident	35
Only somewhat confident	29
Not confident at all—there is no way to beat terrorism	12
Not sure	5

SOURCE: Fox News/Opinion Dynamics, June 4–5, 2002, N=900.

Beliefs about whether bin Laden will be captured or killed. It is worth noting both the increasing degree to which many Americans have defined success in the war on terrorism in terms of killing or capturing Osama bin Laden (Figure 4.9)[51] and the eroding optimism that this will in fact happen (Figure 4.11); this represents a challenge for sustaining public support for the war on terrorism.

As shown in Figure 4.12, a number of polling questions show that an increasing percentage of Americans believe that a necessary condition (but not necessarily a sufficient condition, as only about 10 percent have said it would be enough[52]) for considering the war a success is capturing or killing Osama bin Laden.[53]

---

[51] See, for example, David W. Moore, "Public Uncertain About Success of War in Afghanistan; Half of All Americans Say Success Depends on Capturing Osama bin Laden," The Gallup Organization, July 11, 2002.

[52] On four occasions between November 2001 and August 2002, Newsweek/PSRA asked: "What do you think it will take for the United States to eliminate the threat of future acts of terrorism against this country by Osama bin Laden's organization? Will it be enough to capture or kill bin Laden, or will it also be necessary to capture or kill other top leaders in his organization, or will removing top leaders not eliminate the threat because too many cells and potential leaders would remain?" The percentage who said that capturing or killing bin Laden would be enough ranged from 7 to 11 percent.

[53] The questions were as follows. ABC News/Washington Post: "Do you think the United States has to capture or kill Osama bin Laden for the war on terrorism to be a success, or do you think the war on terrorism can be a success without Osama bin Laden being killed or captured?"; Time/CNN/Harris: "If the U.S. (United States) achieves most of its goals in Afghanistan, but does not capture or kill Osama bin Laden, would you consider the military

Figure 4.11
Percentage Saying bin Laden Must Be Captured or Killed to Win

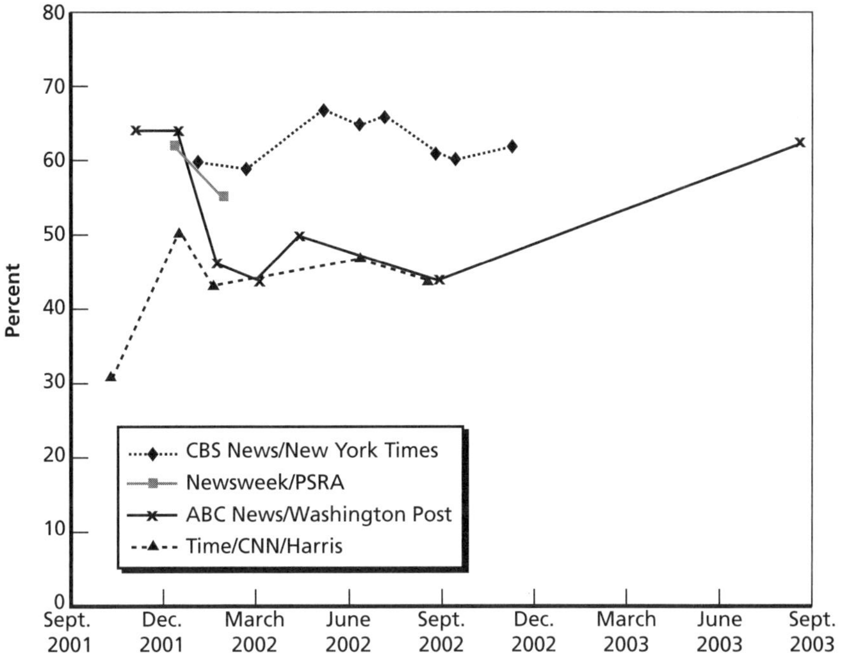

RAND *MG231-A-4.11*

In polling CBS News/New York Times conducted just before and after Saddam Hussein was captured, six in ten said that the United States will not have won the war in Afghanistan unless bin Laden is captured.[54]

action in Afghanistan to be a victory for the U.S. or wouldn't you consider it a victory?"; Newsweek/PSRA: "The Taliban government has been removed from power in Afghanistan but Osama bin Laden and the Mullah Omar, leader of the Taliban, remain at large. Do you think the U.S. (United States) military effort in Afghanistan can be considered a victory if these top leaders of enemy forces are not captured or killed?"; and CBS News/New York Times: "If Osama bin Laden is not captured or killed, then do you think the United States will have won the war in Afghanistan, or not?"

[54] CBS News/New York Times, December 10–13, 2003, N = 1,057, and December 14–15, 2003, N = 635. In polling December 10–13, 63 percent said that the United States will not have won the war in Afghanistan unless bin Laden is killed or captured; polling on December 14–15 found attitudes essentially unchanged: 62 percent felt that way.

Table 4.9
Importance of Killing or Capturing bin Laden and Saddam, September 2003

To protect Americans from another major terrorist attack, how important do you think it is that:

Osama bin Laden is killed or captured: very important, somewhat important, not too important, or not at all important?

Saddam Hussein is killed or captured: very important, somewhat important, not too important, or not at all important? (Pew/PSRA)

	Osama bin Laden	Saddam Hussein
Very important	66%	60%
Somewhat important	20	21
Not too important	7	8
Not at all important	5	9
Don't know	2	2

SOURCE: Pew/PSRA, September 11–12, 2003, N=1,004.

And, as shown in Table 4.9, eight in ten or more of those polled in September 2003 continued to think that capturing or killing Osama bin Laden and Saddam Hussein were important, and six in ten or more of these felt this was very important; as of May 2004, the question was not asked again.

Figure 4.12 shows that a declining percentage of Americans believe that this will happen.[55]

[55] The questions were as follows: CBS News/New York Times: "How much confidence do you have in the ability of the U.S. (United States) government to capture or kill Osama bin Laden, who is believed to have planned the September 11th (2001) attacks on the U.S. (United States) (World Trade Center and the Pentagon): would you say you're very confident he will be caught, somewhat confident, not too confident, or not at all confident?"; NBC News/Wall Street Journal: "Do you think that the United States will ever capture or kill international terrorist Osama bin Laden, or not?"; Gallup/CNN/USA Today: "How likely is it that the U.S. (United States) will be able to capture or kill Osama bin Laden—very likely, somewhat likely, not too likely, or not at all likely?" Newsweek/PSRA: "In your opinion, how likely is it that the current U.S. (United States) military action in Afghanistan will be able to capture or kill Osama bin Laden? Is it very likely, somewhat likely, not too likely, or not at all likely?"; and ABC News/Washington Post: "How confident are you that the United States will capture or kill Osama bin Laden: are you very confident, somewhat confident, not too confident or not at all confident?"

Figure 4.12
Percentage Confident That bin Laden Will Be Captured or Killed

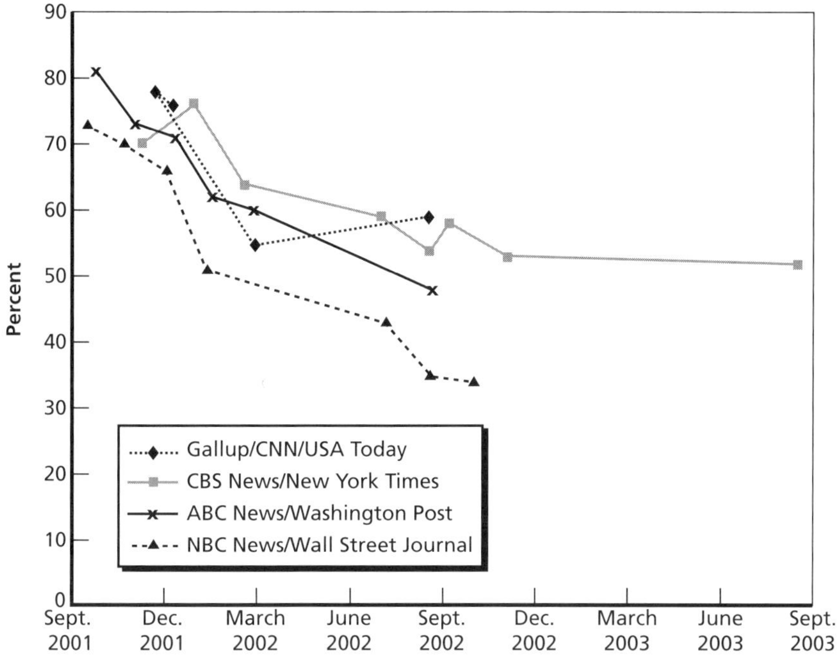

RAND *MG231-A-4.12*

Expected and Actual Costs

As described earlier, a final source of support and opposition to military operations has to do with expected and actual casualties: the basic intuition is that the higher the hypothesized or actual number of casualties, the smaller the percentage of Americans that support the military action. However, the rate at which support declines depends very much on beliefs about the importance of the stakes and the prospects for success, all heavily influenced by partisan leadership. As shown in the previous chapter, prospective support can be highly sensitive to casualties (i.e., show a rapid decline) when the stakes and prospects for success are believed to be low. Having earlier showed that consistent majorities expressed a willingness to tolerate even potentially very large numbers of casualties in the war on terrorism, we now turn to the public's expectations regarding casualty levels in Afghanistan and the war on terrorism.

The data for both are sparse, and they suggest that the public did not have particularly firm expectations regarding casualties in Afghanistan or the larger war on terrorism. For example, one poll in September 2001 found 56 percent who said that they expected a long war in Afghanistan with many casualties,[56] while another poll found only 37 percent who thought large numbers of U.S. troops would be killed or wounded in the military action to come. By November 2001, 51 percent expressed the belief that there would be a large number of U.S. casualties in Afghanistan.[57] The strongest conclusion one can make from these data is that the public wasn't sure what to expect but left open the possibility of large numbers of casualties in Afghanistan and the larger war on terrorism. And, as was shown earlier, regardless of the firmness of their expectations regarding casualties, large majorities expressed a tolerance for casualties into the thousands.

The actual number of casualties sustained in Operation Enduring Freedom in Afghanistan has been quite modest by any measure, but perhaps most importantly, modest relative to the casualties that were expected at the onset of the war on terrorism (see Table 4.10).

Balancing Costs and Benefits

A final measure of the importance of the war on terrorism is the extent to which Americans believed that the war was, in the final analysis, worth the risk or reality of potentially large numbers of casualties.

---

[56] Time/CNN/Harris, October 27–28, 2001, N = 1,055. Twenty-three percent expected a quick victory with few casualties, while 10 percent expected the U.S. to withdraw from Afghanistan without victory.

[57] ABC News/Washington Post, November 27, 2001, N=759.

Table 4.10
Casualty Summary for Operation Enduring Freedom, as of April 8, 2004

Casualty Type	Total
Hostile deaths	
Killed in action	36
Died of wounds	13
Missing in action: declared dead	0
Captured: declared dead	0
Total hostile deaths	49
Nonhostile deaths	
Accident	51
Illness	5
Homicide	0
Self-inflicted	8
Undetermined	2
Pending	0
Total nonhostile deaths	66
Wounded: not mortal	238

SOURCE: Washington Headquarters Services, Directorate for Information Operations and Reports, Department of Defense, "War on Terrorism—Casualty Summary—Operation Enduring Freedom, as of April 8, 2004."

Our analysis suggests that, relative to the past military operations described in the preceding chapter, majorities showed a prospective tolerance for very high U.S. casualties in the war on terrorism: anywhere from about 60 to 75 percent expressed a tolerance for "substantial" casualties—even amounting to thousands of U.S. deaths—and said they still would consider the war to be worth its costs. For example:

- Polling in September 2001 found a generally consistent majority willing to support a war even if there were large numbers of casualties: 53 percent said they would support military action against those responsible for the 9/11 attacks even if it meant getting into a long war with large numbers of U.S. troops killed or injured;[58] 77 percent said they would favor military action, including ground troops, against those responsible for the at-

[58] ABC News/Washington Post, September 13, 2001, N=609.

tacks, even if it meant the U.S. armed forces might suffer thousands of casualties;[59] 65 percent supported taking military action even if it resulted in 1,000 American troops being killed;[60] 76 percent supported military action even if it resulted in 5,000 deaths;[61] and 60–65 percent agreed that a war against countries that harbor or aid terrorists would be worth it even if it involved substantial American casualties.[62]

- In October 2001, 61 percent said that the war would be worth its costs even if several thousand American troops lost their lives,[63] 73 percent said they would favor military action if it resulted in fewer than 100 U.S. soldiers' deaths, 65 percent said they would favor it if it resulted in more than 500 deaths, and 51 percent said that they would support it if it resulted in more than 1,000 deaths;[64] another poll in October 2001 found 51 percent who said the U.S. military should be prepared to lose several thousand or more U.S. soldiers before considering a stop to military action.[65]
- In November 2001, at the height of the fighting in Afghanistan, 52 percent said that they would support sending a significant number of troops into a long war involving large numbers of U.S. troops killed;[66] 74 percent said that the war on terrorism in Afghanistan was worth risking substantial numbers of casualties;[67] 64 percent said they would support the military attacks in

---

[59] Pew/PSRA, September 13–17, 2001, N=1,200.

[60] Gallup, September 14–15, 2001, N=524.

[61] Gallup, September 21–22, 2001, N=517.

[62] Zogby International's polling of September 17–20, 2001, September 23–25, 2001, September 26–29, 2001, September 28–30, 2001, and October 1–3, 2001.

[63] CBS News/New York Times, October 25–28, 2001, N=1,024.

[64] Time/CNN/Harris, October 12, 2001, N=1,044.

[65] Fox News/Opinion Dynamics, October 17–18, 2001, N=900.

[66] ABC News/Washington Post, November 5–6, 2001, N=756.

[67] NBC News/Wall Street Journal, November 9–11, 2001, N=809.

Afghanistan even if they resulted in substantial casualties;[68] 77 percent said they would favor military action, including the use of ground troops, against the attackers, even if it meant the U.S. armed forces might suffer thousands of casualties,[69] and 60 percent said it was worth risking a large number of U.S. military casualties in order to capture or kill Osama bin Laden.[70]

- In December 2001, nearly eight in ten of those polled said that the costs of the war on terrorism were, in some sense, "worth it."[71]
- Finally, in March 2002, 73 percent said they would still support the war if the current trend of increasing casualties in Afghanistan continued.[72]

Figures 4.13 and 4.14 show the results of the two questions that asked respondents whether they would continue to support military action given different hypothesized numbers of casualties.

By any measure—but especially when compared to similarly worded questions that were asked about the various peace operations of the 1990s that were discussed in the last chapter—this is an astonishingly high tolerance for casualties.

Support for Military Action Elsewhere

There has been substantial support for military action against terrorists in other locations such as Yemen, the Philippines, Somalia, and

[68] Los Angeles Times, November 10–13, 2001, N=1,995.

[69] Pew/PSRA, November 13–19, 2001, N=1,500.

[70] ABC News/Washington Post, November 27, 2001, N=759.

[71] ABC News/Washington Post, December 18–19, 2001, N=755.

[72] Fox News/Opinion Dynamics, March 12–13, 2002, N=900.

Figure 4.13
Prospective Willingness to Tolerate Casualties in Afghanistan, October 2001

Would you favor or oppose military action in Afghanistan if it results in the deaths of more than 500/1,000/10,000 Americans? (Time/CNN/Harris, October 12, 2001, N=1,044)

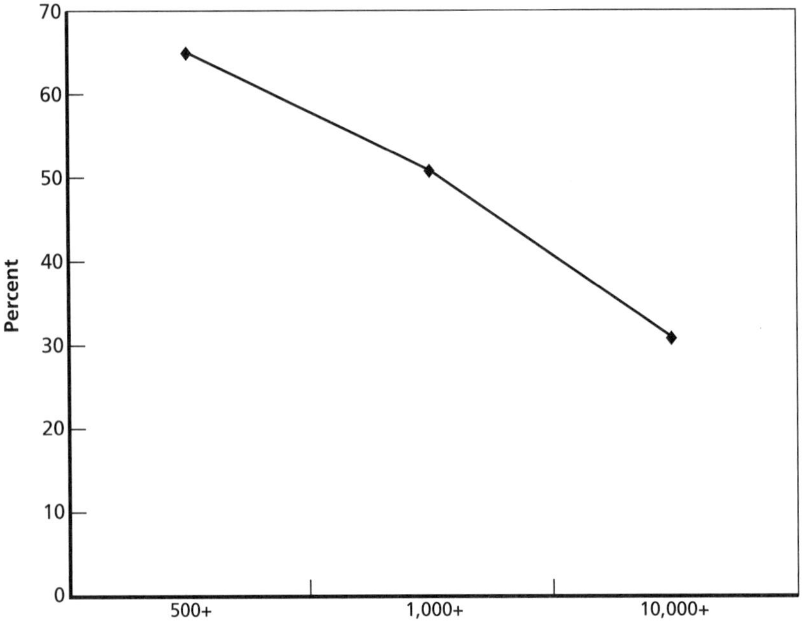

RAND *MG231-A-4.13*

Sudan, with virtually all questions showing strong majorities supporting military action outside of Afghanistan,[73] and most seem to expect other military actions abroad.[74] Below we summarize these data by month:

---

[73] See, for example, Frank Newport, "Taking the War Beyond Afghanistan: Americans Generally Support Military Action in Iran, Iraq, and the Philippines," The Gallup Organization, February 4, 2002, and David W. Moore, "Public Optimistic on Progress of War on Terrorism; Willing to See War Expanded to Other Countries," The Gallup Organization, January 25, 2002.

[74] Steve Crabtree, "Americans See More Military Action Coming," The Gallup Organization, June 17, 2003.

Figure 4.14
Prospective Willingness to Tolerate Casualties in Afghanistan, October 2001

How many soldiers do you think the U.S. military should be prepared to lose in Afghanistan before stopping military involvement: under 100, between 100 and 1,000, several thousand, or as many as it takes to stop terrorism? (Fox News/Opinion Dynamics, October 17–18, 2001, N=900)

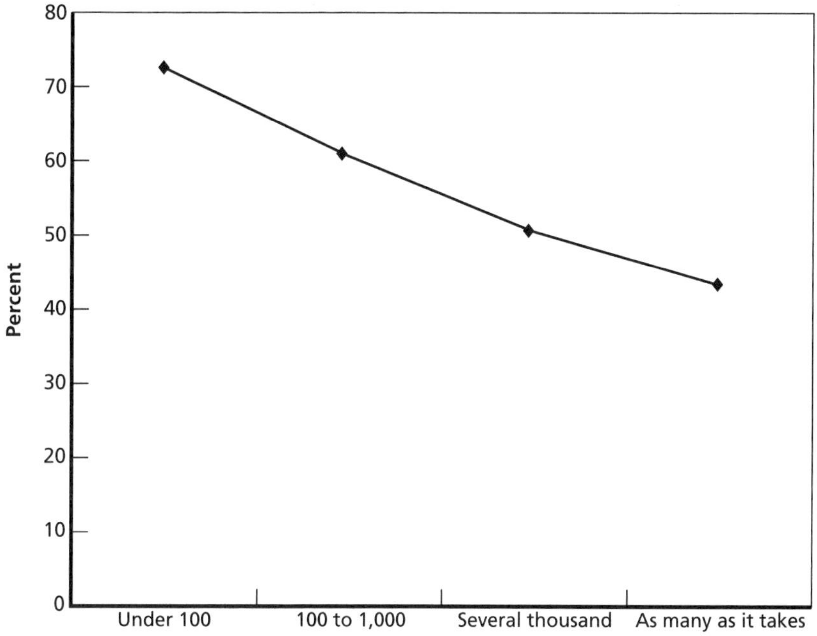

RAND *MG231-A-4.14*

- In October 2001, following the beginning of operations in Afghanistan, support for military action in other locales ranged from 72 to 87 percent,[75] with 86 percent saying they thought

[75] Eighty-seven percent supported military action against other countries that assisted or sheltered terrorists in ABC News, October 8–9, 2001, [N = 1,009] and 72 percent supported military action against terrorists in other countries even if they were not directly connected to the 9/11 attacks in Fox News/Opinion Dynamics, October 17–18, 2001, N=900.

that such military action would be a very or somewhat effective way to fight terrorism.[76]

- In November 2001, support for military action elsewhere ranged from 77 to 81 percent.[77]
- In December, support for military action elsewhere ranged from 64 to 75 percent.[78]
- In January 2002, support was in the 62 to 71 percent range.[79]
- In April 2002, support was in the 58 to 68 percent range.[80]

By May 2003, most expected additional future military action in other locales: nearly eight in ten of those polled in May–June and August 2003 thought that the war on terrorism would require the United States to put military troops in combat situations in other countries as it did in Iraq and Afghanistan.[81]

Chapter Conclusions

To summarize, at its onset, the global war on terrorism was seen by most Americans as a "good war," i.e., one that compared quite fa-

---

[76] Newsweek/PSRA, October 11–12, 2001, N=1,004.

[77] PIPA, November 1–4, 2001, N = 602, found 77 percent who strongly or somewhat favored force against groups in other countries, and ABC News/Washington Post, November 27, 2000, N = 759, found 81 percent who supported military action against other countries besides Afghanistan that assisted or sheltered terrorists.

[78] Newsweek/PSRA, December 13–14, 2001, N = 1,002, Gallup/CNN/USA Today, December 14–16, 2001, N = 1,019, ABC News, December 18–19, 2001, N = 755, and Time/CNN/Harris, December 19–20, 2001, N = 1,008.

[79] Pew/PSRA, January 9–13, 2002, N = 1,201, Gallup/CNN/USA Today, January 11–14, 2002, N = 1,008, Gallup/CNN/USA Today, January 11–14, 2001, N = 1,008, and NBC News/Wall Street Journal, January 18–21, 2002, N = 1,011.

[80] Two questions in CBS News, April 1–2, 2002, N = 616.

[81] Seventy-eight percent said so in Gallup/CNN/USA Today, May 30–June 1, 2003, N = 1,019, and 79 percent said so in Gallup/CNN/USA Today, August 25–26, 2003, N = 1,009. See Steve Crabtree, "Americans See More Military Action Coming," Gallup News Service, June 17, 2003.

vorably in many ways to the last such war—World War II.[82] There was a widespread belief that the United States faced a critical threat that needed to be accorded a high priority, and that, although the campaign was likely to be difficult, the United States would ultimately emerge victorious over its enemy.

Given the prevalence of the beliefs that the stakes involved were critically important and that the United States would be successful, there should be little surprise that the GWOT initially found high levels of support in the already fertile soil of American public opinion; in spite of uncertainties about the road ahead, the level of support for military action in the GWOT has rivaled that for World War II[83] and has shown a robustness in the face of casualties much higher than what was seen during any of the peace operations of the 1990s.[84]

The high level of support for the principle of a global campaign against terrorism and the public's broad—or vague—conception of what actually might be entailed by such a war essentially gave President Bush a free hand in defining which situations should be considered to be part of the GWOT and which should not; as will be shown, high levels of public support could be found for nearly any military action that was tied in some fashion to the larger GWOT. And although most continue to view the war on terrorism as important, the difficulties of demonstrating success in this war, and the resulting erosion in the belief that the United States will win, have created long-term challenges for sustaining support.

In the next chapter we explore the sources and fault lines in the support for the military action in Iraq.

---

[82] The phrase "the good war" is taken from the book of the same name by Studs Terkel.

[83] In December 1941, the Gallup Organization found 97 percent who approved of Congress declaring war on Japan and 91 percent who felt that President Roosevelt should have asked Congress to declare war on Germany as well. Gallup, December 12–17, 1941, N = 1,500. As measured by a Gallup question that asked whether respondents wanted peace as things were then, support for the war ranged between 86 and 92 percent. For an analysis of public support during World War II, see Larson (1996a and 1996b).

[84] This will be described in greater detail in the next section.

CHAPTER FIVE

Operation Iraqi Freedom

The Bush administration frequently justified war with Iraq in two terms: first, as part of the war on terrorism, and second, as part of a larger effort to prevent U.S. adversaries from developing weapons of mass destruction (WMD). A majority of Americans seem to have accepted these arguments: majorities typically have said that they consider the war with Iraq to be part of the war against terrorism,[1] and, as will be seen, they already had longstanding concerns about Iraq developing weapons of mass destruction.

This chapter begins with some background to the war and then describes Americans' attitudes toward renewed military operations against Iraq during four phases: from the end of the first Gulf War to roughly September 2002; during the run-up to the war from September 2002 until the president's announcement of combat operations on March 19, 2003; from the beginning of the war until the president's May 1, 2003 declaration that major combat operations had ended; and during the postconflict efforts to create security and rebuild Iraq.

---

[1] More than three out of four (77 percent) subscribed to this view in ABC News/Washington Post's polling in April 2003; about two out of three continued to view Iraq this way in September 2003. See ABC News/Washington Post, April 16, 2003, September 7, 2003, and September 13, 2003. Polling by CBS News/New York Times showed 52 to 66 percent holding this view. CBS News/New York Times, March 26–27, 2003, N = 868, April 2–3, 2003, N = 950, April 11–13, 2003, N = 898, May 9–12, 2003, N = 910, and September 15–16, 2003, N = 675. The percentage who held this view in polling by Gallup grew from 50 to 57 percent between January and August 2003. Gallup/CNN/USA Today, January 23–25, 2003, N = 1,000 and August 25–26, 2003, N = 1,009.

Background

On September 12, 2002, President Bush addressed the United Nations General Assembly and challenged the UN to enforce the more than a dozen UN Security Council resolutions that had dealt with Iraq's disarmament and its WMD programs. The president put it as follows:

> The conduct of the Iraqi regime is a threat to the authority of the United Nations, and a threat to peace. Iraq has answered a decade of UN demands with a decade of defiance. All the world now faces a test, and the United Nations a difficult and defining moment: Are Security Council resolutions to be honored and enforced, or cast aside without consequence? Will the United Nations serve the purpose of its founding, or will it be irrelevant?[2]

The administration warned the UN that if it failed to meet this challenge, the United States itself would disarm Iraq. Thus began the administration's campaign to press Iraq to disarm and disclose its WMD programs (a condition for ending hostilities in the first Gulf War), to press the UN to act on behalf of its own resolutions on the matter,[3] and to build a case for war if Iraq failed to cooperate.

This campaign involved, on October 10–11, 2002, passage of a joint congressional resolution prospectively authorizing military action against Iraq,[4] which, despite qualms among many lawmakers,[5] enjoyed a wider margin of bipartisan support than had the 1991 stat-

---

[2] George W. Bush, "President's Remarks at the United Nations General Assembly," September 12, 2002.

[3] The White House's case against Iraq also was made in White House, *A Decade of Deception and Defiance*, Washington, D.C., September 12, 2002, released the day of the president's UN speech.

[4] See House Joint Resolution 114, Joint Resolution to Authorize the Use of United States Armed Forces Against Iraq, October 10, 2002. An identical version passed in the Senate.

[5] Congressional Quarterly, "Concerns Linger for Lawmakers Following Difficult Vote for War," *CQ Weekly*, October 12, 2002, pp. 2671–2678.

ute backing the first Gulf War;[6] the measure passed by a better than 3-to-1 margin in the Senate and 2-to-1 in the House.[7] It also involved, on November 8, 2002, unanimous passage of a UNSC resolution (UNSCR 1441) that warned Iraq of "serious consequences"—code for U.S. military action—if it remained in material breach of past UNSC resolutions on the matter.[8]

Secretary of State Powell's February 5, 2003 presentation to the UNSC also was a part of the campaign, aimed to convince fence-sitters in the Security Council of the seriousness of Iraqi WMD and other weapon programs,[9] Iraq's continuing track record of violating its disarmament obligations under UNSCR 1441, and the need for a more effective enforcement mechanism than UN inspections.

Finally, faced with Iraq's continued intransigence in the face of the new resolution, the campaign involved a prolonged—and ultimately unsuccessful—effort to secure a second UNSC resolution authorizing the U.S. use of force, a resolution that was viewed by the administration as desirable but not absolutely necessary.[10] This course

---

[6] The 1991 statute (Public Law 102-1) had been backed by 57 percent of the House and 52 percent of the Senate; the measure that cleared on October 11, 2003 was backed by 69 percent of the House and 77 percent of the Senate. See Gebe Martinez, "Concerns Linger for Lawmakers Following Difficult Vote for War," *CQ Weekly*, October 12, 2002, pp. 2671–2678.

[7] A total of 215 House Republicans (96 percent), 81 House Democrats (39 percent), 48 Senate Republicans (98 percent), and 29 Senate Democrats (58 percent) voted in favor. Ibid.

[8] UNSCR 1441 stated that Iraq had been and remained "in material breach of its obligations under relevant resolutions," especially UNSCR 687 (1991), which called upon Iraq to "unconditionally accept the destruction, removal, or rendering harmless, under international supervision" of weapons of mass destruction and ballistic missiles with a range greater than 150 kilometers.

[9] See Secretary Colin L. Powell, "Remarks to the United Nations Security Council," February 5, 2003, U.S. State Department website, http://www.state.gov/secretary/rm/2003/17300.htm, accessed August 22, 2003.

[10] The United States maintained that UNSCRs 678 and 687 gave the United States and its allies full authority to use force in ridding Iraq of weapons of mass destruction. See White House, "President Says Saddam Hussein Must Leave Iraq Within 48 Hours," March 17, 2003. Moreover, it argued that a second resolution was unnecessary; as Secretary Powell put it: "[E]verybody who signed up, everybody who voted for that resolution, understood that serious consequences meant the likelihood of war." See Secretary Powell's interview with French television channel TF-1, January 29, 2003.

of action essentially failed when, on March 11, 2003, French President Jacques Chirac declared that his country would veto any resolution that opened the way to war,[11] whereupon the United States abandoned any further efforts to secure UN approval for military action.

When Saddam and his sons failed to leave Iraq by the end of a 48-hour deadline set by President Bush on March 17, 2003,[12] the president announced, on March 19, 2003,[13] the beginning of major combat operations in Iraq—dubbed "Operation Iraqi Freedom."[14] On May 1, 2003, the president declared major combat operations to have ended,[15] and the focus shifted to efforts to capture Saddam and his lieutenants and to secure and rebuild Iraq.

Attitudes Since the First Gulf War

In one of the most remarkable—yet least remarked upon—records in American public opinion toward military operations, there has been, since the end of the first Gulf War, consistent majority support for military action against Iraq and for the basic proposition of invading Iraq with ground troops in an effort to remove Saddam Hussein from power.

All of the major U.S. military actions against Iraq since the first Gulf War—in January and June 1993, in October 1994, and in De-

---

[11] As Chirac put it: "No matter what the circumstances we will vote 'no.'" See Paris France-2 Television in French, "France's President Chirac Interviewed on Iraq Crisis," March 10, 2003.

[12] George W. Bush, "President Says Saddam Hussein Must Leave Iraq Within 48 Hours," March 17, 2003.

[13] George W. Bush, "President Bush Addresses the Nation," March 19, 2003.

[14] The president's Gallup approval level rose from 58 to 71 percent. Gallup, March 14–15, 2003, N=1,007 and Gallup, March 22–23, 2003, N=1,019.

[15] George W. Bush, "President Bush Announces Major Combat Operations in Iraq Have Ended," May 1, 2003.

cember 1998—were met with high levels of support,[16] and the public has consistently supported both tougher action against Iraq[17] and Saddam's overthrow, even before the Bush administration campaign against Iraq that began in the fall of 2002.[18]

Indeed, there is not a single instance in the 103 times the question was asked since March 1992—including 38 instances when Gallup asked respondents whether they would support an invasion with ground troops and eight instances when Time/CNN/Harris asked a similar question—that a majority of those polled failed to support a "regime change" in Baghdad by overthrowing Saddam Hussein.[19] Importantly, this was the case during the period *before* the notion of "regime change" even entered into use as a likely military objective for major combat operations.[20]

---

[16] George Gallup, Jr., and Frank Newport, "Support Strong for U.S. Bombing Raid on Iraq," *The Gallup Poll Monthly*, January 1993, p. 7; "Public Backs Air Strike," *The Gallup Poll Monthly*, June 1993, pp. 23–25; David W. Moore and Lydia Saad, "Public Supports Actions Against Iraq," *The Gallup Poll Monthly*, October 1994, pp. 14–15; and David W. Moore, "Public Backs Attack on Iraq," The Gallup Organization, December 19, 1998.

[17] See George Gallup, Jr., and Frank Newport, "Americans Support Military Action in Iraq," *The Gallup Poll Monthly*, July 1992, p. 50; David W. Moore, "Public Supports Stronger Stand Against Iraq; Gives Clinton High Marks for Actions So Far," The Gallup Organization, November 6, 1997; and David W. Moore, "Support Increasing For Military Action Against Iraq; Men in Favor, Women Opposed," The Gallup Organization, February 5, 1998.

[18] See the following publications of The Gallup Organization: Jeffrey M. Jones, "Removing Saddam Considered an Important Foreign Policy Goal; Majority Favors Sending U.S. Troops to Overthrow Iraqi President," June 21, 2002; Lydia Saad, "Do Americans Understand Bush Rationale for Striking Iraq? Fear of Weapons and Terrorism Are Paramount Reasons Given," August 12, 2002; and David W. Moore, "Majority of Americans Favor Attacking Iraq to Oust Saddam Hussein: But Support Has Declined to pre-9/11 level; Four in 10 Now Opposed," August 23, 2002.

[19] We identified a total of 103 instances in which such questions were asked since March 1991: Gallup asked its question 38 times, CBS News/New York Times 21 times, ABC News/Washington Post 20 times, Fox News 10 times, Time/CNN eight times, and NBC News/Wall Street Journal six times. The minimum level of support for invading Iraq was 51 percent.

[20] The 2001 Quadrennial Defense Review created a new construct for shaping forces that was based on four elements: (1) Defending the United States; (2) Deterring aggression and coercion forward in critical regions; (3) Swiftly defeating aggression in overlapping major conflicts while preserving for the President the option to call for a decisive victory in one of those conflicts—including the possibility of regime change or occupation; and (4) Con-

Table 5.1
Support for Military Action to Remove Saddam Hussein

	Full Post–Gulf War March 1991 to April 2003	Pre-9/11 March 1991 to February 2001	9/11 to OIF Nov. 2001 to March 19, 2003	Post-9/11 Nov. 2001 to April 30, 2003
Question count	103	12	80	91
Mean	64	63	62	64
Median	64	64	61	64
Minimum	51	51	51	51
Maximum	82	82	78	81

NOTES: OIF = Operation Iraqi Freedom, i.e., the second Gulf War. Statistics calculated for pooled data including polling by Gallup, ABC News/Washington Post, CBS News/New York Times, Fox News, and NBC News/Wall Street Journal.

Table 5.1 provides summary statistics for data on the question of support for overthrowing Saddam Hussein for four periods: (1) the full 1991–2003 period; (2) the period prior to 9/11 (1991–2001); (3) the period between 9/11 and the beginning of the second Gulf War on March 20, 2003; and (4) the post-9/11 period, including the second Gulf War. As shown in the table, the average level of support for military action against Iraq was in the 60–65 percent range, and the minima and maxima were quite stable across the various time periods.

Figure 5.1 presents Gallup's data on the matter of overthrowing Saddam for the decade from March 1991 to February 2001, a total of 12 questions,[21] and Figure 5.2 presents the data for the 91 times such questions were asked in the two years from March 2001 through April 2003.[22]

ducting a limited number of smaller-scale contingency operations. See DoD, *Quadrennial Defense Review Report,* September 30, 2001, p. 17. For an analysis of military strategy and planning in the three major strategy and force structure reviews since the end of the Cold War that preceded the 2001 QDR—the Base Force, the Bottom-Up Review, and the 1997 Quadrennial Defense Review—see Larson, Orletsky, and Leuschner (2001).

[21] On average, 63.5 percent of those polled favored this option; the minimum percent supporting was 51 percent (in April 1991) and the maximum was 82 percent (in January 1993).

[22] All told, Gallup asked questions 38 times, CBS News/New York Times asked questions 21 times, ABC News/Washington Post asked questions 20 times, Fox News asked questions 10 times, Time/CNN/Harris asked questions 8 times, and NBC News/Wall Street Journal asked questions 6 times.

Figure 5.1
Support for Invading Iraq to Remove Saddam from Power, March 1991–February 2001

February 1991 to January 1993: Would you support or oppose having U.S. forces resume military action against Iraq to force Saddam Hussein from power?

June 1993 to September 2002: Various question wordings.

Late September 2002 forward: Would you favor or oppose sending U.S. ground troops to invade Iraq in order to remove Saddam Hussein from power? (Gallup/CNN/USA Today)

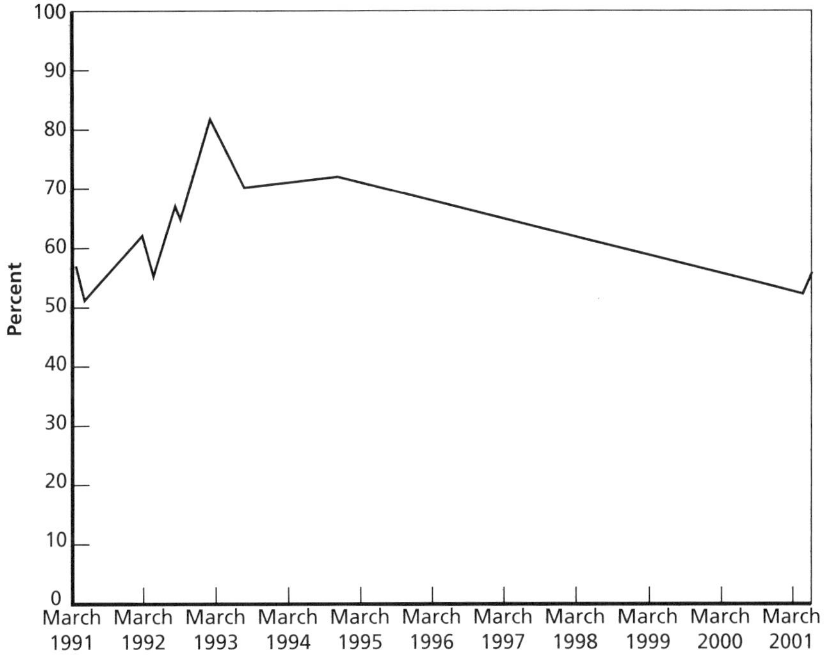

RAND *MG231-A-5.1*

NOTE: Gallup varied the wording of its question somewhat over the period. Details are available from the Roper Center or The Gallup Organization.

As shown, in all cases, a majority supported the basic proposition of taking military action—in many cases including the use of ground troops—to overthrow Saddam's regime. There is, moreover, at least some evidence of growing sentiment in favor of war in the run-up to the war from about January 2003 on.

Figure 5.2
Post-9/11 Support for Invading Iraq to Remove Saddam from Power

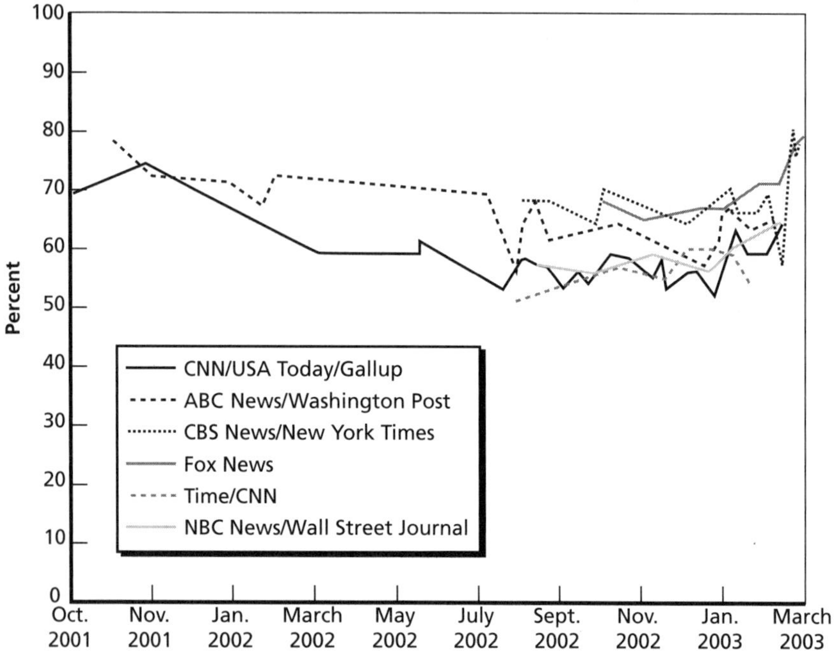

RAND *MG231-A-5.2*

NOTE: Wording for sources other than Gallup typically was as follows. ABC News/Washington Post: "Would you favor or oppose having U.S. forces take military action against Iraq to force Saddam Hussein from power?"; CBS News/New York Times: "Do you approve or disapprove of the United States taking military action against Iraq to try to remove Saddam Hussein from power?"; Fox News: "Do you support or oppose U.S. military action to disarm Iraq and remove Iraqi President Saddam Hussein?"; Time/CNN: "Do you think the U.S. should or should not use military action involving ground troops to attempt to remove Saddam Hussein from power in Iraq?"; NBC News/Wall Street Journal: "Do you think that the United States should or should not take military action to remove Saddam Hussein from power in Iraq?"

This high level of support is all the more impressive in light of the fact that, as was seen in the public opinion data on the peace operations of the 1990s, questions that mentioned ground troops in a combat role in other recent past military interventions typically failed to receive majority support.

This appears to be because of the public's assumption—an entirely reasonable one—that Army soldiers and Marines are likely to be more vulnerable to combat casualties than airmen or naval personnel. In the case of Iraq, however, there is at least some evidence of a very different pattern: a higher willingness to introduce ground troops than to rely solely on bombing (see Figure 5.3).

Although the public opinion data do not illuminate particularly well the reasons for this result, a plausible conjecture is that most believed that ground troops ultimately would be needed to effectuate

Figure 5.3
Support for Bombing Versus Ground Troops

Would you support or oppose a war against Iraq if it were only comprised of bombing the country?

Would you support or oppose a war against Iraq if it included sending in hundreds of thousands of U.S. ground troops? (Zogby International)

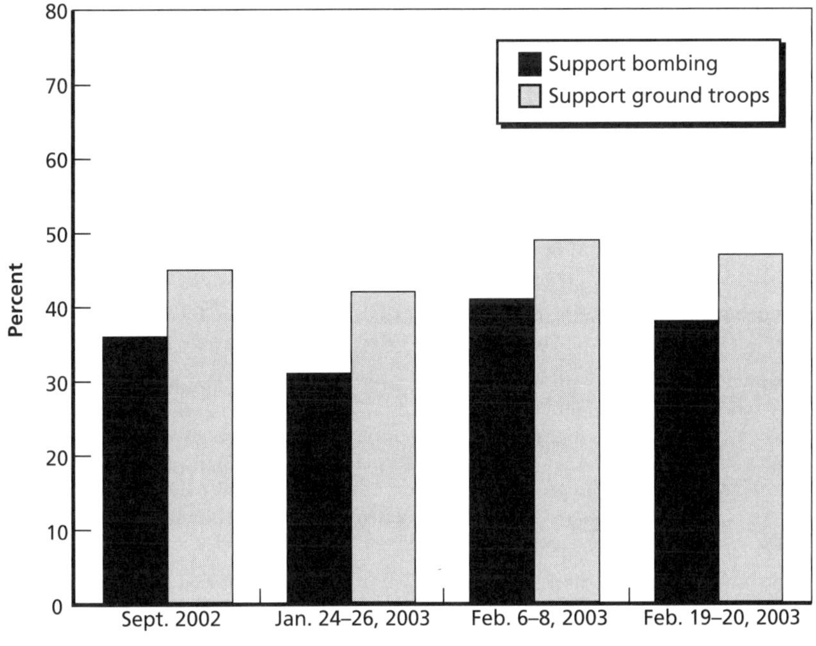

RAND *MG231-A-5.3*

Saddam's ouster, and that there was a greater tolerance for casualties to achieve this outcome.

The public opinion data provide additional evidence that a principal factor animating support for a second Gulf War was the desire that Saddam Hussein be removed from power:[23] majorities of six in ten or more typically expressed dissatisfaction with military operations focused on the limited objective of ensuring Iraqi cooperation with inspections, preferring the more ambitious aim of overthrowing Saddam.[24] In fact, majorities of those polled by ABC News in the fall of 2002 supported continuing U.S. efforts to overthrow Saddam even if Iraq cooperated with inspections.[25]

Attitudes in the Run-Up To War

We now turn to attitudes following the president's speech to the United Nations General Assembly in September 2002. The evidence suggests that the administration's campaign to press Iraq increased the salience of the Iraq issue as early as September.

The Importance of Iraq

Evidence of an increase in the salience of Iraq can be found in the data presented in Figure 5.4, which tracks those mentioning Iraq

---

[23] The desire to remove Saddam was a prominent theme in the first Gulf War, too. See Mueller (1994) and Larson (1996a).

[24] In September 1991, Gallup found only one in four (25 percent) who favored resuming military action against Iraq until Iraq cooperated or WMD sites had been destroyed, and 69 percent who favored resuming military action until Hussein was removed from power; in November 1998, Gallup found one in four (25 percent) who thought the goal of a U.S. attack against Iraq should be pressuring Saddam into complying with UN weapons inspections, while 70 percent favored removing Saddam. Gallup, September 26–29, 1991, N=1,005, and November 13–15, 1998, N=1,039.

[25] Only 31–39 percent of those polled in the fall of 2002 thought that if Iraq cooperated fully with UN inspections that the United States should drop its efforts to force Saddam from power, while 55–66 percent thought that the United States should continue these efforts. ABC News, September 23–26, 2002 and November 13–17, 2002.

Figure 5.4
Importance of Iraq Problem, November 2001–May 2003

Gallup: What is the most important problem facing the country today?

PIPA: Here are five foreign policy problems that the U.S. is facing these days. Thinking about the long term, please select the one that you feel is the most important. [Those mentioning Iraq. First response. Order randomized; question repeated with remaining problems until all ranked.]

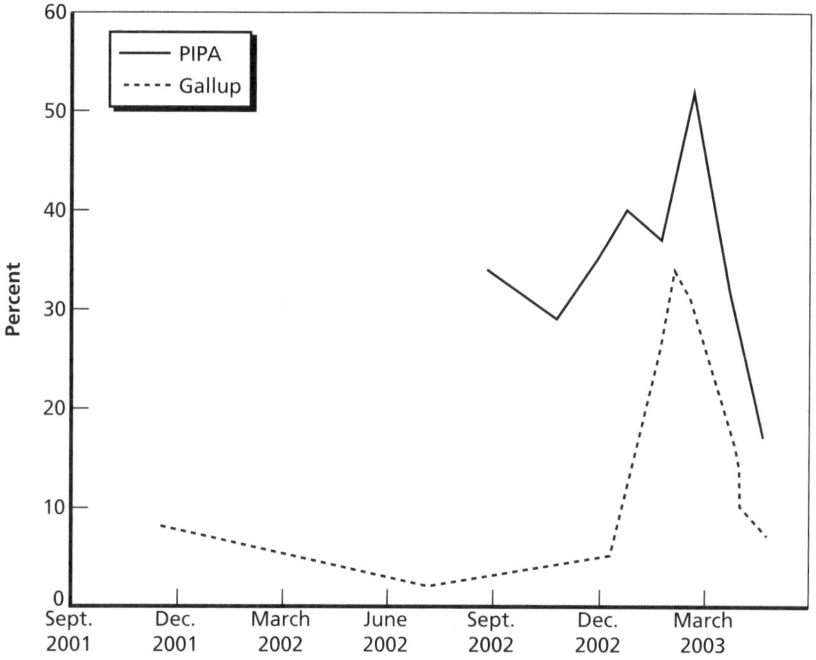

RAND *MG231-A-5.4*

either as the most important issue facing the nation or as the most important foreign policy problem.

The data from the Program on International Policy Attitudes (PIPA) suggest an increase in the salience of the Iraq issue as a foreign policy problem throughout the fall of 2002, while the Gallup data don't show a real increase in the salience of Iraq relative to other

Figure 5.5
Iraq and Terrorism as the Most Important Problem, March 2003–March 2004

What do you think is the most important problem facing this country today? (Gallup)

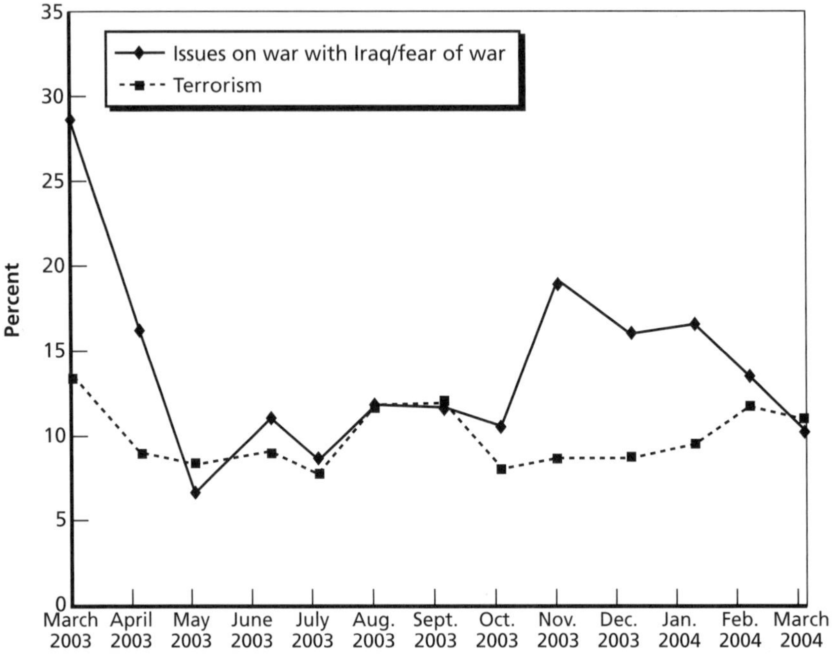

RAND *MG231-A-5.5*

national problems until after December 2002.[26] Also as shown, the salience of Iraq tapered off with the conclusion of major combat.

And as shown in Figure 5.5, there was a significant increase in the percentage who identified Iraq as the country's most important problem over the late summer and fall of 2003, but this has since tapered off from its November peak.

---

[26] The reason the Gallup series is significantly lower than the PIPA series is that the Gallup question asks respondents to consider all national problems facing the country, including domestic economic and social issues, while the PIPA question asks respondents to gauge the relative importance of foreign policy problems alone. The public generally has been most concerned about economic performance over the last couple of years.

Evidence of an increase in the salience of Iraq can also be found in the percentage of those who said that they were following the Iraq issue very closely (see Figures 5.6 and 5.7). Figure 5.6 shows that about 50 percent or more followed Iraq very closely between August 2002 to June 2003, and Figure 5.7 shows that nearly 80 percent were following Iraq very closely when the war began.

As shown, the percentage following Iraq very closely increased from about 30 percent in August 2002 to well over 50 percent in October 2002 and, with a few exceptions, generally remained above 50

Figure 5.6
New York Times Reporting and Percentage Following Iraq Very Closely

Polling by Gallup, Times/Mirror/Pew Research Central/PSRA, CBS News, and Los Angeles Times

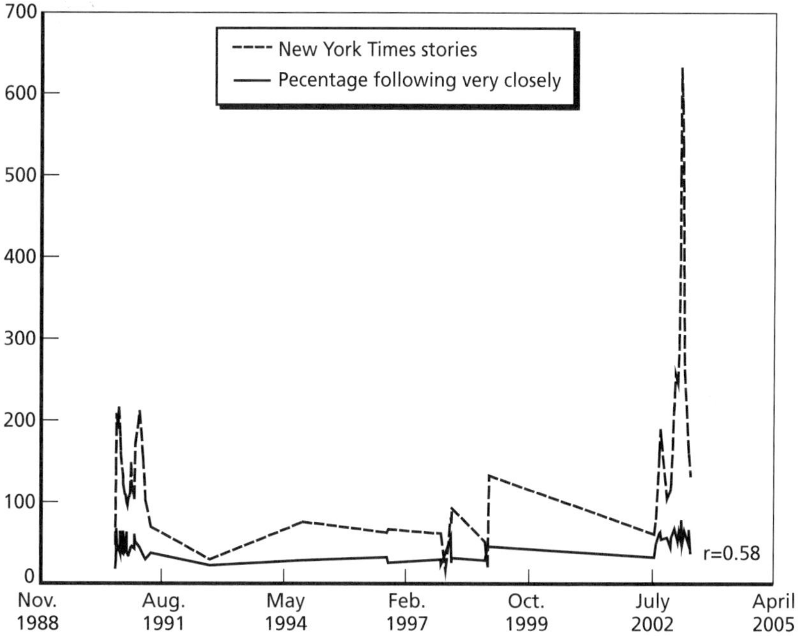

RAND *MG231-A-5.6*

Figure 5.7
Percentage Following Iraq "Very Closely," August 2002–June 2003

Polling by Gallup, Times/Mirror/Pew Research Center/PSRA, CBS News, and Los Angeles Times

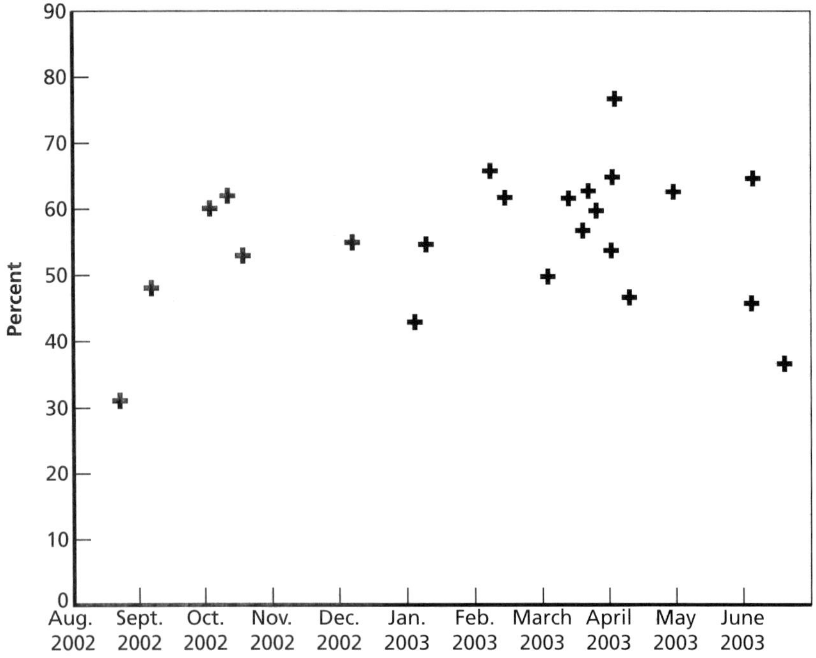

RAND *MG231-A-4.7A*

percent until the conclusion of combat operations in May 2003.[27] The relatively high correlation between the two series (r = 0.58) suggests a relatively strong relationship between media reporting and public attention.[28]

---

[27] Percentages this high are somewhat rare and typically restricted to major wars and crises.

[28] As described in Chapter Two, past research has suggested that the level of media reporting on a topic is a predictor of the likelihood that individuals will mention that topic, i.e., the media does not tell individuals what to think, per se, but tells them what to think *about*.

Figure 5.8
Percentage Following Iraq Very Closely, September 2002–March 2004

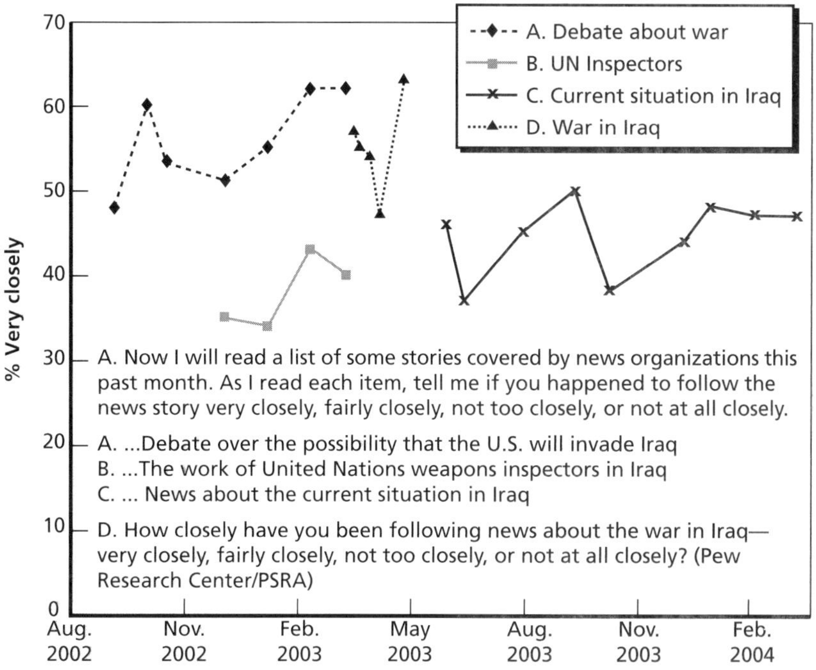

RAND *MG231-A-5.8*

Figure 5.8 presents data from the Pew Research Center on the percentage of Americans who have followed various Iraq-related issues very closely from August 2002 to March 2004; as shown, higher attention was paid to Iraq during the run-up to the war and during major combat operations than during the stability operations that followed it.

The Importance of Removing Saddam

As was described above, well before the war began in March 2003, there was substantial enthusiasm for the prospect of overthrowing Saddam, which provided a relatively firm base of support for military action. Table 5.2 presents data on the public's view of the importance of forcing Saddam Hussein from power from a number of polls conducted between November 2001 and September 2002, at the time of the president's United Nations speech.

Table 5.2
Importance of Forcing Saddam Hussein from Power, November 2001–September 2002

(I'm going to read you some objectives of the current war against terrorism. For each one, please tell me how important you think it is for the United States to meet that objective, using a five-point scale on which a '5' means that it is extremely important, and a '1' means that it is not important.) . . . Invading Iraq to remove Saddam Hussein and end his support of terrorism (NBC News/Wall Street Journal, November 9–11, 2001, N = 809)

5: Extremely important	52%
4	19
3	16
2	5
1: Not important	7
Cannot rate	1

How important do you think it is for the United States to force Saddam Hussein from power: very important, somewhat important, not too important, or not important at all? (ABC News, August 29, 2002, N = 504, and September 12–14, 2002, N = 760)

	August 29, 2002	September 12–14, 2002
Very important	56%	68%
Somewhat important	30	23
Not too important	7	6
Not at all important	5	3
No opinion	3	1

(Now moving on to the topic of terrorist attacks (on the World Trade Center and the Pentagon, September 11, 2001) . . . I'm going to read you a list of different things that the United States could do in its fight against terrorism. As I read each one, please tell me how important you think the action is as a response to terrorism. We'll use a scale from 1 to 7 where 1 is Not at all important and 7 is Very important.) Okay . . . How important is . . . removing Saddam Hussein from power? (Investors Business Daily/Christian Science Monitor, September 3–8, 2002, N = 9014)

7: Very important	47%
6	14
5	12
4	7
3	5
2	6
1: Not at all important	7
Not sure	3

As shown in the table: polling by NBC News/Wall Street Journal in November 2001 found 71 percent who considered overthrowing Saddam to be at least somewhat important to the success of the war on terrorism, with 52 percent calling it "extremely important"; two polls by ABC News, one before and one after the president's September 12, 2002 UN General Assembly speech, show that even before the speech, 86 percent thought that forcing Saddam from power was an important goal, and more than half considered it to be very important.

Also as shown, that percentage grew to 91 percent immediately following the president's UN General Assembly speech, with nearly 70 percent considering it very important. While the change in the overall percentage who believed in the importance of the goal was modest (from 86 to 91 percent), there clearly was fairly substantial movement into the "very important" category in the wake of the campaign's kickoff speech at the UN: the percentage in this category increased from 56 to 68 percent. Finally, 73 percent of those polled by Investors Business Daily/Christian Science Monitor in September 2002 thought removing Saddam to be at least somewhat important to the fight against terrorism, with 47 percent rating it "very important."

Inspections as an Alternative to War

There was a striking parallel between the run-up to the first and second Gulf Wars; in both cases, members of the public were asked to choose between two options—war and something else—and in both cases, members of the public lost faith in the efficacy of the nonmilitary option.

In the first Gulf War, of course, the choice was between war and continuing the program of economic sanctions that had been imposed on Baghdad. The data from that period suggest that over the fall of 1990 and early January 1991 the American public became increasingly pessimistic that this course of action was likely to yield the desired result of Iraq decamping from Kuwait; as a result, ultimately eight in ten came to support the first Gulf War.[29]

In the case of the second Gulf War, Iraq failed to voluntarily provide a full and complete disclosure of its WMD programs and had undertaken fairly blatant efforts to hide its program from the UN inspectors. In this case, then, the choice essentially was between war on the one hand, and continuing with the United Nations inspectors' efforts to search for evidence of Iraq's WMD program on the other. As they had before the first Gulf War, Americans became increasingly skeptical that the nonmilitary course of action was likely to yield the desired result, i.e., dismantlement of the Iraqi WMD program; not incidentally, many Americans also seemed more interested in overthrowing Saddam at that point than simply eliminating his WMD program.[30]

Figure 5.9 presents data on the matter of support for military action and for inspections. As shown in the figure, the percentage who favored giving the UN inspectors more time declined pretty dramatically in February 2003, while the percentage favoring military action increased, especially in March 2003; a growing percentage also became convinced that the president had done enough to win international support for the war.[31]

Also like the first Gulf War, the policy alternatives in the debate were partisan ones: a Republican president offered a policy that would take the nation to war if Iraq failed to comply with the UN

---

[29] For data and analysis on this point, see Larson (1996a, 1996b) and Mueller (1994).

[30] For example, in December 1998 when Iraq expelled the UN inspectors, CBS News/New York Times asked: "Do you think the U.S. (United States) should continue air strikes against Iraq only until Saddam Hussein cooperates with the United Nations weapons inspectors, or should the air strikes continue until Saddam Hussein is removed from power?" Only 28 percent said that air strikes should continue until Saddam cooperated, whereas 62 percent said that they should continue until Saddam was removed. CBS News/New York Times, December 13–17, 1998, N=1,992.

[31] The belief that the president had done enough to win international support for the war grew from 54 percent in mid-September 2002, to 66 percent in mid-December, to 72 percent on March 17, 2003. See ABC News/Washington Post Poll, "Support for War Spikes as Bush Sets a Deadline," March 18, 2003.

Figure 5.9
Declining Faith in UN Inspections

Left: Should the U.S. take military action against Iraq fairly soon, or should the U.S. wait and give the UN and weapons inspectors more time? (CBS News/New York Times)

Right: Which of these comes closest to your opinion? Iraq's development of weapons is a threat to the U.S. that requires military action right now. OR, Iraq's development of weapons is a threat that can be contained with inpections for now. OR, Iraq's development of weapons is not a threat to the U.S. at all. (CBS News/New York Times)

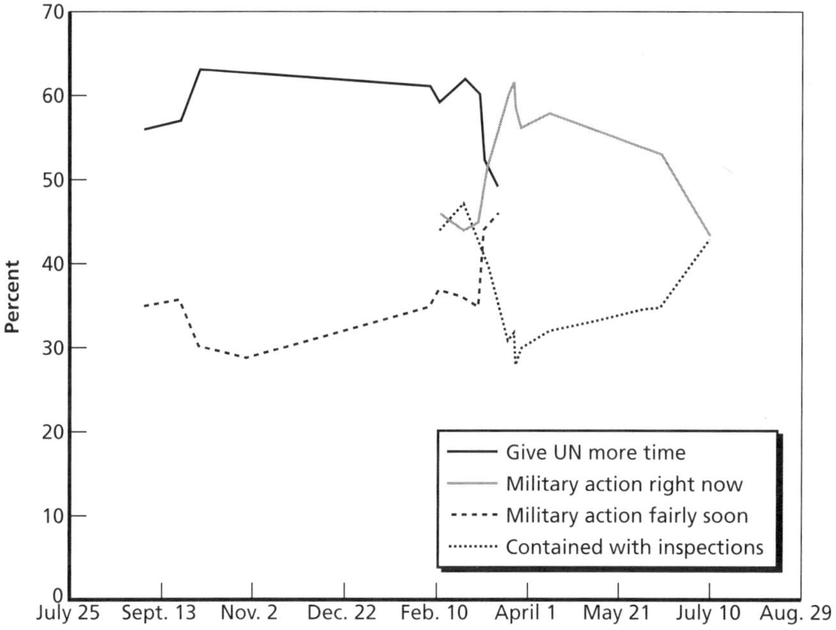

RAND *MG231-A-5.9*

resolutions demanding that it disclose its WMD program and disarm, and its alternative, promoted by some Democratic leaders, advocated the continuation of the inspection regime for an indeterminate period in the hope both that war might be avoided and that UN inspections might turn something up.

Not surprisingly, public preferences for these alternatives also were partisan in nature: as shown in Figure 5.10, about two-thirds of

Figure 5.10
Partisan Divisions on Military Action or Giving UN Inspectors More Time

Should the U.S. take military action against Iraq fairly soon, or should the U.S. wait and give the UN and weapons inspectors more time? (CBS News, March 15–16, 2003, N=1,049)

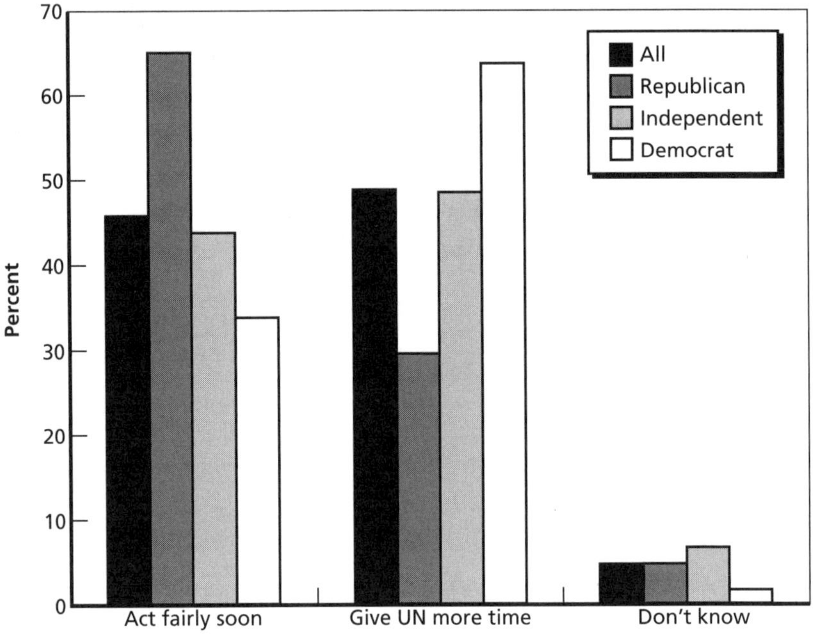

RAND *MG231-A-5.10*

the Republicans polled by CBS News on March 15–16, 2003 preferred military action, while about two-thirds of the Democrats polled preferred giving the United Nations more time.

United Nations Authorization and the Participation of Allies

The second major issue in the run-up to the war was the importance of United Nations authorization for U.S. military action and the number of countries that would join the United States in its "coalition of the willing."

Some polling—and even more commentary—seemed to suggest that the American public would not support a U.S. war in Iraq without a United Nations authorization.[32] As suggested by the data presented earlier, however, this conclusion turned out to be quite wrong—strong majorities supported the war, and support for the combat phase of the war appeared to be fairly robust.

In fact, what seems to be clear is that while most Americans would have *preferred* United Nations authorization as well as the participation of a number of the United States' major allies with whom the burden might be shared, it was not a condition for supporting the war (see Table 5.3).[33]

As shown in the table, 56 percent of those polled by ABC News on March 5–9, 2003 indicated that UN Security Council support was desirable, but not necessary, and 23 percent of the 35 percent who said that Security Council authorization was necessary indicated that they would support the war if the United States had support from the governments of the United Kingdom, Australia, and Spain. Taken together, this suggested support approaching eight in ten, about the levels actually observed during the war.

---

[32] See, for example, Frank Newport, "Public Wants Congressional and U.N. Approval Before Iraq Action; Majority Support for Removing Saddam Hussein Remains, but Many Feel President Bush Needs to Do Better Job of Explaining Rationale for Such Action," The Gallup Organization, September 6, 2002; Pew Research Center, "Bush Engages and Persuades Public on Iraq," polling report, September 19, 2002; "Nine Key Questions About Public Opinion on Iraq; Support for Invading Iraq Remains High—But With Conditions," The Gallup Organization, October 1, 2002; Lydia, Saad, "Top Ten Findings About Public Opinion and Iraq; Public Still Supportive of Iraq Invasion, But With Reservations," The Gallup Organization, October 8, 2002; Joseph Carroll, "Americans on Iraq: Military Action or Diplomacy?" The Gallup Organization, October 8, 2002; David W. Moore, "Support for Invasion of Iraq Remains Contingent on U.N. Approval; Most Americans Doubt Saddam Hussein Will Comply With U.N. Resolutions," The Gallup Organization, November 12, 2002; and David W. Moore, "Public Rallying Around Bush's Call for War; But Less Than Majority Support War Without New U.N. Vote," The Gallup Organization, February 11, 2003.

[33] See ABC News/Washington Post Poll, "Most Support Allied Attack Even Without U.N. Support," February 10, 2003.

Table 5.3
Support With and Without UN and Allies, March 2003

Do you think that getting support from the United Nations Security Council is necessary before the United States goes to war with Iraq, or is support from the United Nations Security Council desirable, but not necessary?

(If necessary, ask:) What if the United States has support from the governments of other countries, such as Great Britain, Australia and Spain . . . in that case is getting support from the United Nations Security Council necessary (before the United States goes to war with Iraq), or desirable, but not necessary?

Desirable, not necessary	56%
Necessary, of which	35
Desirable, not necessary	23
Necessary	8
Not desirable (volunteered)	2
No opinion	2
Not desirable (volunteered)	5
No opinion	4

NOTE: ABC News, March 5–9, 2003, N=1,032.

Attitudes toward the importance of UN approval were heavily partisan: as shown in Figure 5.11, large majorities of Republicans generally supported U.S. military action whether or not the United Nations approved, while only about a third of the Democrats and four in ten Independents took this position.

Support for Military Action in Iraq

The average overall support for military action against Iraq appears generally to have been unaffected until after December 2002, however. As suggested by Figure 5.12, which presents the average monthly support for military action from 82 polling questions from various organizations, average support for military action appears to have remained within a few points of 60 percent from August 2002 until January 2003, but it rose by about seven points between January and March 18, 2003; a rally of about 12 percentage points occurred once combat operations were underway that carried on through April 2003.

Figure 5.11
Importance of UN Authorization to Support for Military Action by Party, March 15–16, 2003

Which of these comes closer to your point of view about the U.S. taking military action against Iraq? (1) The U.S. should take military action against Iraq even if the UN opposes that action. (2) The U.S. should take military action ONLY if the UN supports the action. OR (3) The U.S. should not take military action against Iraq at all. (CBS News, March 15–16, 2003, N=1,049)

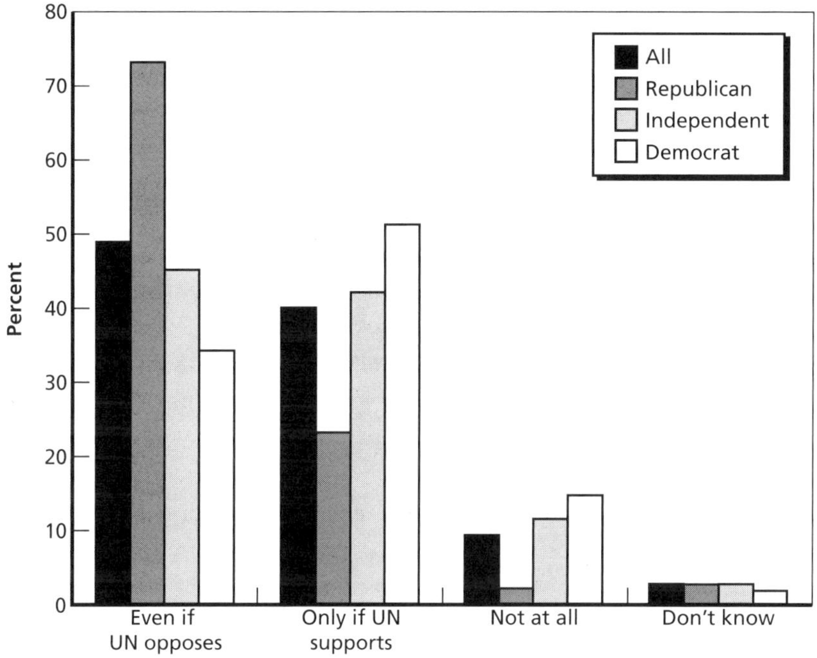

RAND *MG231-A-5.11*

As a result of uncertainties about the possible outcome of UN inspections in the face of continued Iraqi intransigence, whether UN authorization would be forthcoming, and other matters, it seems that most Americans were hedging their bets on committing themselves to an invasion of Iraq. But a full rally seems to have been underway just

Figure 5.12
Average Support for Military Action in Iraq, by Month

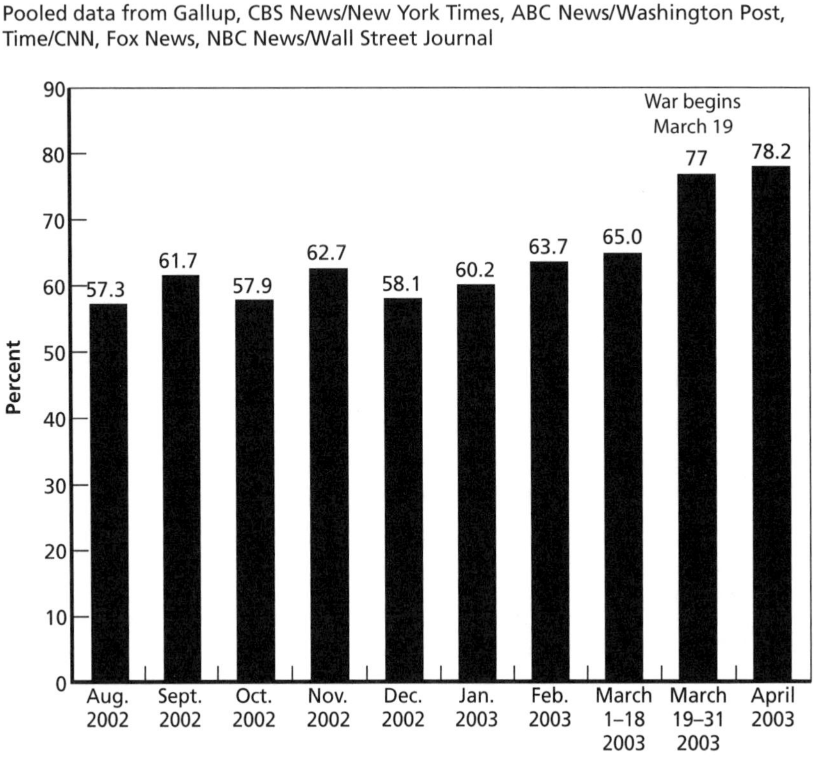

RAND *MG231-A-5.12*

after the president's 48-hour ultimatum to Saddam but before military action began.[34]

Figure 5.13 presents data from polling done in January and February 2003 that asked respondents whether they had made up their minds on the matter of invading Iraq. As shown, by about a two-to-one margin, those who favored invasion and had made up their

[34] ABC News/Washington Post Poll, "Support for War Spikes As Bush Sets a Deadline," March 18, 2003.

Figure 5.13
Firmness of Support or Opposition to War, January–March 2003

Would you favor or oppose invading Iraq with U.S. ground troops in an attempt to remove Saddam Hussein from power? (Gallup/CNN/USA Today)

A. (If Favor/Oppose, ask:) Would you say—your opinion will not change no matter what the outcome of the United Nations weapons inspections in Iraq, or your opinion could change depending on the outcome of the United Nations weapons inspections in Iraq?

B. (If Favor/Oppose, ask:) Would you say—your mind is made up about invading Iraq, or you could change your mind about invading Iraq?

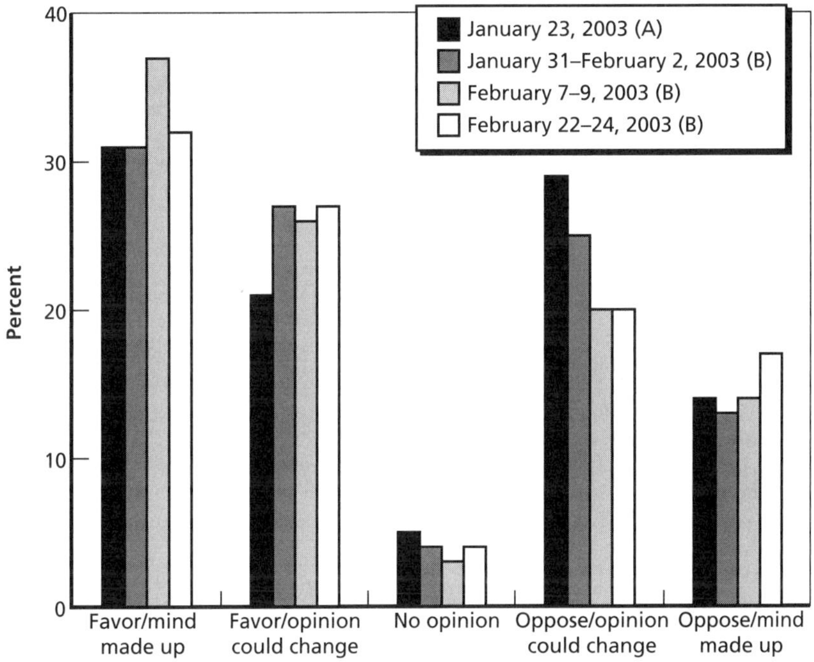

RAND *MG231-A-4.13A*

minds outnumbered those who opposed and had made up their minds, but roughly half of those polled said they could still change their minds on the matter.

In light of this hedging, the structure of support for a prospective war in Iraq during this period was also surprisingly robust. Figure 5.14 portrays the results of 16 polling questions that ABC News/

Washington Post and Fox News/Opinion Dynamics asked about the strength of support or opposition to military action between December 2002 and April 2003.

Figure 5.14
The Structure of Support for Prospective War in Iraq, December 2002–April 2003

ABC News/Washington Post (light): Would you favor or oppose having U.S. forces take military action against Iraq to force Saddam Hussein from power? (If favor/oppose, ask:) Would you say you favor/oppose military action against Iraq strongly or only somewhat? OR, Would you support or oppose the U.S. going to war with Iraq? Would you support/oppose it strongly or only somewhat?

Fox News (dark): Do you support or oppose the United States having taken military action to disarm Iraq and remove Iraqi President Saddam Hussein? (If support/oppose, ask:) Is that strongly support/oppose or only somewhat support/oppose?

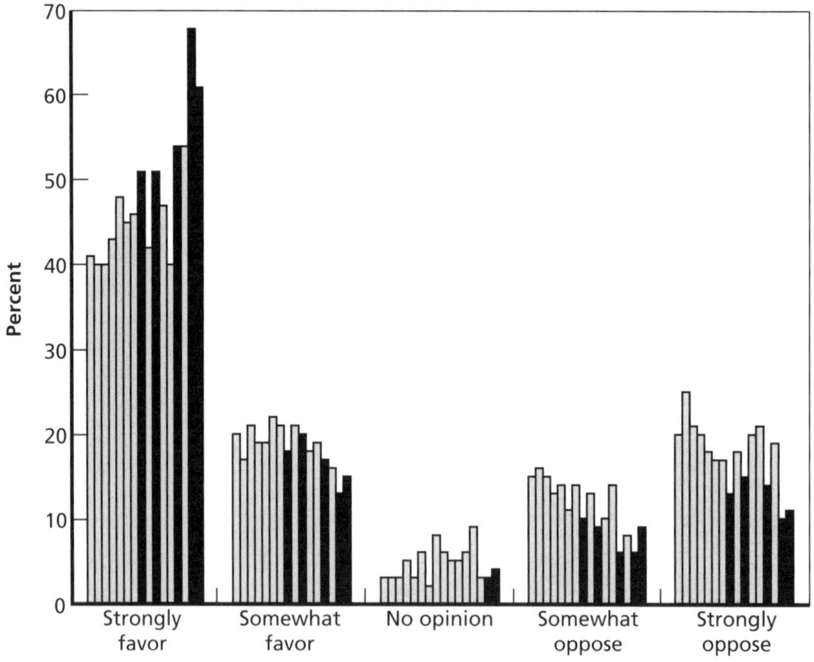

RAND *MG231-A-5.14*

As shown in the figure, respondents were twice as likely to strongly favor military action as strongly oppose it, and in every case those strongly favoring military action constituted a plurality; in four cases those strongly supporting actually constituted a majority.[35]

If one assumes that support fails gracefully (i.e., those who strongly favor and become disillusioned yield to growing doubts by shifting to a somewhat favorable position, and so on), the 10–20 percent margin over and above a simple majority and the structure of support for the war in Iraq appear to have provided a fairly substantial cushion of support for the war. It was also a clearly more favorable structure for support than that observed in Haiti, Bosnia, or Kosovo.

Although majorities in each party, and self-described independents, ultimately favored military action, there were important partisan differences in support (see Figure 5.15): there was an approximately 25–30 percent difference between Republicans on the one hand and Independents and Democrats on the other in support for the war. This difference reflected an important potential fault line in support, discussed further later in this chapter.

Taken together, and in spite of the hedging and partisan differences that were apparent, the administration had good reason to believe that a robust majority ultimately would favor military action if that course was chosen.

Questions on whether the war was likely to be worth its costs. Although support levels are sensitive to question wording, before and during the war majorities typically indicated that a war to remove Saddam would be worth the casualties and other costs (see Figure 5.16);[36] the peak in September 2003 is probably due to a rally in

---

[35] The average percentage who strongly favored military action was 48 percent, and the average percentage somewhat favoring military action was 19 percent.

[36] In fact, 50 percent of those polled just before the war said that they would even support a war against Iraq if it meant sending their son or daughter to war. Zogby International, March 14–15, 2003, N=1,129.

Figure 5.15
Approval of Military Action by Party, March 2003

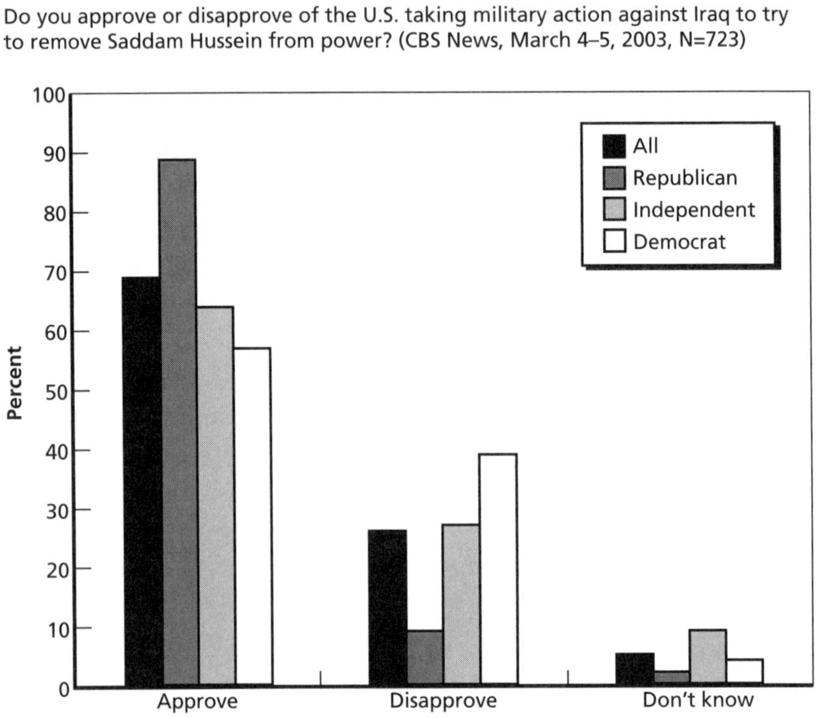

RAND *MG231-A-5.15*

support for war following President Bush's UN speech on Iraq, as well as Secretary of State Colin Powell's February 2003 presentation to the UN Security Council.

Participation in Demonstrations

Another indicator of support or opposition is participation in demonstrations or rallies related to the war. Despite the extensive media coverage devoted to demonstrations in the run-up to the war, it appears

Figure 5.16
Is Removing Saddam Worth Its Potential Costs?

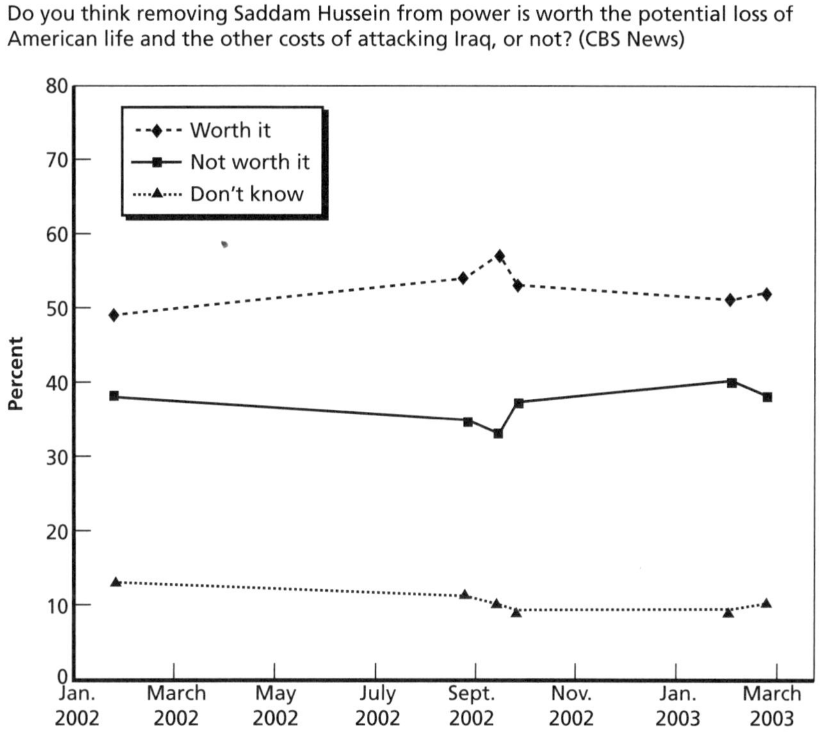

RAND *MG231-A-5.16*

as though only a very small fraction of Americans actually demonstrated against the approaching war: perhaps 2 percent.[37]

The Los Angeles Times' polling in late January 2003 found that only 3 percent of those polled said they themselves or someone they knew had participated in anti-war demonstrations, while ABC News/ Washington Post's polling in late March 2003 found that only 2 percent of those polled had actually attended any anti-war demonstra-

[37] Polling during the Vietnam War also found that only small percentages of Americans had participated in anti-war demonstrations.

tions.[38] According to the Los Angeles Times data, whereas 3 percent of Democrats and Independents had themselves participated in demonstrations, 5 percent of Republicans had; additionally, 11 percent of Democrats knew someone else who had demonstrated, whereas only 1 percent of Republicans said that they knew someone who had done so.

There appears to have been somewhat greater interest than actual participation in demonstrations: 5 percent of those polled by Pew/PSRA said that they had used the web to get information on local rallies or demonstrations.[39] And according to polling by the Los Angeles Times in early April 2003, a total of only 6 percent of those polled had expressed their opinion by demonstrating, sending emails or letters to congressional representatives, or other forms of communicating their positions.[40] The implication seems to be that since participating in a demonstration can be costly in personal time and other ways, two-thirds of those who expressed any interest at all in demonstrations ultimately balked at participating and instead wrote letters.

Moreover, the demonstrations may not have had their intended effect of creating sympathy for the demonstrators' cause, much less a bandwagon in opposition to the war: while 7 percent of those polled by ABC News/Washington Post said that the demonstrations had made them more likely to oppose the war, nearly three times as many—20 percent—said that it made them more likely to support

---

[38] ABC News/Washington Post asked: "Have you yourself attended any anti-war demonstrations, or have you attended any pro-war demonstrations, since the war with Iraq began?" Two percent said that they had attended anti-war demonstrations, half as many (1 percent) said they had attended pro-war demonstrations, and 96 percent said that they had not attended any demonstrations. ABC News/Washington Post, March 23, 2003, N=580.

[39] Pew/PSRA asked: "Thinking about the war in Iraq, in the last week, have you used the web to . . . get information about how to get involved politically, including local rallies or demonstrations?" Five percent said that they had done this, while 95 percent said they had not. Pew/PSRA, March 20–25, 2003, N=1,600.

[40] Los Angeles Times, April 2–3, 2003, N=745.

the war, and 71 percent said that it made no difference at all.[41] Other polling found even less sympathy for the demonstrators.[42]

Attitudes During the War

There was a substantial increase in support for the war—a "rally" of perhaps ten points—once military action actually began on March 19, 2003 (see Figure 5.17).[43] Once begun, support for the war typically was in the 70–75 percent range (Figures 5.17 and 5.18), a level of support not seen since the first Gulf War and the initial intervention in Somalia.[44]

CBS News' question on approval or disapproval for the war showed an increase in support for military action from about 65 percent to nearly 80 percent; various versions of what is commonly called the "mistake" question suggest consistent support from 70 percent or more from February through July 2003; and the Pew Research Center's question on whether the United States made the right decision in going to war (Figure 5.19) suggests support peaking above 70 percent during the combat phase and trending down to just a bit above 60 percent in July 2003, a time in which U.S. forces were increasingly under attack by irregulars and the administration was

[41] Ibid.

[42] Gallup/CNN/USA Today asked: "In recent days, some people protesting the war (with Iraq) have tied up traffic in major cities. Does this type of protest make you: more sympathetic to the protestors' cause, less sympathetic to the protestors' cause, or does it not make any difference to you either way?" Five percent said that the protests made them more sympathetic, 67 percent said less sympathetic, and 27 percent said it made no difference. Gallup/CNN/USA Today, March 22–23, 2003, N = 1,020. Polling during the Vietnam War also found a fair amount of hostility toward anti-war demonstrators.

[43] Most of the academic research on the so-called "rally effect" focuses on changes in the Gallup presidential approval rating.

[44] See the appendix in Larson (1996a) for question wording and data.

Figure 5.17
Approval of Military Action Against Iraq, March 17–April 27, 2003

Do you approve or disapprove of the United States taking military action against Iraq to try to remove Saddam Hussein from power? (CBS News)

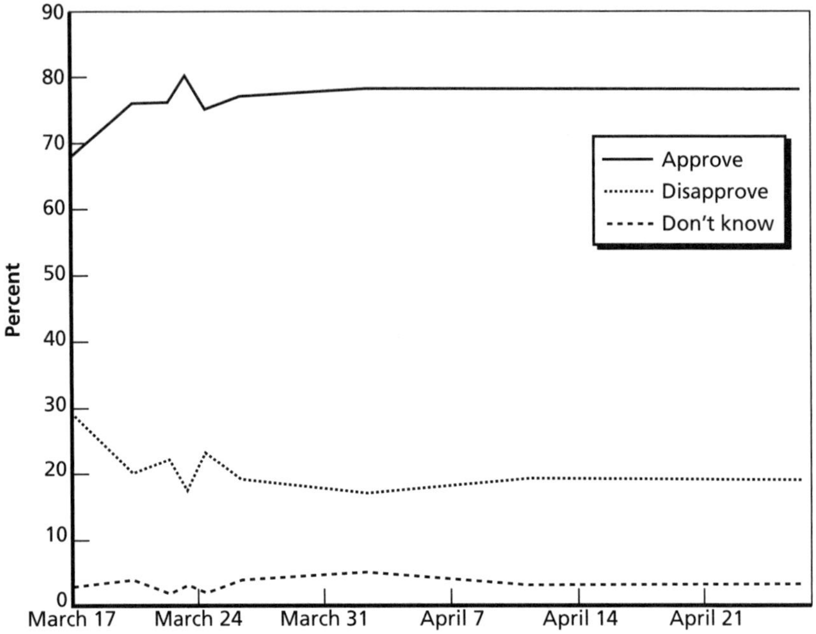

RAND *MG231-A-5.17*

under attack by critics at home for its pre-war claims regarding weapons of mass destruction.[45]

[45] See David W. Moore, "Little Concern About Lack of WMD in Iraq; Public Rejects Charges of Deliberate Deception by Bush Administration," The Gallup Organization, June 4, 2003, and David W. Moore, "Fewer Say Iraq Worth Going to War Over; Failure to Find Weapons of Mass Destruction, Continuing Conflict Appear to Have Major Impact," The Gallup Organization, July 1, 2003.

Figure 5.18
Various Versions of the "Mistake" Question on Iraq, March–July 2003

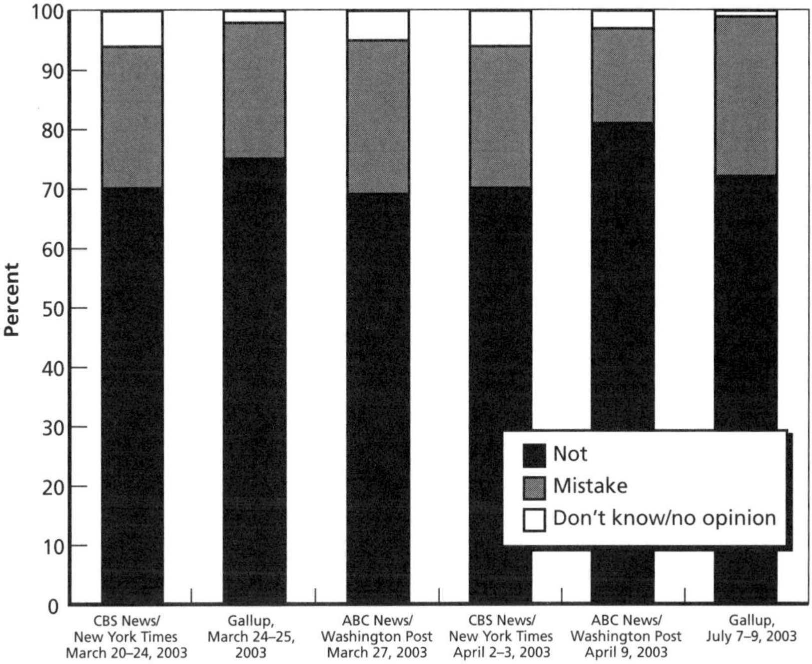

RAND *MG231-A-5.18*

NOTE: Question wordings were as follows. CBS News: "Do you think the United States made a mistake getting involved in the current war with Iraq, or not?"; Gallup: "In view of the developments since we first sent our troops to Iraq, do you think the United States made a mistake in sending troops to Iraq, or not?"; ABC News/Washington Post: "Considering everything, do you think the United States did the right thing in going to war with Iraq, or do you think it was a mistake?"

Moreover, initial support for the war appears to have been relatively robust (see Figure 5.20); the overall distribution of results is heavily weighted in favor of strong approval, while fewer than one in five strongly disapproved.

Figure 5.19
Did the U.S. Make the Right or Wrong Decision in Using Force with Iraq?

Do you think the U.S. made the right decision or the wrong decision in using military force against Iraq? (Pew Research Center)

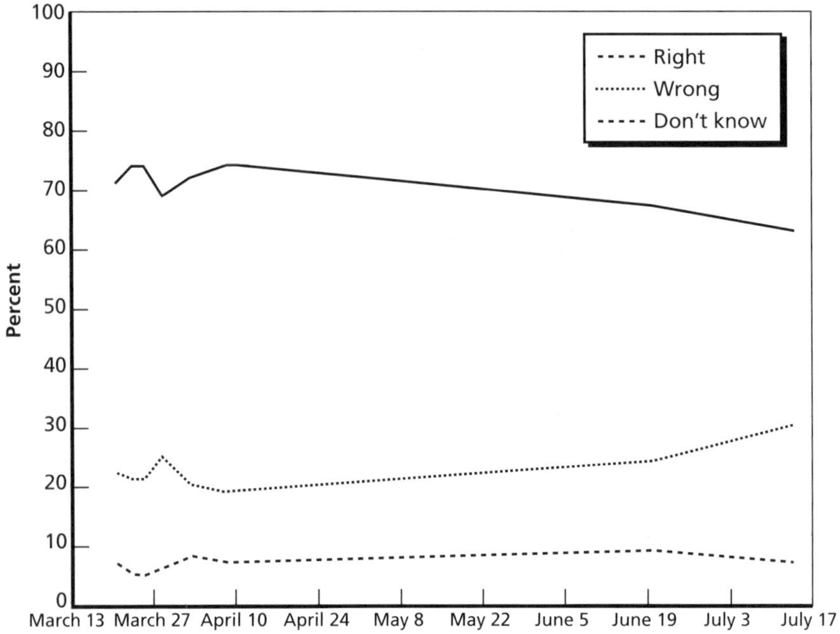

RAND *MG231-A-5.19*

Indeed, the data in the figure show that the structure of support—the distribution of respondents based upon the strength of their approval or disapproval—was even more favorable than that during the pre-war polling: by a three-to-one or better ratio, majorities strongly approved, while the percentage strongly disapproving remained below 20 percent. Thus, support was not only much higher but also far more robust in the Iraq case than for Haiti, Bosnia, or Kosovo.

Figure 5.20
The Structure of Support for the War in Iraq, Late March 2003

Do you approve or disapprove of the U.S. decision to go to war with Iraq? (If approve/disapprove, ask:) Do you approve/disapprove strongly or not strongly? (Gallup, March 20, 2003)

In general, do you approve or disapprove of current U.S. military actions in Iraq? (If approve/disapprove, ask:) Do you feel that way strongly or just somewhat? (Time/CNN/Harris, March 27, 2003)

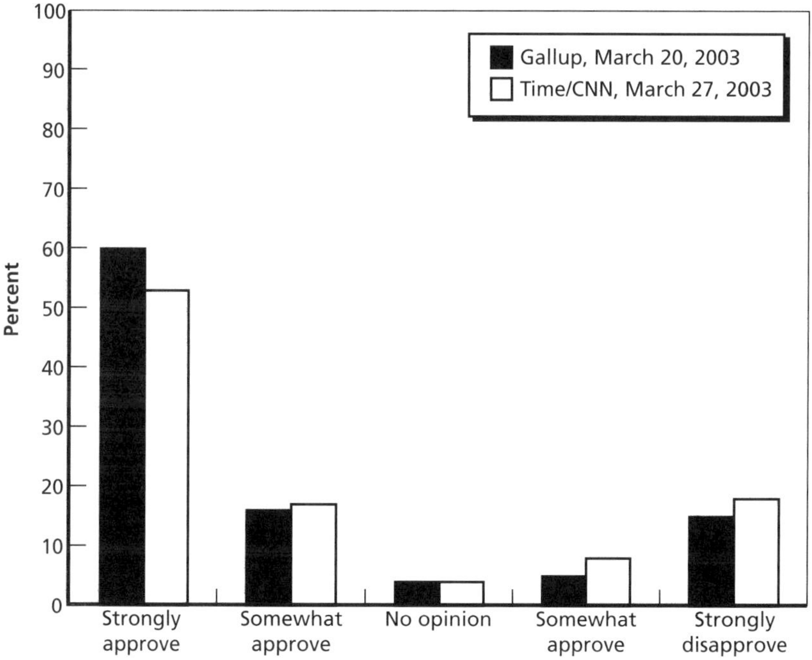

RAND *MG231-A-5.20*

Attitudes Since the End of Major Combat Operations

The public opinion data present a mixed picture of attitudes since the end of major combat operations; by some measures, support has remained reasonably steadfast, but some other measures, and changes in some of the key underlying beliefs, suggest an erosion in the foundations of support. We begin with a summary of support and opposition for U.S. operations in Iraq since the conclusion of major combat operations, and then turn to the sources of support.

As of April–May 2004, there is ample evidence of erosion in most measures of support for the war.

"Mistake" Questions

Questions that asked whether the war had been a mistake, and whether it had been the right decision to go to war, suggested that, as of April–May 2004, a little over half of Americans continued to approve of the war in Iraq.

At the only time Gallup asked its "mistake" question during the war, three in four (75 percent) indicated their support by saying that sending troops had not been a mistake. Between July 2003 and May 2004, those saying that the United States had not made a mistake in sending troops to Iraq fell from about seven in ten to a little over half (Figure 5.21).[46]

Meanwhile, those saying it had been the right decision to use force against Iraq also fell, from nearly seven in ten to a little over six in ten.[47] Thus, questions that asked whether the United States had made the right decision in going to war with Iraq typically found somewhat higher support than questions that asked whether the United States had made a mistake in using force, until these trends converged in mid-April 2004 at slightly more than half.[48]

---

[46] Fifty-four percent said that the United States had not made a mistake in sending troops to Iraq in Gallup, May 7–9, 2004, N=1,003.

[47] Two questions: Pew/PSRA, June 19–July 2, 2003, N = 1,201, and July 14–August 5, 2003, N = 2,528.

[48] Fifty-four percent said that the United States had made the right decision in using military force against Iraq in Pew Research Center/PSRA, April 21–25, 2004, N=1,000.

Figure 5.21
Various "Mistake" Questions, March 2003–May 2004

Gallup: In view of the developments since we first sent our troops to Iraq, do you think the U.S. made a mistake in sending troops to Iraq, or not?

Pew/PSRA: Do you think the U.S. made the right decision or the wrong decision in using military force against Iraq?

AP/MSNBC/IPSOS: All in all, thinking about how things have gone in Iraq since the U.S. went to war there in March 2003, do you think the United States/Bush administration...made the right decision in going to war in Iraq, or made a mistake in going to war in Iraq?

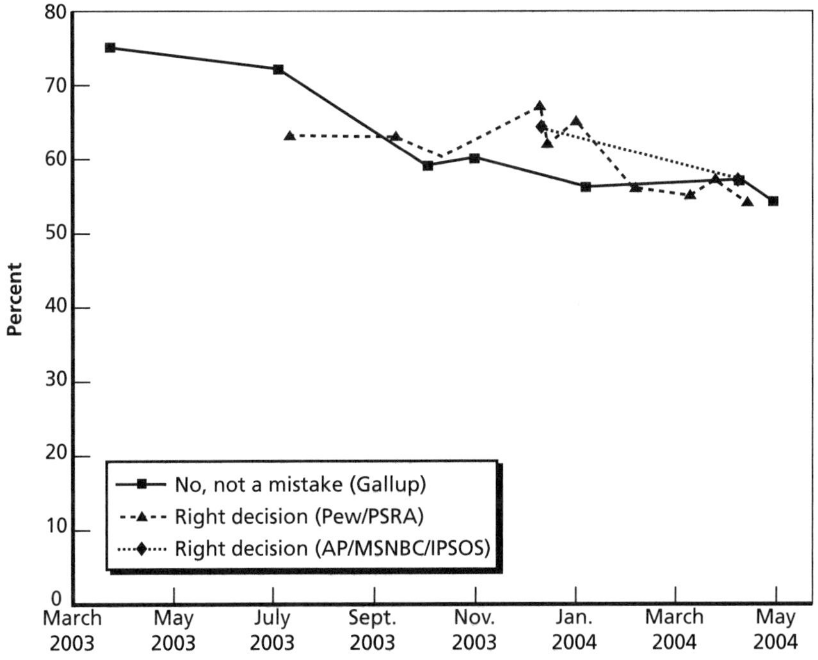

RAND *MG231-A-5.21*

Approval of U.S. Forces in Iraq

Support for the presence of U.S. forces in Iraq has varied with question wording, and most recently has ranged between about 45 and 65 percent, depending on question wording (Figure 5.22).

Figure 5.22
Support for a U.S. Military Presence in Iraq, July 2003–April 2004

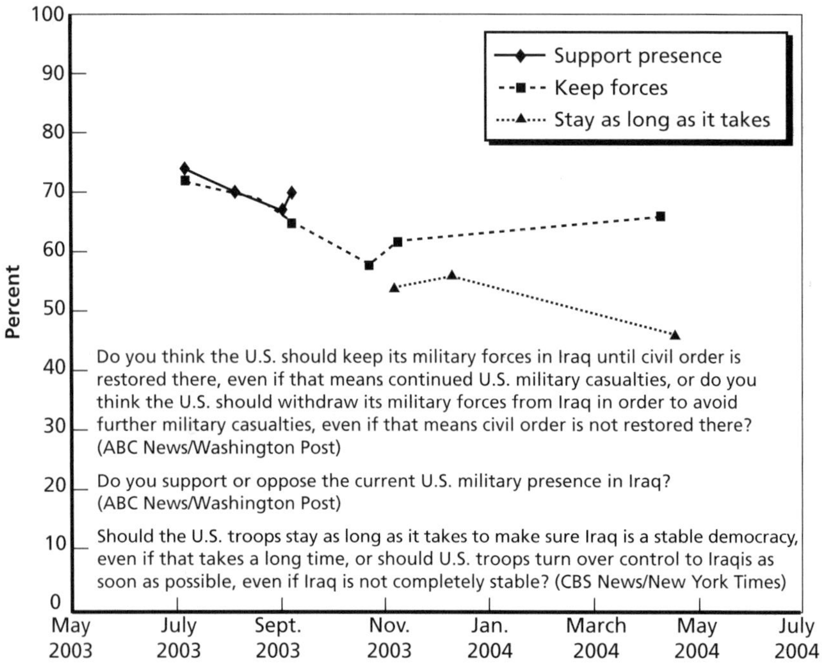

RAND *MG231-A-5.22*

The best available time series suggests a decline in support for keeping U.S. forces in Iraq until civil order was restored from the summer of 2003 until October 2003, and then a recovery (see Figure 5.22); the most recent reading by ABC News and the Washington Post in mid-April 2004 found 66 percent who thought the United States should keep military forces in Iraq until civil order is restored. Also as shown, there has been some erosion in the percentage that believe U.S. forces should stay as long as it takes to ensure that a stable democracy can be created in Iraq; fewer than half took this position in April 2004.

Questions on Whether the War Was Worth Its Costs

Since the end of the war, however, a number of measures suggest that doubts have increased as to whether it was worth going to war, whether the war was worth its costs, and other similar reflections of the public's deliberations over costs and benefits.

Figure 5.23 reports the results of polling by a number of polling organizations that asked respondents whether the situation in Iraq had been worth going to war. As shown, favorable sentiment was in the 70 percent range in April 2003 and, with the exception of a bump up in late July, since declined. By late April–early May 2004, the belief that the war had been worth its costs generally was held by around 50 percent, although CBS News/New York Times found only one in three in late April who thought that the end result of the war had been worth its costs.[49]

As early as June 2003, partisan differences had emerged in judgments about whether it had been worth going to war: 56 percent of Democrats said that the war had not been worth fighting, while only 39 percent of Independents and 10 percent of Republicans said they felt this way;[50] by May 2004, 80 percent of Republicans but just 27 percent of Democrats said the war in Iraq had been worth it.[51]

A combination of the failure to find weapons of mass destruction,[52] renewed partisanship following the war and as a result of the presidential campaign, the continuing unstable security situation, and the growing toll of American dead and wounded have all been at work in eroding Americans' belief that the war was worth its costs.

---

[49] CBS News/New York Times, April 23–27, 2004, N=1,042.

[50] ABC News/Washington Post Poll, "Public Disquiet Grows With Casualties in Iraq," June 23, 2003.

[51] Jeffrey M. Jones, "Half of Americans Continue to Say Iraq War 'Worth It'; One in Four Cite Situation in Iraq as Most Important Problem Facing Country," Gallup News Service, May 7, 2004.

[52] The change in attitudes toward WMD can be followed in David W. Moore, "Little Concern About Lack of WMD in Iraq; Public Rejects Charges of Deliberate Deception by Bush Administration," The Gallup Organization, June 4, 2003, and David W. Moore, "Fewer Say Iraq Worth Going to War Over; Failure to Find Weapons of Mass Destruction, Continuing Conflict Appear to Have Major Impact," The Gallup Organization, July 1, 2003.

Figure 5.23
Was It Worth Going to War in Iraq?

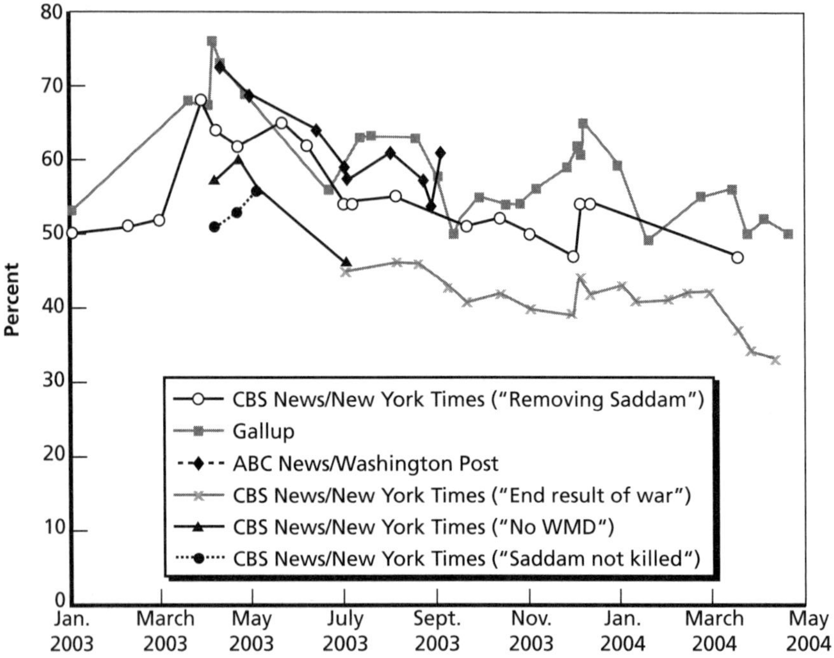

RAND *MG231-A-5.23*

Presidential Handling of Iraq

As shown in Figure 5.24, approval of the president's handling of the Iraq situation peaked in April 2003 and has since declined; indeed, several polls at the end of August suggest that a majority no longer approves of the president's handling of the Iraq situation.[53]

[53] For example, CBS News' September 15 poll found 46 percent who approved of the president's handling of Iraq; Newsweek/PSRA's September 18–19, 2003 and September 25–26, 2003 polls found 46 and 47 percent respectively approving of the president's handling of Iraq; and ABC News/Washington Post's September 26–29, 2003 poll found just 50 percent approving.

Figure 5.24
Approval of Presidential Handling of Situation with Iraq

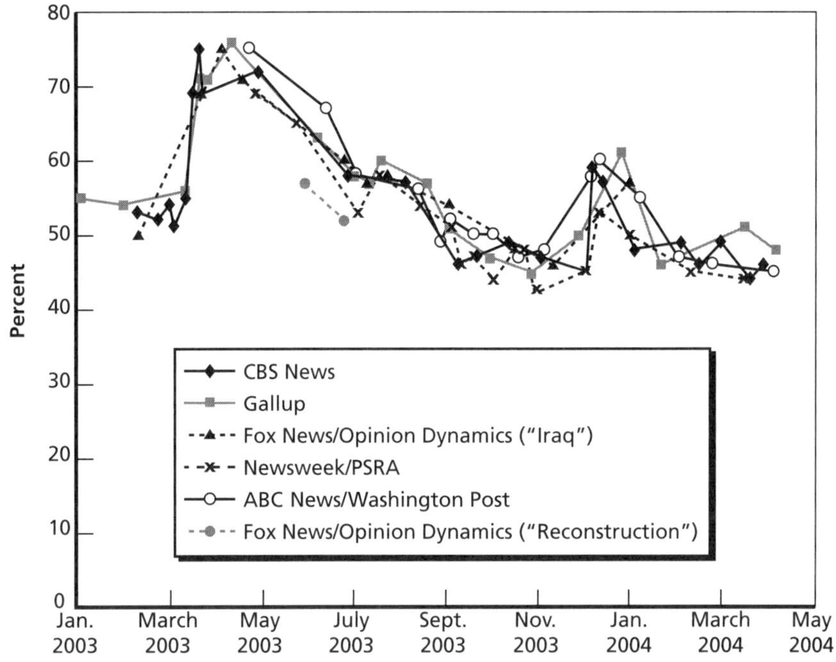

RAND *MG231-A-5.24*

The public opinion data also suggest that fewer than half believe that the administration has a clear plan for postwar Iraq; as shown in Figure 5.25, the percentage of respondents believing the administration has a clear plan as of April 2004 ranged from about one in three to slightly fewer than half.

Preferences Regarding Escalation or Withdrawal

As described in Chapter Two, when support for a military operation declines, it frequently leads to reduced support for maintaining the current level of troops and increased polarization over the level of commitment: some who have come to oppose the operation believe

Figure 5.25
Percent Believing Bush Administration Has a Clear Plan for Iraq

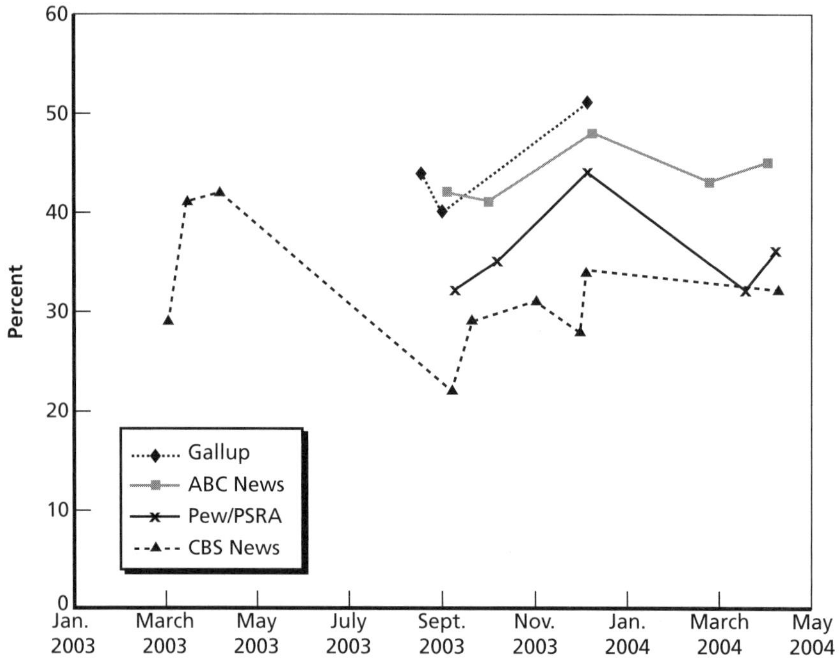

RAND *MG231-A-5.25*

that the best course of action is escalation and/or an increased commitment, whereas others believe the best course is for the United States to cut its losses and reduce its commitment by withdrawing. Our analyses suggest that preferences hinge primarily on the perceived importance of the stakes that are involved: in high-stakes operations (e.g., the first Gulf War, Afghanistan, and Iraq), most members of the public are loath to cut and run, while low-stakes operations (e.g., Somalia, Haiti, Bosnia, and Kosovo) are simply not deemed important enough to justify a costly commitment in blood and treasure.

Figure 5.26
Polarization over the Level of Commitment to Iraq, mid-April 2004

Which comes closest to your view about what the U.S. should now do about the number of U.S. troops in Iraq? The U.S. should send more troops to Iraq, the U.S. should keep the number of troops as it is now, the U.S. should withdraw some troops from Iraq, or the U.S. should withdraw all of its troops from Iraq? (Gallup)

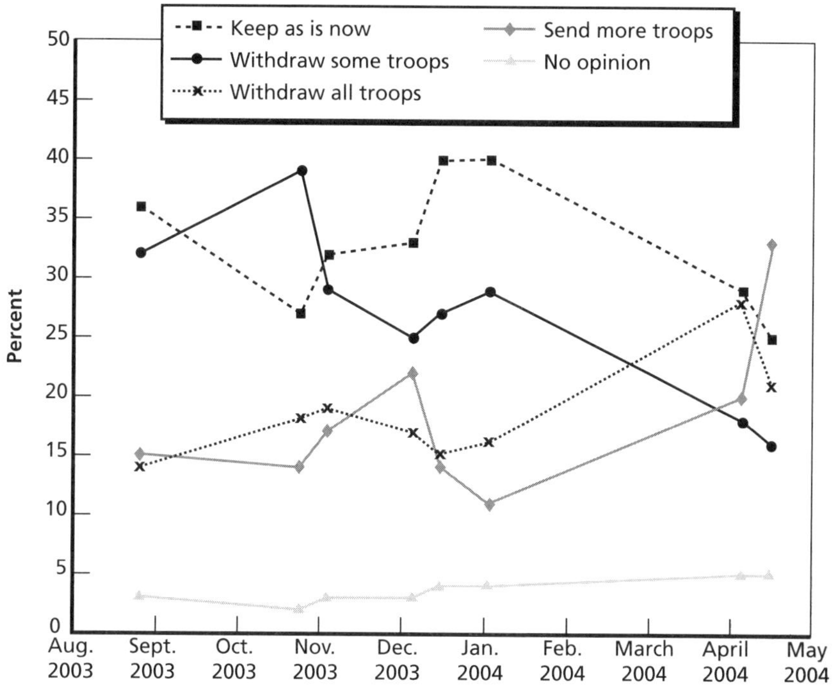

RAND *MG231-A-5.26*

As of April 2004, the public opinion data on Iraq were showing signs of just this sort of polarization over the level of commitment in Iraq (Figure 5.26).

As shown in the figure, since about December 2003, the percentages who have favored maintaining troop levels or favored the withdrawal of some troops have declined, while those favoring send-

Figure 5.27
Polarization over the Level of Commitment to Iraq, mid-April 2004

Which comes closest to your view about what the U.S. should now do about the number of U.S. troops in Iraq? The U.S. should send more troops to Iraq, the U.S. should keep the number of troops as it is now, the U.S. should withdraw some troops from Iraq, or the U.S. should withdraw all of its troops from Iraq? (Gallup)

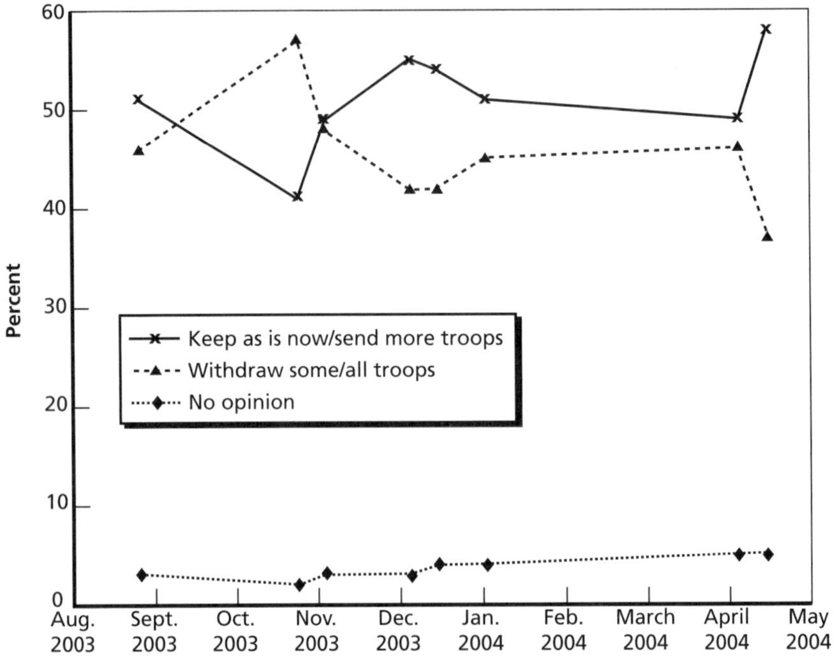

RAND *MG231-A-5.27*

ing more troops and favoring withdrawal of all troops has increased In mid-April, however, the percentage favoring sending more troops jumped, while those favoring maintaining troops or withdrawal of some or all troops have declined.

When we combine support for the withdrawal options and support for maintaining or increasing troop levels, it becomes clear that from early November 2003 to early April 2004, the administration continued to have a permissive majority in favor of current or increased troop levels in Iraq, and that the margin favoring this position grew to more than 20 percentage points by April 2004 (Figure 5.27).

The Response to Casualties in Iraq Has Been Very Different from That in Somalia

In early November 2003, the shoot down of a helicopter transporting troops resulted in the largest single incident of hostile deaths among U.S. service personnel since the end of major combat operations (16 died), approaching the 18 who died in the firefight in Mogadishu.[54] Nevertheless, the response to this incident was very different from the response to the firefight in Mogadishu (see Table 5.4).

Table 5.4
Withdrawal Sentiment Before and After U.S. Deaths in Iraq, November 2003

Which comes closest to your view about what the U.S. should now do about the number of U.S. troops in Iraq [ROTATED: the U.S. should send more troops to Iraq, the U.S. should keep the number of troops as it is now, the U.S. should begin to withdraw some troops from Iraq, (or) the U.S. should withdraw all of its troops from Iraq]? (Gallup, October 24–26, 2003, and November 3–5, 2003)

	Late October	Early November
Send more troops	14	17
Keep as it is now	27	32
Withdraw troops	57	48
Begin to withdraw some troops	39	29
Withdraw all troops	18	19
No opinion	2	3

Do you think the U.S. should keep military troops in Iraq until a stable government is established there, or do you think the U.S. should bring its troops home as soon as possible? (Pew Research Center/PSRA, October 15–19, 2003, N = 1,515 and December 19, 2003–January 4, 2004, N=1,506)

	October	Early January
Keep troops in Iraq	58	63
More troops needed	32	29
Have enough there to do the job	21	26
Reduce number of troops (volunteered)	*	*
Don't know/refused (volunteered)	5	5
Bring troops home	39	32
Don't know/refused	3	5

* = Less than 0.5.

[54] On November 2, 16 U.S. service personnel were killed when a CH-47 Chinook transport helicopter crashed, apparently shot down by small arms fire or a rocket-propelled grenade.

As shown in the table, and as would be predicted for a case in which, unlike Somalia, the U.S. stakes were deemed by most to be quite important, the response to the deaths in Iraq was a perceptible stiffening of resolve and strengthening of support for the U.S. presence in Iraq: whereas 41 percent in Gallup's polling wanted to keep troop levels as they were or even send more troops before the incident, 49 percent held this view after the incident. And whereas 58 percent preferred either a gradual or complete withdrawal in late October before the incident, only 48 percent preferred this option after the incident. In Pew's polling, support for keeping troops in Iraq increased by five points, from 58 to 63 percent.

Moreover, in the case of Iraq, majority support for the operation appeared to hold, whereas support for the venture in Somalia fell further, from a little over four in ten to the mid-30s. That most viewed the stakes in Somalia as relatively modest while most have viewed those in Iraq as quite important strongly suggests the critical importance of the perceived stakes in regulating preferences for withdrawal or escalation sentiment.

Table 5.5
Support Before and After U.S. Deaths in Iraq, November 2003

In view of developments since we first sent our troops to Iraq, do you think the United States made a mistake in sending troops to Iraq, or not?

	Late October	Early November
No	59	60
Yes	40	39
No opinion	1	1

Do you think the situation in Iraq was worth going to war over, or not?

	Late October	Early November	Early December
Worth going to war	54	54	59
Not worth going to war	44	44	39
No opinion	2	2	2

SOURCE: Gallup, October 24–26, 2003, N = 1,006, November 3–5, 2003, N = 1,007, and December 5–7, 2003, N=1,004.

Following this incident, the percentage of those polled by Gallup who continued to say that the United States had *not* made a mistake in sending troops to Iraq remained essentially unchanged at 60 percent, and the percentage saying that the situation in Iraq had been worth going to war over was unchanged at 54 percent in late October and early November but grew to 59 percent in early December (see Table 5.5). By comparison, the reader will recall that support for Somalia was only a little over four in ten even before the firefight in Mogadishu, and that this support slipped further, into the mid-30s, following the incident.

Taken together, while the case of Iraq presents some worrisome signs, it has demonstrated much more robust support in the face of casualties than was observed in Somalia.

The Importance of Capturing or Killing Saddam Hussein

After the war, Americans seem increasingly to have defined success in Iraq as including the capture or death of Saddam Hussein. The best time series available, from ABC News/Washington Post, suggests that the importance of capturing or killing Saddam Hussein increased since the war began in March 2003 (see Figure 5.28).

As shown, the percentage who said that Saddam must be captured or killed for the war to be considered a success increased from around 50 percent to a little over 60 percent;[55] other polling showed about 70 percent saying that capturing or killing Saddam was "very important."[56]

Meanwhile, confidence that Saddam would be captured or killed declined, recovered following the deaths of Saddam's sons Uday and Qusay in July 2003, and then declined again (Figure 5.29).

---

[55] A question by Gallup/CNN/USA Today in early October 2003 found a comparable result: 58 percent said they thought it was necessary for the United States to capture or kill Saddam for the war to be a success. Gallup/CNN/USA Today, October 10–12, 2003, N=1,004.

[56] The Pew Research Center's polling in April and July 2003 found the percentage who thought it was "very important" for the United States to capture or kill Saddam to be virtually unchanged: 67 percent in April, and 69 percent in July. Pew/PSRA, April 10–11, 2003, N=1,000, and July 24–25, 2003, N=1,002.

Figure 5.28
Capturing or Killing Saddam Hussein as Definition of Success for War

Do you think the U.S. has to kill or capture Saddam Hussein for the war in Iraq to be a success, or do you think the war in Iraq can be a success if Saddam Hussein is removed from power, but not killed or captured? (ABC News/Washington Post)

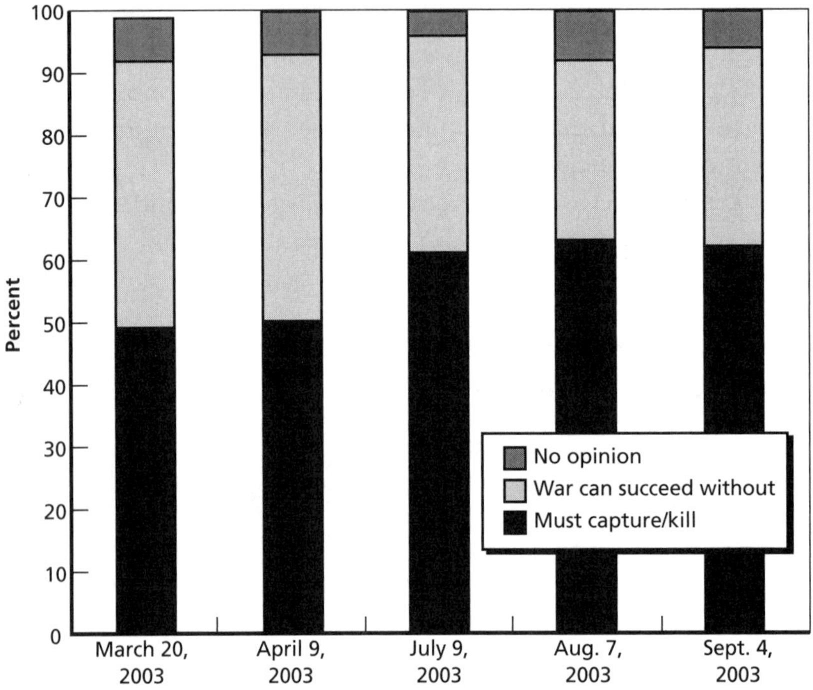

RAND *MG231-A-5.28*

There is mixed evidence as to whether Saddam's mid-December 2003 capture resulted in a rally in support for the war (Table 5.6).

As shown, whereas three of the four questions we examined that were asked before and after Saddam's capture showed an increase in favorable sentiment, only the first question in the table actually exhibited a change that was statistically significant. Because this ques-

Figure 5.29
Confidence That Saddam Hussein Will Be Captured

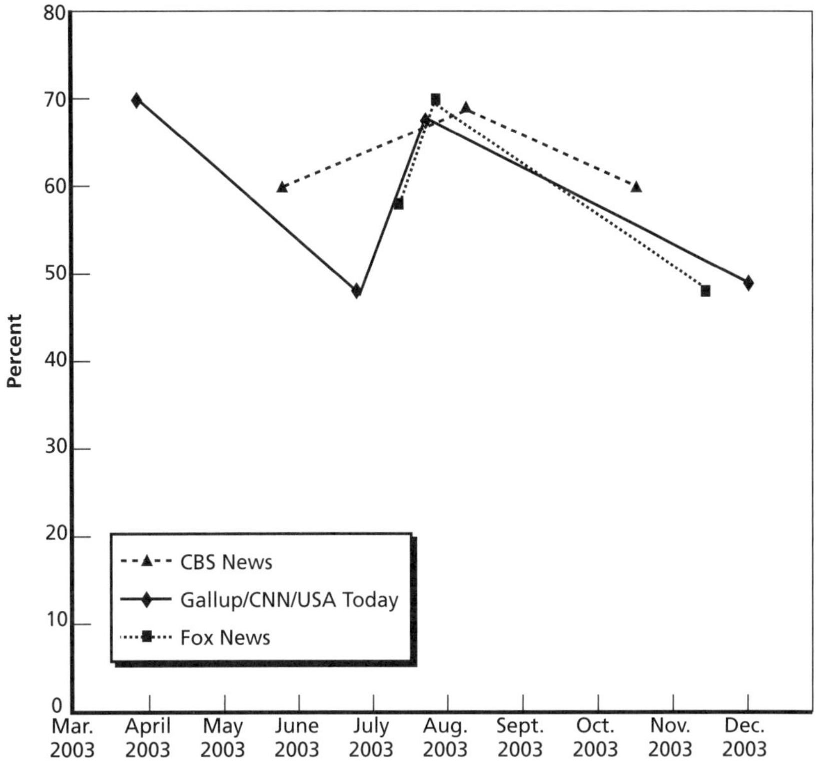

RAND *MG231-A-5.29*

tion was asked just before and just after Saddam's capture, however, it probably makes for the best comparison.[57]

---

[57] Although a before-after comparison is not possible, according to polling by ABC News/ Washington Post just after Saddam's capture, 80 percent thought that the United States should keep its military forces in Iraq until a stable government was in place, while 18 percent favored withdrawal. ABC News/Washington Post, December 14, 2003, N=506.

Table 5.6
Support Before and After Saddam Hussein's Capture in December 2003

Do you think the United States made a mistake getting involved in the current war with Iraq, or not? (CBS News/New York Times, December 10–13, 2003, N = 1,057, and December 14–16, 2003, N=857) (Difference statistically significant at .001 level)

	December 10–13, 2003	December 14–16, 2003
No	53	64
Yes	43	29
No opinion	4	7

All in all, do you think the situation in Iraq was worth going to war over, or not? (Gallup/CNN/USA Today, December 5–7, 2003, N = 1,004, and December 14, 2003, N=664)

	December 5–7, 2003	December 14, 2003
Worth going to war	59	62
Not worth going to war	39	33
No opinion	2	5

All in all, considering the costs to the United States versus the benefits to the United States, do you think the war with Iraq was worth fighting, or not? (ABC News/Washington Post, November 12–16, 2003, N = 1,023, and December 14, 2003, N=506)

	November 12–16, 2003	December 14, 2003
Worth fighting	52	53
Not worth fighting	44	42
No opinion	4	5

In view of developments since we first sent our troops to Iraq, do you think the United States made a mistake in sending troops to Iraq, or not? (Gallup/CNN/USA Today, November 3–5, 2003, N=1,007, and January 12–15, 2004, N=1,004)

	November 3–5, 2003	January 12–15, 2004
No	60	56
Yes	39	42
No opinion	1	2

Sources and Fault Lines in Support

Statistical Modeling Results

Our probit regression models did quite a good job in predicting approval or disapproval of a war in Iraq using respondent-level data from two polls, one done before the war and one after it was underway: using different combinations of questions from different surveys, the models correctly predicted support or opposition for 75–78 percent of the respondents, with all of the variables of interest assuming values in the predicted direction.

The results of the probit regression (Table 5.7) suggest that most of the bivariate relationships that were demonstrated in cross-tabulations of the data also stood up in the multivariate analysis.

As shown, members of the president's Republican party were much more likely than Democrats or Independents to support the war. Additionally, the belief that the United States had important security interests involved—as illustrated by the belief that Iraq's weapons capabilities were a serious threat to the United States—was the most important belief in predicting support for the war in Iraq: it increased the probability of supporting the war by about a third (.32). The perceived prospects for success of the campaign were also predic-

Table 5.7
Iraq: Marginal Probability from Probit Estimates of Approval (Q9)

Variables	Change in Probability at Mean Values
Stakes (Q10)	0.322 (0.055)***
Prospects (Q12)	0.099 (0.068)
Casualties (Q13)	–0.028 (0.012)**
Information consumption (Q7)	–0.026 (0.050)
Party 1 if Independent†	–0.351 (0.079)***
Party 1 if Democrat†	–0.165 (0.079)**
Race 1 if black†	–0.010 (0.106)
Gender 1 if female†	–0.143 (0.065)**
Wald Chi-square (Prod > Chi2)	78.65 (0.000)
Log likelihood	–194.28
Observations	369
Correctly specified	76%

† dF/dx is for discrete change of dummy variable from 0 to 1.
* Significant at 10%.
** Significant at 5%.
*** Significant at 1%.
Robust standard error in parentheses.
SOURCE: Gallup, January 3–5, 2003, N = 1,000.

tive of support for the war; the belief that the war had good prospects increased the probability of supporting by about 10 percent, suggesting that those who thought the United States and its allies could win the war were also more likely to support the campaign. At the same time, an increase in the expected casualties was associated with decreased support for the campaign, although casualties were a less important consideration than the perceived stakes and prospects for success.

We also modeled support and opposition to the war in Iraq once the war was underway (Table 5.8). Again, party was the most important predictor—members of the president's party were more likely than Democrats or Independents to support the war—and the belief that the United States had vital interests or good prospects each increased the probability of supporting the war by about a third.

As in the other cases, partisanship—in the form of membership in the president's party—played an important role both in overall

Table 5.8
Iraq: Marginal Probability from Probit Estimates of Approval (Q3)

Variables	Change in Probability at Mean Values
Vital interests (Q11)	0.314 (0.054)***
Prospects (Q13)	0.033 (0.021)
Casualties (Q14)	–0.135 (0.050)***
Party 1 if Independent†	–0.381 (0.065)***
Party 1 if Democrat†	–0.159 (0.063)**
Gender 1 if female†	–0.097 (0.045)**
Wald Chi-square (Prod > Chi2)	92.58
Log likelihood	–178.89
Observations	407
Correctly specified	75%

† dF/dx is for discrete change of dummy variable from 0 to 1.
* Significant at 10%.
** Significant at 5%.
*** Significant at 1%.
Robust standard error in parentheses.
SOURCE: ABC News/Washington Post March 20, 2003, N = 506.

support and opposition and in key beliefs about the nature of the stakes, prospect for success, and costs. Accordingly, we begin with a discussion of the role of partisanship in support.

Partisan Leadership and Followership

To understand the partisan nature of support, it is important to first understand the anatomy of the rally that led to the high levels of support observed during the war. To yield the high levels of support described earlier, the president needed to draw support from outside of his natural constituency of Republicans and pull in support from Independents and Democrats as well. As shown in Figure 5.30, the president not only generated support from his Republican base, but also managed to reach outside of his base, ultimately getting support from about 70 percent of the Independents and Democrats.

The critical point to understand, however, is that the support from these quarters was always expected to be less robust than the support that came from the president's own natural constituency. Put another way, if support was going to erode, it was likely to erode at a faster rate for those least committed to the president and his policies on Iraq, i.e., Democrats.

In fact, this is what has happened: approval, and the belief that the situation in Iraq was worth going to war over, were both closely related to partisanship. As a result of the contretemps that arose in June and July 2003, when some administration critics claimed that the administration had misled the public about Iraqi WMD, and other factors such as an eroding belief that the United States would be successful and the growing toll in casualties, support for the U.S. venture in Iraq from Democrats collapsed.[58] As a result, and as shown

[58] The president's exact words in his State of the Union address were: "The British government has learned that Saddam Hussein recently sought significant quantities of uranium from Africa." See George W. Bush, "State of the Union Address," January 28, 2003. Critics pointed to a previously discredited forgery that purported to be evidence of a sale of yellow cake uranium from Niger. The British continue to believe that Iraq was making efforts to acquire uranium from Africa, which one can infer stems from intelligence sources and methods other than the forgery.

Figure 5.30
Anatomy of the Rally in Support for the War by Party, April 2–3, 2003

Do you support or oppose the Bush administration's decision to take military action against Iraq at this time? (Los Angeles Times, April 2–3, 2003)

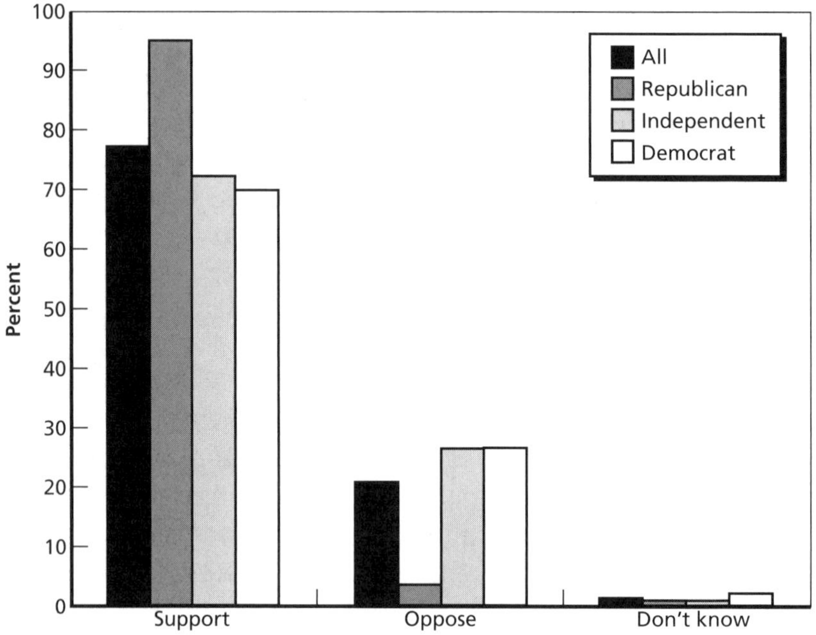

RAND *MG231-A-5.30*

in Figure 5.31, by July 2003 nearly 90 percent of Republicans—but fewer than 40 percent of Democrats—said that the situation in Iraq had been worth going to war over.

Thus, partisan divisions—both among national leaders and within the electorate—constitute an important fault line both in the key underlying beliefs about Iraq and, ultimately, the willingness to support the U.S. action there.

Polling by CBS News showed that by late April 2004, partisan differences existed on various measures of approval and the sorts of underlying beliefs that are associated with approval (Figure 5.32).

Figure 5.31
Partisan Differences About the Worth of Going to War in Iraq, July 2003

All in all, do you think the situation in Iraq is/was worth going to war over, or not?
(Gallup, July 18–20, 2003, N=1,003)

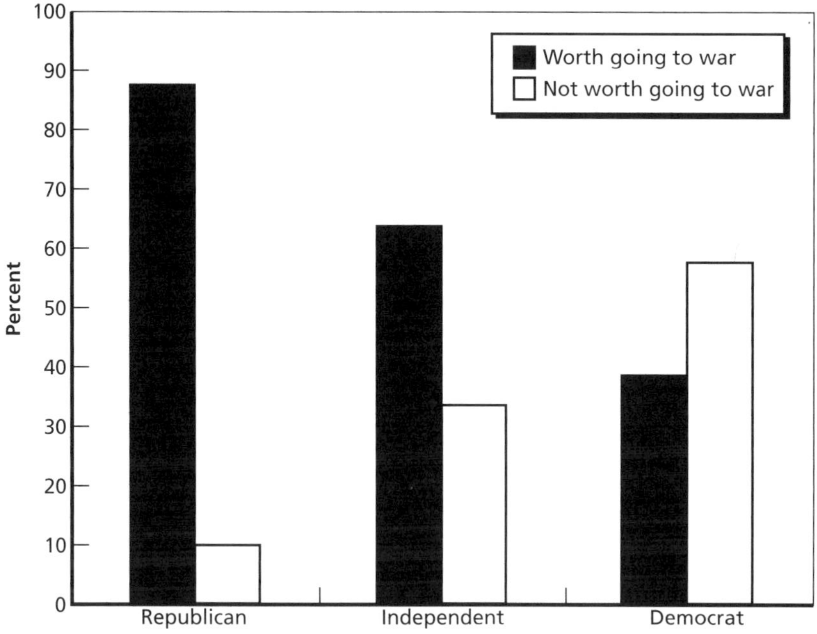

RAND *MG231-A-5.31*

As shown, Republicans were two times or more likely than Democrats to believe that the war had not been a mistake, that it had been the right thing to do, that the United States should stay as long as it took to stabilize Iraq, and that the war had been worth the costs, to approve President Bush's handling of Iraq, to believe that the situation was going very or somewhat well, and to believe that it was very or somewhat likely that the United States ultimately would succeed in Iraq.

Figure 5.32
Partisan Differences in Approval and Beliefs About Iraq, Late April 2004

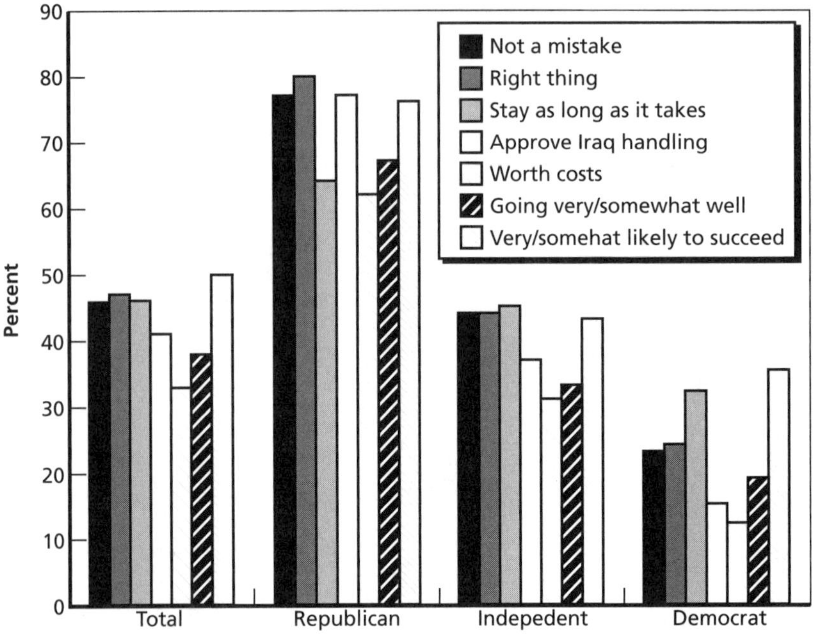

RAND *MG231-A-5-32*

Assessment of Stakes

Security interests. Prior to the war, most Americans appeared to feel that the United States had important stakes in Iraq. Between 1997 and 1998, for example, the percentage who said that what happened in Iraq was very important to the interests of the United States was in the 62–67 percent range,[59] and in 1999, the percentage believing that the United States had vital interests in Iraq ranged be-

[59] CBS News, November 23–24, 1997, N = 953, February 19–21, 1998, N = 1,153, and November 15, 1998, N = 762.

tween 67 and 76 percent;[60] moreover, 86 percent of those polled in June 2002 rated the possible future Iraqi development of weapons of mass destruction a critical threat to the vital interests of the United States,[61] 66 percent of those polled in late September 2002 said that they believed the Iraqi regime posed an imminent threat to U.S. interests,[62] and 72 percent of those who supported the war in early April said that a major reason was that Iraq posed an imminent threat to the United States.[63]

It is more difficult to gain a sense of how the United States' postwar security interests are perceived. By July 2003, for example, 62 percent expressed the belief that U.S. national security had improved as a result of the war because a potential threat had been removed,[64] although that belief soon stabilized at about four in ten: only 40 percent of those polled in September 2003 thought that the U.S. presence in Iraq would lead to greater stability in the Middle East.[65] On the other hand, polling by ABC News/Washington Post from mid-January to mid-April 2004 found nearly six in ten consistently saying that the war with Iraq had contributed to the long-term security of the United States.[66] The contribution of the war in Iraq to the war on terrorism was less direct, however: only 41 percent of those polled in January 2004 said that going to war with Iraq had made Americans safer from terrorism, and in April 2004, 40 percent of those polled took that position.[67]

---

[60] Three questions: Potomac Associates/Opinion Dynamics, June 15–28, 1999, N = 1,200, Chicago Council on Foreign Relations/German Marshall Fund/Harris, June 1–30, 2002, N = 3,262, and ABC News/Washington Post, March 20, 2003, N = 506.

[61] Chicago Council on Foreign Relations/German Marshall Fund/Harris, June 1–30, 2002, N=3,262.

[62] Newsweek/PSRA, September 26–27, 2002, N = 1,011.

[63] Investor's Business Daily/Christian Science Monitor/TIPP, April 1–6, 2003, N = 906.

[64] Newsweek/PSRA, July 24–25, 2003, N = 1,002.

[65] CBS News, September 15–16, 2003, N = 675.

[66] ABC News/Washington Post, April 15–18, 2004, N = 1,201.

[67] Newsweek/PSRA, January 29–30, 2004, N = 1,259 and Time/CNN/Harris, April 8, 2004, N = 1,005.

Moral justification. There was also widespread belief that attacks on Iraq were morally justified. Fifty-nine percent considered an attack on Iraq in February 1998 to be morally justified,[68] for example, and between August 2002 and January 2003, about two out of three of those polled said using the U.S. military to remove Saddam would be morally justified;[69] in March–April 2003, seven in ten of those polled considered U.S. military action against Iraq to be morally justified.[70] Questions on the matter of the United States' moral justification for postwar action are unavailable.

Reasons for supporting war. Americans ultimately appear to have believed that they had many good reasons for supporting the war. As shown in Table 5.9, only one reason offered by Gallup in its March 14–15, 2003 polling question—lowering fuel prices—was viewed by less than a majority as a good reason for taking military action against Iraq.[71]

Table 5.10 presents the results of an open-ended question asked by ABC News on March 5–9, 2003, which asked respondents to explain why they supported or opposed going to war with Iraq. The responses suggest that the 59 percent who supported going to war had a diverse set of reasons for supporting the U.S. move to war with Iraq, but they were dominated by the desire to remove Saddam or deal with the threat posed by Iraq. As shown, the dominant reason cited for going to war was to remove Saddam, offered by 15 percent of those polled or about one-quarter of those who favored war. Next most frequently cited were various formulations of threat, the belief that the inspections were unlikely to work, and that Iraq was defying the United Nations. The 35 percent who opposed war also had a fairly diverse set of reasons for doing so.

---

[68] Gallup/CNN/USA Today, February 20–22, 1998, N = 1,005.

[69] The percentages were 65 and 66 percent in Time/CNN/Harris, August 28–29, 2002, N = 1,004, and January 15–16, 2003, N = 1,010.

[70] The percentages were 73 and 70 percent in Time/CNN/Harris, January 15–16, 2003, N = 1,010, and Los Angeles Times, April 2–3, 2003, N = 745.

[71] This seems to have reflected a sensitivity to the "no blood for oil" arguments of opponents, as 63 percent viewed protecting oil supplies as a very good or good reason.

Table 5.9
Reasons For and Against Taking Military Action Against Iraq, March 14–15, 2003

Now, here are some statements people have given as reasons to *favor* taking military action against Iraq. Regardless of how likely you think it might be to happen, for each, please say whether it is: a very good reason, a good reason, a bad reason, or a very bad reason for taking military action against Iraq? How about that . . .

Reasons for taking military action	Very Good	Good	Bad	Very Bad	No Opinion
Prevent Iraqi WMD	52	33	11	3	1
Iraqi people freed	43	41	13	2	1
U.S. must play leadership role	37	40	18	5	*
Groups that hate U.S. discouraged from attacking U.S.	25	32	27	13	3
Lower fuel prices	21	21	39	17	2
Encourage political change	18	50	20	7	5
Oil supplies protected	18	45	25	10	2

Now, here are some statements people have given as reasons to *oppose* military action against Iraq. Regardless of how likely you think it might be to happen, for each, please say whether it is: a very good reason, a good reason, a bad reason or a very bad reason for not taking military action against Iraq? How about that . . .

Reasons for not taking military action	Very Good	Good	Bad	Very Bad	No Opinion
Innocent deaths	23	34	29	11	3
More urgent problems	18	27	40	14	1
Iraq retaliate w/WMD	18	27	34	17	4
Many soldiers would die	18	32	35	11	4
Inspectors more time	17	31	30	19	3
Terrorist attacks	15	24	40	18	3
Negative world response	12	25	44	16	3
Inspections can solve	12	30	34	19	5
Saddam not a threat	11	19	33	34	3

NOTE: Gallup, March 14–15, 2003, N=1,007
* = Less than 0.5

Table 5.10
Main Reasons For and Against Going to War, March 2003

What's the main reason you'd support going to war with Iraq/favor military action against Iraq? [Asked of the 59 percent who favored going to war]

Favored going to war, giving as their first response the following:	59%
Remove Saddam	15
Threat to the U.S.	13
Iraq has dangerous weapons/disarmament/inspections don't work/ defying the UN	9
Threat (general)	8
Supports terrorism	8
Moral obligation/have to act/unfinished business	6
Support (George W.) Bush	4
In military/support military	3
Help Iraqis/Mideast peace	3
Other	2
No opinion	2

What's the main reason you'd oppose going to war with Iraq/military action against Iraq? [Asked of the 35 percent who opposed going to war]

Opposed going to war, giving as their first response the following:	35%
Think it's unjustified/insufficient threat	6
Need the support of the UN/need more international support	5
Have other problems here at home/bad economy	5
Moving too fast/too aggressive	4
Anti-war in general	4
Afraid of more terrorist attacks in U.S.	4
Human cost/loss of life (civilian/military)	4
Inspections are working/give inspectors more time	2
Keep trying diplomacy	2
Economic cost/not worth the money	2
Fear a wider war/broader complications	2
Don't trust (George W.) Bush/government	1
No opinion	1
Other	*

* = Less than 0.5.
SOURCE: ABC News, March 5–9, 2003, N=1,032.

Clarity regarding reasons for war. As early as August 2002, 56 percent of respondents said they had a clear idea of why the United States was considering new military action against Iraq.[72] A growing percentage of Americans appear to have given the question of using military force to remove Saddam a great deal of thought: 46 percent in August 2002, 54–55 percent in September and October, 56–58 percent in December 2002 through February 2003, and 64 percent in March 2003.[73]

As shown in Tables 5.11 and 5.12, support was closely related to the amount of thought individuals had given to the question of using

Table 5.11
Cross-Tabulation of Support and Thought Given to Military Action in Iraq, October 2002

Would you favor or oppose taking military action in Iraq to end Saddam Hussein's rule?

How much have you yourself thought about whether the U.S. should use military force to remove Saddam Hussein from power in Iraq?

	Favor	Oppose	N
A great deal	66	28	813
Some	64	24	479
Only a little	52	36	123
Not at all	31	49	82
Don't know/refused	36	10	15
All	62	28	1,513

NOTE: $p < 0.001$ in a Chi-square test of independence.
SOURCE: Pew October 2–6, 2002.

[72] Gallup, August 5–8, 2002, N = 1,007. This was somewhat lower than the 74 percent who said that they had a clear idea of what the U.S. military involvement in Iraq was about in late 1990, and the 81 percent who said they had a clear idea in July 1991. Gallup, December 13–16, 1990, and July 18–21, 1991, N = 1,002.

[73] Pew/PSRA, August 14–25, 2002, N = 1,001, September 12–16, 2002, N = 1,150, October 2–6, 2002, N = 1,513; December 4–8, 2002, N = 1,205; January 8–12, 2003, N = 1,218; February 12–18, 2003, N = 1,254; and March 13–16, 2003, N = 1,032.

Table 5.12
Cross-Tabulation of Party and Thought Given to Military Action in Iraq, October 2002

How much have you yourself thought about whether the U.S. should use military force to remove Saddam Hussein from power in Iraq?

In politics today, do you consider yourself a Republican, Democrat, or Independent?

	A great deal	Some	Only a little	Not at all	N
Republican	58	33	6	2	442
Independent	50	36	8	6	443
Democrat	54	29	9	6	501
No preference	57	15	11	17	71
Other	67	19	13	0	11
Don't know/refused	36	34	15	15	45
All	54	32	8	5	1,513

NOTE: $p < 0.001$ in a Chi-square test of independence.
SOURCE: Pew October 2–6, 2002.

military force, and that amount of thought exhibited important partisan differences; support rose as an increasing percentage of Americans considered the matter, although Republicans were somewhat more likely than Democrats or Independents to have given the issue thought.

Iraq as the most important problem facing the nation. Gallup regularly asks respondents to identify the most important problem facing the nation; not surprisingly, the war in Iraq has been a prominent response (Figure 5.33).

As shown in the figure, concern about the war in Iraq peaked in March 2003 and plummeted in early May following the conclusion of major combat operations; it rose again, however, peaking again in November 2003 and declining thereafter. In the last (March 2004) reading, concern about the economy had once again eclipsed concern about Iraq, and concern about the war in Iraq rivaled that for terrorism.

Figure 5.33
The Most Important Problem Facing the Country, March 2003–March 2004

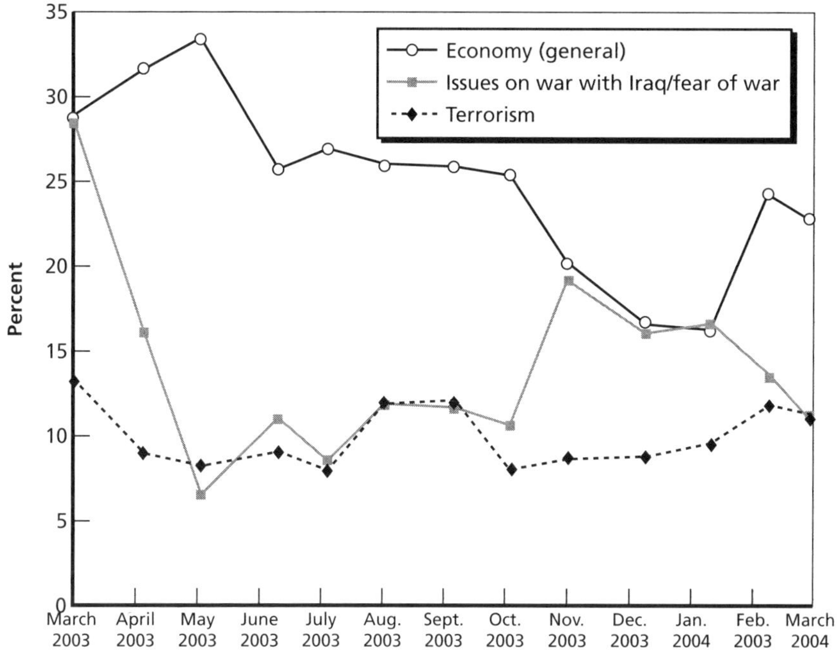

RAND *MG231-A-5.33*

Support and weapons of mass destruction. Finally, because the issue of Iraqi weapons of mass destruction was so prominent before and after the war, it is worth summarizing the results of our analyses of the evolving relationship between support and beliefs about Iraqi WMD.[74] These analyses suggested that beliefs about Iraqi WMD became increasingly important in support from Democrats but played a less important role in determining support or opposition for Republicans.

[74] Additional details can be found in Appendix G of the technical appendix, published separately.

In October 2002, about two-thirds of those who believed that Iraq was close to acquiring or already had nuclear weapons supported military action, whereas fewer than four in ten of those who did not believe this supported such action. At the same time, beliefs about the presence of WMD in Iraq in October 2002 did not differ in a statistically significant fashion by party.[75]

By March 2003, about two-thirds (64 percent) of those who felt that the United States would only be able to justify the war if it found Iraqi WMD supported going to war, whereas more than eight in ten (85 percent) of those who felt the United States could justify the war for other reasons supported action. Statistically significant differences by party also had emerged: Republicans were far more likely than Democrats or Independents to believe that the war could be justified even if WMD were not found.[76] By April, more than eight in ten (84 percent) of those who thought the United States could justify the war for other reasons continued to support the war, while only slightly more than half (53 percent) of those who felt that finding WMD was necessary to justify the war supported it. However, nearly seven in ten (69 percent) Independents and more than half (56 percent) of Democrats expressed the belief that the war could be justified for reasons other than WMD, more than in the March poll.

By June 2003, whereas more than three out of four (77 percent) Republicans and six in ten (62 percent) of Independents continued to say that they thought the war could be justified even if WMD were not found, fewer than half (48 percent) of Democrats said so.[77] And by January 2004, 48 percent continued to say that the war could be justified even if no weapons of mass destruction were found, and an-

---

[75] Pew Research Center/PSRA, October 2–6, 2002. Our analyses showed that the probability of supporting military action also was higher among those who believed that Iraq assisted the 9/11 terrorists, and that that belief also had a partisan cast to it: Republicans were far more likely than Democrats to believe that Iraq had helped the terrorists.

[76] ABC News/Washington Post, March 20, 2003.

[77] ABC News/Washington Post Poll, "Public Disquiet Grows With Casualties in Iraq," June 23, 2003.

other 48 percent felt that the war could be justified only if weapons were found (23 percent) or could not be justified at all (25 percent).[78]

Not surprisingly, beliefs about Iraqi WMD differ greatly by party. CBS News' polling in late April 2004, for example, found that 52 percent of all Americans believed Iraq probably still had weapons of mass destruction that had not yet been found; 73 percent of Republicans believed this, as opposed to only 33 percent of Democrats.[79]

Prospects for Success

As shown in Figure 5.34, there has been an erosion in those who have a favorable view of how well things have been going for the United States in Iraq, and as suggested by the modeling results reported earlier, there is a high likelihood that this long-term decline in optimism about the likely success of the mission has been having a corrosive effect on support.[80]

Eighty percent or more typically felt that things were going very or fairly well during the major combat phase of the war, but this had slipped to about 60 percent by July 2003 and to 50 percent or less by September. Equally striking was that the percentage who said that the

---

[78] Gallup, January 29–February 1, 2004, N=1,001.

[79] CBS News, April 23–27, 2004, N=1,042.

[80] The question from Pew was "How well is the U.S. military effort in Iraq going?"; it was asked 17 times between March 2003 and April 2004. Gallup Question A was "How would you say the war with Iraq has gone for the U.S. so far—very well, moderately well, moderately badly, or very badly?"; it was asked seven times between March 22–23 and April 14–16, 2003. Gallup Question B was "How would you say things are going for the U.S. in Iraq now that the major fighting has ended—very well, moderately well, moderately badly, or very badly?"; it was asked 13 times between April 2003 and May 2004. ABC News/Washington Post's question was "How would you say the war (with Iraq) is going for the United States and its allies: very well, fairly well, not too well, or not well at all?"; it was asked four times between March 23 and April 9, 2003. CBS News' question was "How would you say things are going for the U.S. (United States) in its efforts to bring stability and order to Iraq? Would you say things are going very well, somewhat well, somewhat badly, or very badly?"; it was asked 11 times between May 2003 and April 2004.

Figure 5.34
Percentage Saying U.S. Doing Very or Somewhat Well in Iraq

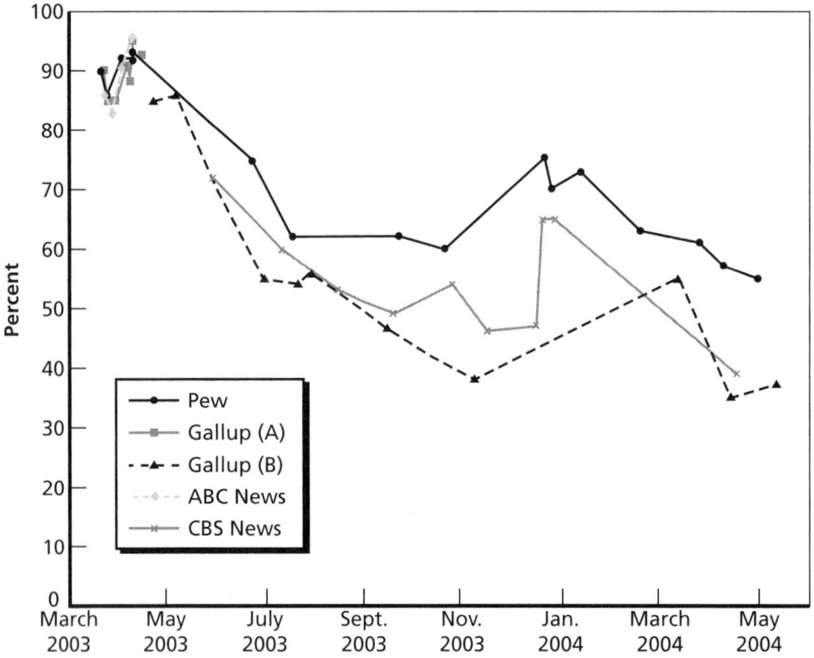

RAND *MG231-A-5.34*

war was basically over fell from 41 percent in early May to 10 percent in mid-September.[81]

Another indicator of how Americans are judging the prospects for the operation is the percentage who said they were "very concerned" that the United States will get "bogged down" in Iraq (Figure 5.35).

According to ABC News/Washington Post's polling, by mid-April, nearly six in ten said that they believed the United States had gotten bogged down in Iraq, while only four in ten thought the

[81] Gallup, May 5–7, 2003, N=1,005, and September 19–21, 2003, N=1,003.

Figure 5.35
Percent Very Concerned About Getting Bogged Down in Iraq

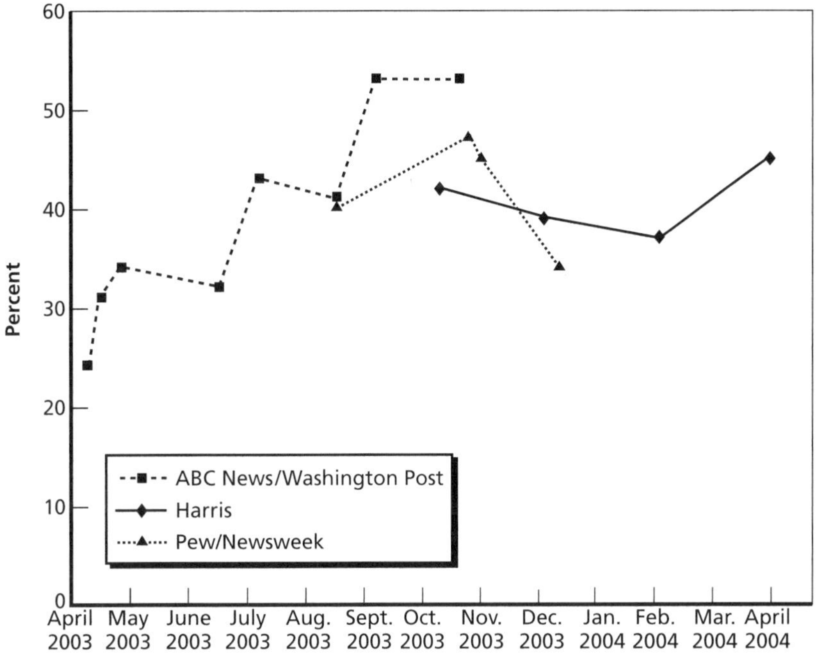

RAND *MG231-A-5.35*

United States was making good progress.[82] And as shown in Figure 5.35, the belief that the United States would become bogged down has spread from about one in four in early April 2003 to a slight majority in early September 2003. These beliefs have also been partisan-coded: by June 2003, 51 percent of Democrats and 31 percent of Independents said they were "very concerned"; by comparison, fewer than one in five (17 percent) of Republicans said so.[83]

---

[82] ABC News/Washington Post, April 15–18, 2004, N=1,201.

[83] ABC News/Washington Post Poll, "Public Disquiet Grows With Casualties in Iraq," June 23, 2003.

Although confidence that Saddam would be captured appears to have grown after the deaths of his sons,[84] and there may have been a rally following his December 2003 capture, other indicators suggested skepticism about the overall mission's prospects. For example, by September 2003, only two to four in ten said that they thought that the administration had a clear plan for handling the postwar situation in Iraq.[85]

Expected and Actual Costs

There are some data to suggest that the public expected lower casualties in OIF than in the first (1991) Gulf War (see Figure 5.36); other data suggest that the combat operations resulted in fewer deaths than most had expected, and that most Americans continued to expect deaths to occur during the postwar phase.[86] According to these data, a slight majority (51 percent) expected 3,000 or fewer casualties in the war; for the 55 percent who were willing to venture a guess about potential deaths in the first Gulf War, the average guess was 30,000 or fewer.

Table 5.13 reports the casualties that have been incurred in Operation Iraqi Freedom through October 22, 2003 by type. As shown,

---

[84] Gallup/CNN/USA Today's polling showed an increase from 18 to 31 percent in those very confident that Saddam would be captured, CBS News showed an increase from 19 to 32 percent, and Fox News showed an increase from 20 to 34 percent. Gallup/CNN/USA Today, March 29–30, 2003, N = 1,012, June 27–29, 2003, N = 1,003, and July 25–27, 2003, N = 1,006; CBS News, May 27–28, 2003, N = 758 and August 11–12, 2003, N = 798; and Fox News, July 15–16, 2003, N = 900 and July 29–30, 2003, N = 900.

[85] CBS News, September 15–16, 2003, N = 675 found only 22 percent who thought the administration had developed a clear plan for rebuilding Iraq, Pew/PSRA, September 17–22, 2003, N = 1,500 found only 32 percent who said that the president had a clear plan for bringing the situation to a successful conclusion, NBC News/Wall Street Journal, September 20–22, 2003, N = 1,007 found only 43 percent who thought the administration had a clear plan for handling the situation, ABC News/Washington Post, September 10–13, 2003, N = 1,104 found 42 percent who thought the administration had a clear plan for handing the situation, and Gallup/CNN/USA Today found 40 percent who thought the administration had a clear plan.

[86] See Darren K. Carlson, "Americans Expected Postwar Military Deaths," The Gallup Organization, July 15, 2003.

Figure 5.36
Expected Casualties in 1991 and 2003 Wars with Iraq[87]

How many Americans do you think would be killed before the war (with Iraq) was over? (Gallup, January 3–6, 1991, N=1,006 and January 3–5, 2003, N=1,000)

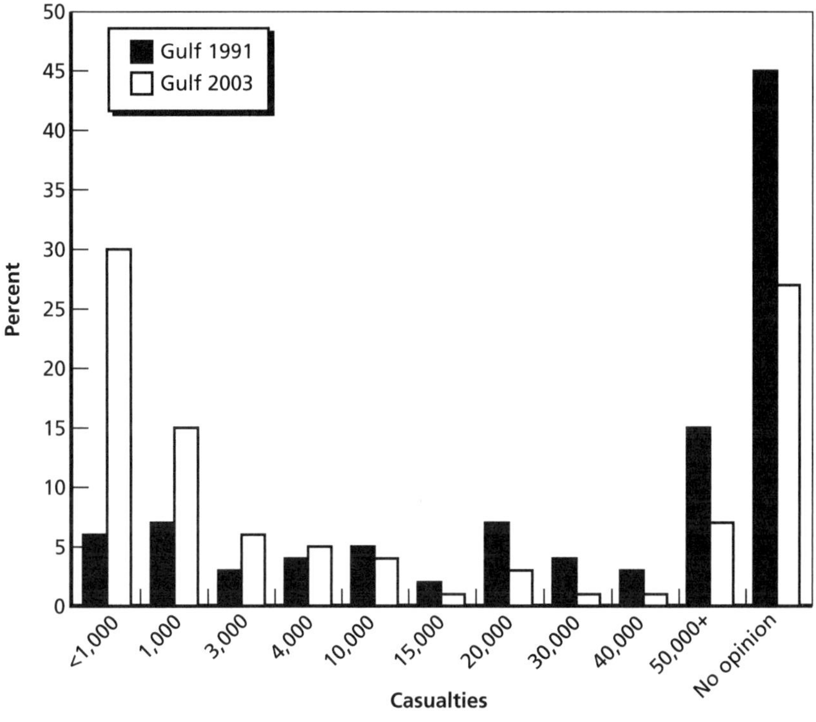

RAND *MG231-A-5.36*

as of October 22, 2003, there had been a total of 219 deaths due to hostile action; 115 of these occurred during major combat operations, and the remaining 104 took place during stability operations in the postconflict period. Another 123 deaths have occurred due to non-hostile causes, mostly accidents, and there have been 1,519 wounded in action.

---

[87] Data are from Los Angeles Times, December 12–15, 2002, N=1,305.

Table 5.13
Casualty Summary for Operation Iraqi Freedom, as of May 1, 2004

Casualty Type	Total
Hostile deaths	
Killed in action	417
Died of wounds	106
Missing in action: declared dead	10
Captured: declared dead	1
Total hostile deaths	534
Nonhostile deaths	
Accident	135
Illness	25
Homicide	5
Self-inflicted	24
Undetermined	0
Pending	14
Total nonhostile deaths	203
Wounded: not mortal	4,133

SOURCE: Washington Headquarters Services, Directorate for Information Operations and Reports, Department of Defense, "War on Terrorism—Operation Iraqi Freedom—By Casualty Category," as of May 1, 2004."

And as suggested by Figure 5.37, since April 2003, the United States has been incurring casualties in Iraq at a fairly steady rate; in September 2003, a total of 18 deaths were due to hostile action and 12 to nonhostile causes, and 209 service personnel were wounded in action, more than four times the low of 51 wounded in May 2003.[88]

Balancing Costs and Benefits

As shown in Figure 5.38, there was, at least relative to the peace operations of the 1990s, a relatively high tolerance for American losses in Iraq: the average American expressed a willingness to tolerate perhaps 500 to 1,000 deaths to accomplish U.S. objectives in Iraq, depending on polling.

[88] The American public generally has shown itself to be more concerned with the number of servicemen killed in action than the number who die due to non-hostile causes, or the number of wounded.

Figure 5.37
Cumulative Deaths in OIF by Type, March 2003–May 2004

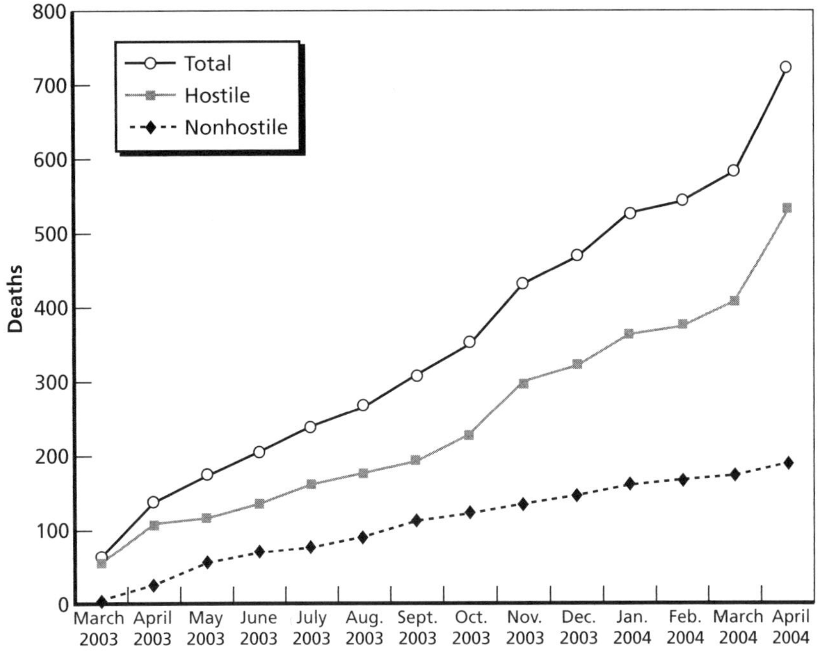

SOURCE: Directorate for Information Operations and Reports (DIOR), Department of Defense, May 1, 2004.

RAND *MG231-A-5.37*

Polling by Gallup in October 2002 suggested that the average American would support a war with 100 to 1,000 casualties.[89] In December 2002, 51 percent of those who supported a ground attack

[89] Gallup asked: "Would you favor or oppose invading Iraq with U.S. (United States) ground troops in an attempt to remove Saddam Hussein from power if you knew that . . . there would be 100 U.S. casualties? . . . there would be 1,000 U.S. casualties? . . . there would be 5,000 U.S. casualties?" Fifty-three percent indicated support in a prior question that did not mention casualties, 51 percent supported with 100 casualties, 46 percent with 1,000 casualties, and 33 percent with 5,000 casualties. Gallup/CNN/USA Today, October 3–6, 2002.

Figure 5.38
Prospective Willingness to Tolerate Casualties in Iraq, December 2002

The number of possible casualties in a ground war with Iraq has been estimated at between 100 American soldiers, if the Iraqi military offers little resistance, to as many as 5,000 American soldiers if the Iraqi Republican Guard fight an effective urban defense. With this in mind...would you still support sending ground troops to fight in Iraq if it meant up to 100 American soldiers would be killed in battle, or not? (If Yes, ask:) Would you still support sending ground troops if up to 500 American soldiers were killed in battle, or not? (If Yes, ask:) Up to 1,000? (If Yes, ask:) Up to 5,000? (If yes, ask:) Would you say you would support sending ground troops to fight in Iraq no matter what it cost in American casualties, or not? (Los Angeles Times, December 12–15, 2002, N=1,305)

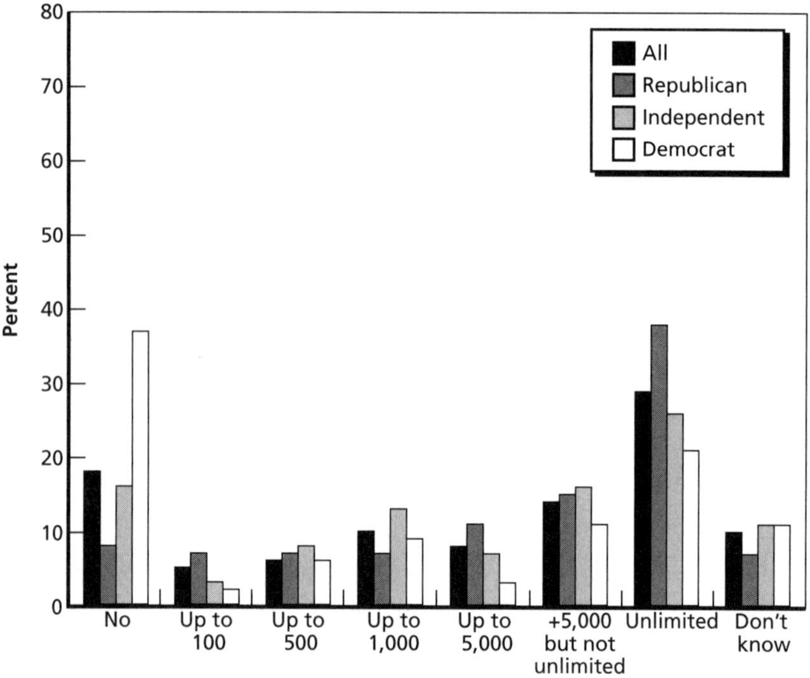

RAND *MG231-A-5.38*

said that they would still support a war if there were more than 1,000 casualties, although the usual partisan differences were also evident: 64 percent of Republicans who supported a ground attack, 49 percent of Independents, and 35 percent of Democrats all said they would still support a war with casualty levels this high. And in April 2003, 53 percent said that they would consider the war in Iraq to be successful if it removed Saddam from power at a cost of 500 or more American soldiers killed.[90]

Figures 5.39 and 5.40 present two questions from polls by the Los Angeles Times that asked about support given different levels of hypothesized casualties.

Figure 5.39 presents the total percentages in December 2002 saying they would support a ground attack of Iraq at different levels of hypothesized casualties, broken out by party. As would be expected, as the hypothesized casualty levels are increased, support falls. And given a more prevalent belief among Republicans that important stakes were involved and that the war had good prospects for success, Republicans were the most likely to support a ground attack of Iraq at each level of hypothesized casualties—majorities supported up to 5,000 killed—followed by Independents and, finally, Democrats.

Figure 5.40 shows the percentages in April 2003 saying they would consider a war in Iraq to be successful given different levels of hypothesized casualties; as shown in the figure, the partisan gap had largely closed by early April, probably benefiting from the rally in support described earlier.

Again, the percentages decline as the hypothesized casualty levels increase, and although question wording cannot be entirely ruled out, the willingness to tolerate casualties appears to have increased from the December poll: whereas only a majority of Republicans supported war at any level of casualties in December 2002, by April 2003 a majority of Republicans, Independents, and Democrats said they would consider the war a success if there were 500 soldiers killed.[91]

---

[90] The Los Angeles Times asked: "Would you say the war in Iraq was successful if it removed Saddam Hussein from power and fewer than 100 American soldiers were killed in battle, or would you not say it was successful in that case? (If Yes, ask:) Would you still say it was successful if up to 500 American soldiers were killed in battle? (If Yes, ask:) Up to 1,000? (If Yes, ask:) Up to 5,000? (If Yes, ask:) Would you say that the military action against Iraq had been successful if Saddam Hussein was removed from power, no matter what it costs in American casualties?" Los Angeles Times, April 2–3, 2003, N=745.

[91] A total of 60 percent of Republicans, 56 percent of Independents, and 54 percent of Democrats said that they would consider the war successful if 500 American soldiers were killed in battle.

Figure 5.39
Prospective Willingness to Tolerate Casualties in Iraq by Party, December 2002

The number of possible casualties in a ground war with Iraq has been estimated at between 100 American soldiers, if the Iraqi military offers little resistance, to as many as 5,000 American soldiers if the Iraqi Republican Guard fight an effective urban defense. With this in mind...would you still support sending ground troops to fight in Iraq if it meant up to 100 American soldiers would be killed in battle, or not? (If Yes, ask:) Would you still support sending ground troops if up to 500 American soldiers were killed in battle, or not? (If Yes, ask:) Up to 1,000? (If Yes, ask:) Up to 5,000? (If yes, ask:) Would you say you would support sending ground troops to fight in Iraq no matter what it cost in American casualties, or not? (Los Angeles Times, December 12–15, 2002, N=1,305)

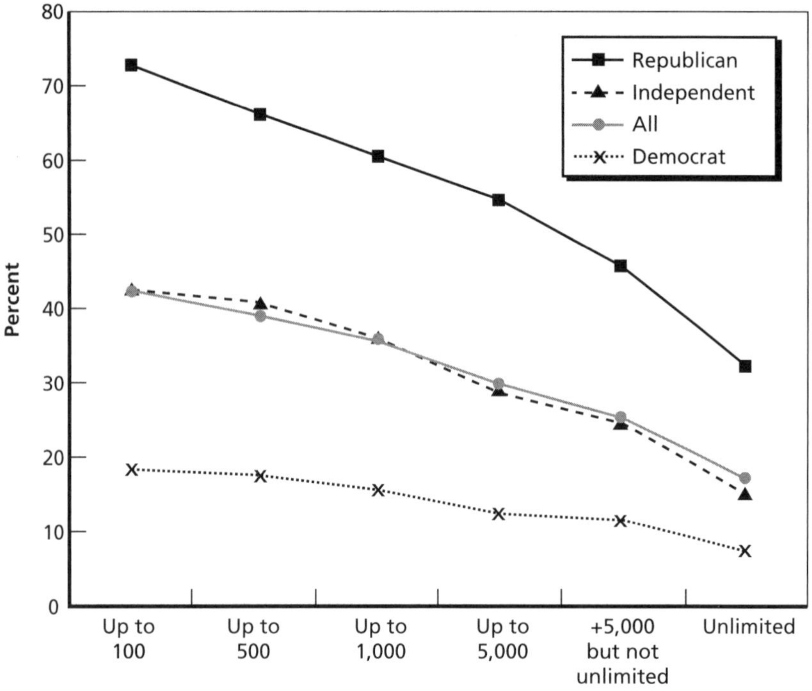

RAND *MG231-A-5.39*

While the casualties incurred during major combat operations in Iraq appeared to be acceptable to most, this appears not to have carried over into the postconflict stability operations (Figure 5.41): the

Figure 5.40
Prospective Willingness to Tolerate Casualties in Iraq by Party, April 2003

Would you say the war in Iraq was successful if it removed Saddam Hussein from power and fewer than 100 American soldiers were killed in battle, or would you not say it was successful in that case? (If Yes, ask:) Would you still say it was successful if up to 500 American soldiers were killed in battle? (If Yes, ask:) Up to 1,000? (If Yes, ask:) Up to 5,000? (If Yes, ask:) Would you say that the military action against Iraq had been successful if Saddam Hussein was removed from power, no matter what it costs in American casualties? (Los Angeles Times, April 2–3, 2003, N=745)

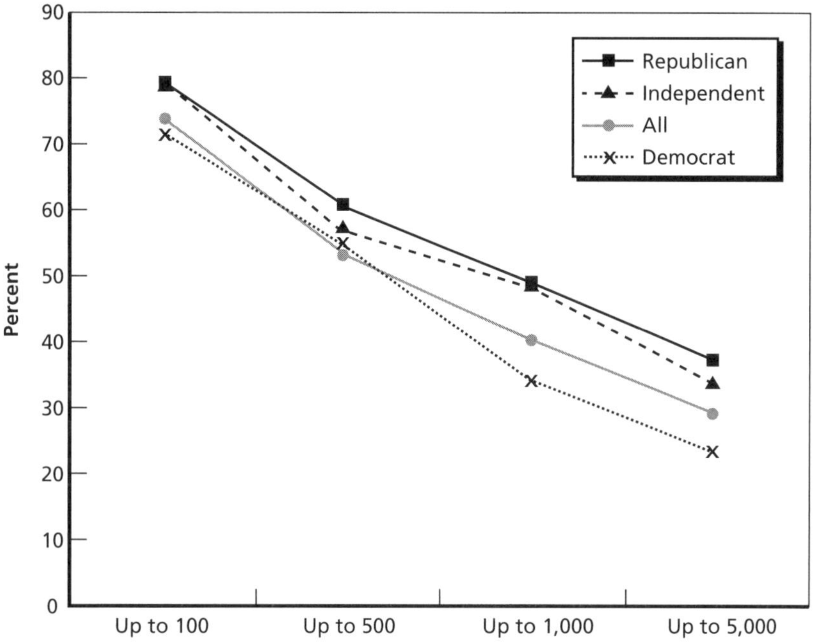

RAND *MG231-A-5.40*

belief that casualties have been acceptable declined over the spring and summer of 2003 to the point where, in September, only about four in ten any longer considered the casualties acceptable.

The acceptability of casualties was also partisan-coded: By June 2003, 60 percent of Democrats and 53 percent of Independents—

Figure 5.41
Acceptability of Casualties in Iraq

Again thinking about the goals versus the costs of the war, so far in your opinion has there been an acceptable or unacceptable number of U.S. military casualties in Iraq? (ABC News/Washington Post)

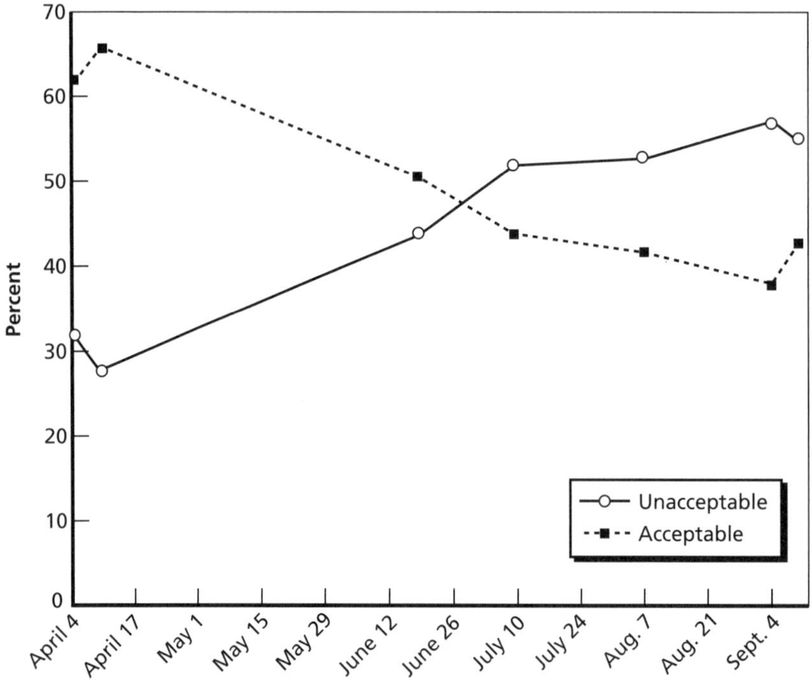

RAND *MG231-A-5.41*

but only 21 percent of Republicans—said that the casualties incurred in Iraq had become unacceptable.[92]

It is important to note that the number of deaths incurred in Iraq to date are well within the envelope of the maximum casualty tolerance suggested by some of the polling data: 500 to 1,000 dead. Whether we should still consider these data points to be a reasonable

[92] ABC News/Washington Post Poll, "Public Disquiet Grows with Casualties in Iraq," June 23, 2003.

estimate of the maximum tolerance of the American public for casualties in Iraq is not clear; there has been only one relatively old case (Vietnam) where the public indicated the maximum number of casualties it considered acceptable and the actual casualties climbed to that level, enabling a comparison.[93] In all other cases, casualty levels were never large enough to compare actual with hypothesized support.

Nor is it clear how many members of the public know with any precision how many casualties the United States actually has incurred in Iraq; although there is daily reporting on the U.S. casualties, there are at least some indications that the media have generally focused their Iraq reporting more on the issues of terrorism and weapons of mass destruction than on casualties (see Figure 5.42). Anecdotally at least, the media seem to have focused on new casualties each day rather than providing a sense of the cumulative tally. Moreover, past polling work suggests that the public has a tendency to overestimate the actual number of dead and wounded.[94] Taken together with the other data presented earlier, it seems likely that casualties are having a corrosive effect on support, but they may be less important than other factors, and their contribution to the decline in support is nearly impossible to tease out from the effects of other factors.

Sources and Fault Lines in Escalation and Withdrawal Sentiment

While most Republican leaders have generally supported the U.S. presence in Iraq, they have divided on the question of whether troop levels are adequate, with some leaders favoring more troops and others accepting the administration's argument that force levels are adequate. Democratic leaders have also divided somewhat on the ques-

---

[93] About one in four indicated that they would still support the Vietnam War if the number of casualties reached the levels reached in the Korean War; when the actual casualty levels surpassed the Korean War tally, only about one in four remained as supporters.

[94] Polling by the Program on International Policy Attitudes during some of the peace operations of the 1990s suggested that Americans believed that the United States had incurred deaths due to hostile action, when in fact it had not.

Figure 5.42
New York Times Stories on Various Iraq-Related Topics, as of October 29, 2003

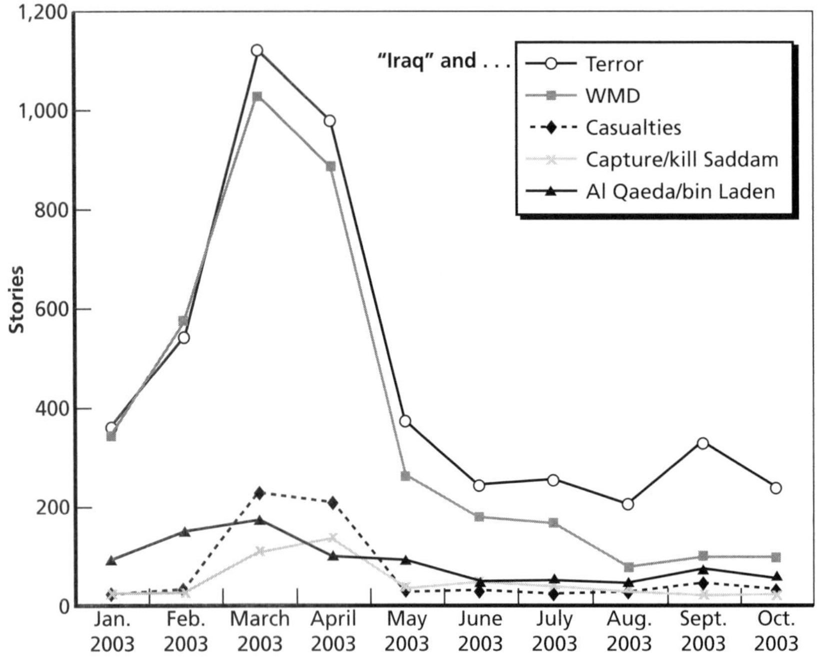

RAND *MG231-A-5.42*

tion of what to do in Iraq, with some moderate Democratic leaders suggesting that force levels in Iraq are inadequate and that additional forces should be sent to Iraq, and some more liberal members suggesting that the United States should withdraw more quickly. Public preferences regarding escalation in or withdrawal from Iraq have also had a strong partisan flavor; as was described earlier, this constitutes a major fault line in support for the continued presence there.

Table 5.14 reports on escalation and withdrawal sentiment for Iraq before and after the November 2003 shoot down of a Chinook helicopter that killed 16 U.S. military personnel.

Table 5.14
Withdrawal Sentiment Before and After Early November Casualties in Iraq, by Party

Which comes closest to your view about what the U.S. should now do about the number of U.S. troops in Iraq? The U.S. should . . .

Gallup, October 24–26, 2003	Total	Rep	Ind	Dem
Send more troops to Iraq	14	18	14	10
Keep the number of troops as it is now	27	37	25	19
Begin to withdraw some troops from Iraq	39	36	41	38
Withdraw all of its troops from Iraq	18	7	17	32
Don't know/refused	2	2	3	1
Gallup, November 3–5, 2003	Total	Rep	Ind	Dem
Send more troops to Iraq	17	21	16	14
Keep the number of troops as it is now	32	47	29	18
Begin to withdraw some troops from Iraq	29	21	30	37
Withdraw all of its troops from Iraq	19	8	21	28
Don't know/refused	3	3	4	3
Change	Total	Rep	Ind	Dem
Send more troops to Iraq	+3	+3	+2	+4
Keep the number of troops as it is now	+5	+10	+4	–1
Begin to withdraw some troops from Iraq	–10	–15	–11	–1
Withdraw all of its troops from Iraq	+1	+1	+4	–4
Don't know/refused	+1	+1	+1	+2

The data in the table also show that, following the "rally" that occurred after the 16 deaths in the shoot down of the helicopter in early November 2003, most of the increased support for staying the course in Iraq came from Republicans and Independents; Democrats showed only modest movements, and only at the extremes: 4 percent fewer supported complete withdrawal, and 4 percent more supported sending more troops. This result is consistent with past work suggesting that increased support typically comes from a president's core constituency, and that only in cases where there is a rally in support from the leadership of the opposing party—as was the case immediately after 9/11—will full-blown rallies occur that yield significant increases in public support.[95] As just described, the modest rally in support in early November 2003 drew in some Independents but did not benefit greatly from Democrats.

This result also casts additional doubt on the counterfactual argument offered by some academics that the public would have rallied in support of President Clinton had he simply advocated staying the course in Somalia: there was far higher support for the Bush administration's Iraq policy in November 2003 than for the Clinton administration's Somalia policy in October 1993, and yet President Bush was able to move only about 8–10 percent of those who supported withdrawal to supporting the continued presence of U.S. forces. For President Clinton to have generated a rally for a more assertive Somalia policy after the firefight in Mogadishu along the lines suggested by these academics would have required a change in support that could only have resulted if large percentages had crossed party boundaries to support President Clinton, even as Republican and Democratic leaders opposed him. Their claim that the public would have rallied in favor of a more assertive Somalia policy seems increasingly dubious in light of the public opinion data on Iraq.

Chapter Conclusions

It appears that the hardening of partisan divisions among national leaders over Iraq, largely manifested in criticism of the credibility of the justifications given for the war, has been the principal fault line in support for the operation: as described above, while we observed recurring partisan differences in beliefs about the stakes, prospects for success, and acceptability of casualties, and ultimately, support for the operation, it was not until major combat operations had concluded that these divisions affected support; nor do these divisions seem

[95] Brody (1991, pp. 70–73) shows that the rally in presidential approval for President Carter during the Iran hostage crisis was bipartisan in nature, but only a majority of Democrats and Independents actually approved of the president. Michael Kagay (1992) provides a nice analysis of the rally in support for the ground war in the first Gulf War.

likely to go away any time in the near future, especially with the presidential electoral season underway.

As of late August 2004, as this report was about to go to press, attitudes toward Iraq were quite mixed, with support depending very much on the question being asked:

- 55 percent supported U.S. military action in Iraq,[96] and 53 percent said that the country had made the right decision in using military force against Iraq.[97]
- 50 percent said they believed that the United States had made a mistake in sending troops to Iraq, while 47 percent said it had not.[98]
- Between 43 and 49 percent felt that it had been worth going to war in Iraq.[99]
- Between 43 and 45 percent approved of President Bush's handling of the situation in Iraq.[100]
- Between 40 and 54 percent thought that the United States should keep troops in Iraq until the situation stabilized.[101]
- Between 45 and 53 percent thought the military effort in Iraq was going very or fairly well.[102]

---

[96] August 2–5, 2004, N = 938.

[97] Pew, August 5–10, 2004, N = 773.

[98] Gallup/CNN/USA Today, July 19–21, 2004, N = 1,005.

[99] Forty-three percent in an NBC/Wall Street Journal poll felt that removing Saddam Hussein had been worth the U.S. military casualties and the financial cost of the war, while 49 percent told Gallup that they thought it had been worth going to war. NBC/Wall Street Journal, August 23–25, 2004, N=806, and Gallup, August 9–11, 2004, N=499.

[100] The Pew Research Center's poll of August 5–10, 2004, found 43 percent approving, while Time's poll found 45 percent approving. Pew, August 5–10, 2004, N = 773, and Time, August 3–5, 2004, N=976.

[101] Pew (August 5–10, 2004, N = 1,512) found 54 percent who thought that the United States should keep troops in Iraq until the situation had stabilized, while The Harris Poll (August 10–15, 2004, N=1,012) found 40 percent who thought the United States should wait until a stable government had been established before withdrawing troops.

[102] Gallup (August 9–11, 2004, N = 499) found 45 percent who thought that things in Iraq were going very or moderately well, while Pew (August 5–10, 2004, N = 1,512) found 53 percent who thought the U.S. military effort was going very or fairly well.

- Between 36 and 45 percent thought that the president had a clear plan for bringing the situation in Iraq to a successful conclusion.[103]

There remains a risk that the proportion of people who believe the United States made a mistake and has ended up in a losing situation in Iraq could continue to grow, even as casualties continue to be incurred. Past experience suggests that further erosion in beliefs about the importance of Iraq or the progress being made would be expected to drive support down, opposition up, and further polarize the public over the question of whether to increase the U.S. commitment in Iraq or begin to withdraw.

On the other hand, recent polling suggests a decline in some negative perceptions regarding the Iraq situation, and a concomitant increase in some measures of support. Gallup's polling, for example, reveals that the percentages disapproving of President Bush's handling of the Iraq situation, saying the Iraq war was not worth it, and believing that things were going badly for the United States in Iraq had all declined in the three months from June to August 2004.[104] It remains to be seen whether this trend will continue, as it will depend largely on the flow of positive developments that can buoy support.

Preeminent among these would be evidence that Iraq actually is becoming more stable, and that there is a growing Iraqi distaste for the insurgency and growing support for the Iraqi interim government and the emerging democratic process. Although it is too early to judge their impact on public support, the recent peaceful resolution of the situation in Najaf and the conclusion of the Iraqi National Conference are potentially important developments in this respect. Somewhat anecdotally, the rather pessimistic tone of much commentary and media reporting on Iraq seems to have minimized U.S. suc-

---

[103] Pew (August 5–10, 2004, N = 1,512) found 36 percent who said the president had a clear plan, while Gallup/CNN/USA Today (July 19–21, 2004, N = 506) found 33 percent who said so.

[104] See Lydia Saad, "Public Remains Split on Iraq; No Indication That Early Fighting in Najaf Soured Attitudes," Gallup Poll News Service, August 20, 2004.

cesses, while concentrating on combat, bombings, beheadings, kidnappings of foreigners, and other mediagenic events. Although there is little reason to believe that "spin" trumps "the facts on the ground," an improving situation on the ground, were it to penetrate the media's veil and reach the American public, would also be expected to shore up support somewhat.

Finally, with the 2004 presidential campaign concluded, the acute partisan nature of support and opposition on Iraq, evidenced by the 84 percent of Republicans—but only 18 percent of Democrats—who in an August 2004 Los Angeles Times national poll said they thought that the situation in Iraq had been worth going to war over,[105] could diminish and result in somewhat higher support; in fact, both candidates' support for the war, and their positions on the fundamental question of whether the United States should withdraw before the mission in Iraq is completed, suggested that relatively modest differences in policies would have resulted whatever the election outcome.[106]

---

[105] See Los Angeles Times, "Kerry Feels Negative Effect of Attack Ads; Bush the Beneficiary," Los Angeles Times Poll Alert, Study No. 505, August 25, 2004.

[106] See Jim VandeHei, "In Hindsight, Kerry Says He'd Still Vote for War," *Washington Post*, August 10, 2004, p. A1. Senator Kerry has stated his belief that U.S. troops might be reduced by August 2005, as a result of alliance contributions and efforts to more quickly build Iraqi military and police capabilities.

CHAPTER SIX

Main Findings and Implications

Main Findings

The Key Predictors of Support and Opposition

Based upon our analyses of the available public opinion data, including bivariate and multivariate analyses of individual-level data from polling datasets, the most important predictors of support or opposition for military actions in the GWOT—and the peace operations of the 1990s as well—are a small set of key beliefs that are linked to support or opposition in a very sensible fashion:

- **Importance of the stakes.** Beliefs about the importance of the U.S. stakes in a situation are systematically associated with support and opposition for military operations there: those who believe the United States has important stakes—whether in terms of vital national interests, security interests, or moral or humanitarian interests—are more likely to support the operation than those who don't believe the United States has important stakes involved.
- **Prospects for success.** Beliefs about the prospects for a successful outcome in the operation are also systematically associated with support or opposition: those who are more confident in a successful outcome are more likely to support the operation than those who are less confident.
- **Expected and actual casualties and other costs.** Beliefs about the likely costs, especially in casualties, are also associated with sup-

port: those who expect few casualties typically are more likely to support the operation than those who expect many casualties.

Additionally, leadership and what we call "followership"—the tendency to follow one's natural party or ideological leaders—was consistently associated both with beliefs about the merits of the operation—the stakes, prospects for success, and likely costs—and with support and opposition: individuals who are members of the president's party are more likely to support a president's use of force than those who are not, and within each party, those who are the best informed are more likely to take the same positions as their partisan leaders than those who are less well informed.

Using respondent-level datasets from polls done on various operations (Haiti, Bosnia, Kosovo, Operation Enduring Freedom (OEF) in Afghanistan, and Operation Iraqi Freedom), our bivariate analyses consistently demonstrated a statistically significant relationship between support and these predictors. And, using a family of statistical techniques called probit regression, we were able to correctly predict the support or opposition of anywhere from 60 to 80 percent of the respondents based largely upon these predictors; our modeling of respondent-level public opinion data on Somalia after the October firefight correctly predicted the preferences for escalation and withdrawal of over 60 percent of the respondents.

The Relative Importance of the Predictors

Our multivariate modeling suggested that the belief that the United States had important stakes in a situation—whether conceived in terms of traditional security interests such as vital interests or in terms of humanitarian or moral equities—was the most important predictor of support or opposition to military operations, more important even than judgments about the prospects for success, which was the second most important factor.

This finding lends additional empirical support to the basic conclusion of the research reported here: that the higher support for the use of troops and the willingness to accept casualties and stay the course in Afghanistan and Iraq, compared with the peace operations of the 1990s, is due largely to the belief that the United States has important stakes in more recent situations, a belief that was generally lacking in the earlier ones.

When we compared the distribution of coefficients for the key independent variables for GWOT-related operations with those for the peace operations of the 1990s, these differences become somewhat more apparent:

- In the case of the GWOT-related operations, perceptions of the stakes were more important than either the prospects for success or the likely costs of the operation, whereas in the case of the peace operations of the 1990s, perceptions of the stakes, prospects for success, and costs were all of roughly comparable importance, and a belief in important moral interests seemed to be more important than a belief that important security interests were involved (as shown in the case studies, few actually believed the latter). The higher correlation between support and the perceived stakes suggests that beliefs about the importance of the stakes—and not the operations' prospects—have been the most important factor shaping support or opposition to the use of troops in the GWOT, and probably the tolerance for casualties as well.[1] It also helps to explain the greater willingness to accept casualties in the GWOT-related operations than the peace operations—the stakes, being higher, mean that higher costs would also be deemed acceptable.
- As just suggested, the prospects for success were more important predictors of support and opposition for the peace operations than for GWOT-related operations, and they rivaled the importance of the stakes. This is consistent with our case studies, which showed that even in cases where the expected casualties were low, fewer than a majority supported some operations;

[1] This effect is usually intensified by the personification of the wordings of questions that were asked. For example, focused questions that asked about the importance of killing or capturing Osama bin Laden had a higher correlation with support than broader questions asking about the importance of U.S. involvement in the campaign.

doubts about the probability of a successful outcome of an operation of even modest value would appear to be the reason.

- In the peace operations the coefficients for party were generally in the same range as those for the other variables (importance of the interests, prospects for success, and expected costs), suggesting that all of these variables played comparably important roles in determining support or opposition. This is consistent with the case studies, which demonstrated the recurring partisan divisions over peace operations. Finally, the extreme importance of party in Afghanistan was somewhat puzzling given the bipartisan leadership support for that operation, and it seems to be a curious artifact of the data: although supermajorities of both Republicans and Democrats supported the use of force in the GWOT, there were still significant partisan differences. One conjecture is that a small group of those who would be expected to oppose the war (pacifists, leftists, and other anti-war activists, liberals, those who dislike President Bush) were more likely to self-identify with the Democratic party and remained indifferent to support for the war from their would-be Democratic leaders. The high correlation between party and support for Iraq was much easier to explain, as partisan differences clearly existed among national leaders. It also suggests that partisan leadership and followership continue to play an important role in the shaping of public opinion on the GWOT.

Americans' Tolerance for Casualties

Moreover, the data from polling done at the time of actual military operations suggests that some of the more tumescent predictions regarding the public's willingness to tolerate casualties greatly exaggerate the public's casualty tolerance (see Table 6.1).

While the rankings are probably about right—Iraqi WMD being viewed as more important than Taiwan, Taiwan more important than civil war in the Congo—the results seem to be off the mark by one or more orders of magnitude. Polling done before and during the recent war in Iraq, for example, suggests that the authors' prediction

Table 6.1
Feaver and Gelpi's Estimates of the American Public's Casualty Acceptance

Mission	Military Elite	Civilian Elite	Mass Public
Prevent Iraqi WMD	6,016	19,045	29,853
Defend Taiwan	17,425	17,554	20,172
Stabilize Congo	284	484	6,861

SOURCE: Peter D. Feaver and Christopher Gelpi, "A Look at Casualty Aversion: How Many Deaths Are Acceptable? A Surprising Answer," *The Washington Post*, November 7, 1999, p. B3, cited in Charles K. Hyde, "Casualty Aversion: Implications for Policymakers and Senior Military Officers," *Essays 2000*, Chairman of the Joint Chiefs of Staff Strategy Essay Competition, Washington, D.C., 2000.

that the average American would be willing to accept nearly 30,000 casualties in a war against Iraqi weapons of mass destruction was off by a factor of 30 to 60,[2] and the prediction that the average American would tolerate nearly 7,000 casualties in an African civil conflict would seem to be off by a factor of somewhere between 100 and 1,000.[3]

---

[2] As reported here, actual polling prior to and during the recent war in Iraq suggested that the average American might tolerate casualties in the 500–1,000 range in a war to eliminate Iraq's weapons of mass destruction.

[3] We can infer a low casualty tolerance for civil conflicts in Africa from two bits of evidence a decade apart: First, support fell below 50 percent in Somalia in the late summer or early fall of 1993 after only seven deaths there, and fell further after the 18 servicemen died in the firefight on October 3–4, 1993. Second, polling by ABC News/Washington Post found that only 41 percent supported sending U.S. troops to Liberia as part of an international force to help enforce a cease-fire in the civil war, while higher percentages favored the use of U.S. ground troops in an international peacekeeping force in Liberia. As described in one analysis: "Finally, many people express skepticism with another, far smaller, possible military mission: Fifty-one percent say they'd oppose sending up to 2,000 U.S. troops to Liberia as part of an international force to help enforce a cease-fire in the civil war there; just 41 percent say they'd support it. Conflict clearly is the concern: Other polls have found higher support for sending U.S. troops when it's posed as a 'peacekeeping' force, a considerably more benign description." ABC News/Washington Post Poll, "Bush Faces Rising Public Doubts on Credibility and Casualties Alike," news release, July 11, 2003. See also Darren K. Carlson, "Should the U.S. Keep the Peace in Liberia?" August 5, 2003, and David W. Moore, "Americans Favor U.S. Peacekeeping Force in Liberia; Still Strong Support for U.S. Troops in Iraq," July 11, 2003. Put another way, polling done on this question during actual civil conflicts does not suggest that the American public's tolerance for casualties there would be particularly high.

The results in the table—an experimental result from a one-off academic survey conducted in the equivalent of a controlled, hot-house environment—are not credible when compared to actual public opinion data collected during relevant historical episodes. Further, the use of the *mean* number of casualties rather than the *median*—only the latter is robust to outliers, and the authors' results have a long right-hand tail—does not foster confidence in the analysis or the result. As appealing as such results may be to some audiences, the policy community should not give them much credence until they are shown to predict support and opposition for prospective uses of force with some level of accuracy;[4] until then, they are only of passing academic interest.

"Casualty Phobia" or "Defeat Phobia"?

Our reanalysis of the data from Somalia and data from the November 2003 shoot down of a helicopter in Iraq affirms that when support is lost, those who oppose an operation may do so either because they want to cut their losses and withdraw or because they believe that greater effort is warranted. Individuals' specific beliefs about the expected benefits and costs of escalation or withdrawal predict their positions on the matter: those who believe that the expected benefits are high and the costs low are more likely to support escalation, while those holding the opposite beliefs are more likely to support withdrawal. Specifically, our reanalysis of the data regarding preferences for withdrawal and escalation in Somalia following the October 1993 firefight confirmed that most wanted to leave Somalia, although not before U.S. servicemen held hostage were recovered. And the data on the public's response to the deaths of 16 servicemen in Iraq in early November also confirms this interpretation: there was a perceptible stiffening of resolve among Americans after this incident. The reason is that in the case of Somalia, few viewed the stakes as very important, whereas in the case of Iraq, most did.

---

[4] The "Lakatos Criteria"—Imre Lakatos' suggestion that the actual ability of a theory or model to correctly predict outcomes in its domain of application should be a key criterion for evaluating its utility—applies as well here as it does in other areas of research.

Thus, the present research does not support the contention, as some have suggested, that the public is "defeat-phobic" rather than "casualty-phobic," except in the limiting condition where most Americans *actually believe* that the stakes are very important *and* the prospects for success good; in cases where the United States' stakes are not deemed to be particularly important (as in Somalia) and the prospects for a successful outcome poor, Americans have proved themselves more than willing to cut their losses, so long as U.S. servicemen held hostage were recovered. In the case of Somalia, the data are clear: the American public preferred an orderly withdrawal, i.e., a withdrawal following the recovery of captured and killed servicemen, and were willing to entertain a wide range of options for accomplishing that, while eschewing either an immediate withdrawal or some sort of increased commitment in Somalia. In the case of Iraq, which involved far more important stakes than Somalia had, the data are also clear: there was a greater reluctance to withdraw in the face of casualties, and even a tendency among some toward escalation.[5]

To put a finer point on it, it is because Iraq is believed by most to involve much more important stakes than Somalia did that Americans are more likely to be prone to be "defeat-phobic" in Iraq, even where they showed themselves to be "casualty-phobic" in Somalia after the firefight.

We now turn to the main implications of this research for the Army and national political leaders.

Implications for the Army

The main implication for the Army is that Americans have proved themselves far more willing to use ground troops—to put "boots on the ground"—and to accept casualties in operations conducted under the GWOT than in any of the peace operations in the preceding decade (see Figure 6.1).

---

[5] For a description of the conditions under which escalation and withdrawal are preferred, see Chapter Two of this report.

Figure 6.1
Approval for the Presence of U.S. Troops in Various Operations

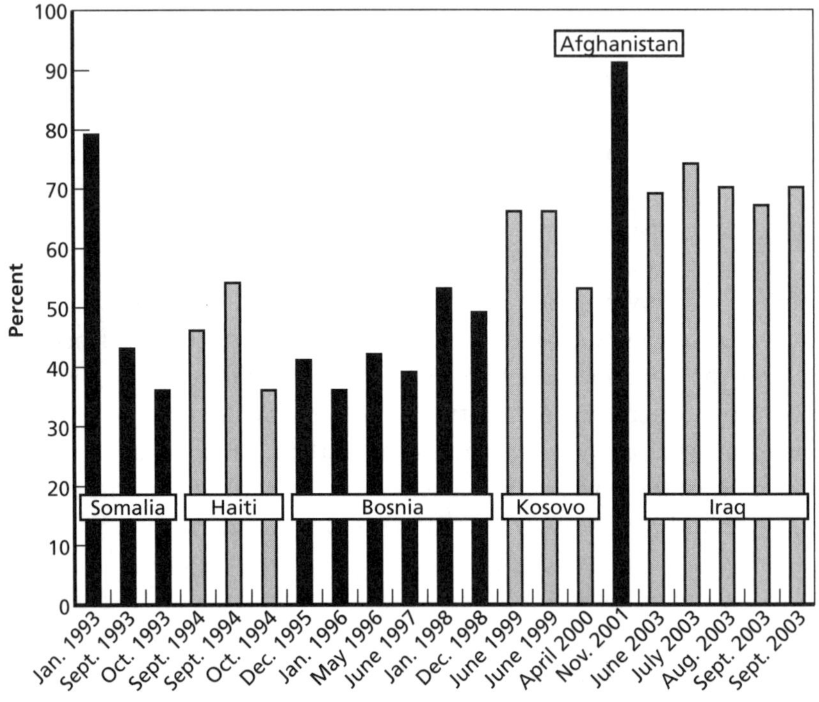

SOURCES: ABC News/Washington Post, Chicago Council on Foreign Relations, Christian Science Monitor/Investors Business Daily, Fox News, Gallup, Newsweek/PSRA, Time/CNN/Harris.

RAND *MG231-A-6.1*

As suggested by the figure, only in the cases of the wars in Afghanistan and Iraq have majorities in the last decade approved of the presence of U.S. troops for combat operations; majorities also supported the presence of U.S. troops for the initial (humanitarian) phase of the Somalia operation and the peacekeeping operation following the air war in Kosovo, but they generally failed to support the presence of U.S. troops during the latter ("nation building") phase of Somalia and the U.S. interventions in Haiti and Bosnia.[6]

This suggests more support for an Army role than was observed in the peace operations of the 1990s, at least to the extent that the specific military operations that are proposed under the GWOT are judged to be relevant to the GWOT, and that they have good prospects for a successful outcome.

To the extent that national leaders are able to link specific operations to the larger GWOT in the public mind, they can expect a relatively permissive public opinion environment for taking military action, including the use of ground forces.

It is an open question, however, whether as a result of questions that have arisen about the existence and nature of any connections between Al Qaeda and Saddam's Iraq, about Iraq's prewar weapons of mass destruction program, and about how the operations in Iraq might possibly have hindered the campaign against Al Qaeda, Americans will unquestioningly accept the argument that new military operations that are proposed are necessarily part of the GWOT.

Implications for National Leaders

More broadly, the immediate aftermath of 9/11 initially seemed to offer at least one bright prospect: that a post–Cold War consensus regarding the focus of national security and defense policies had finally emerged among national leaders in the executive and legislative branches. For the foreseeable future, it seemed at the time, leaders in both parties would support a focus for U.S. national security on terrorist groups with global reach, their sponsors, and those providing them refuge.

The U.S. action in Afghanistan generally received overwhelming bipartisan support from national leaders, and public support accordingly was preternaturally high. Bipartisan support for the war in Iraq

---

[6] As shown, two out of three questions that asked respondents whether they approved of the presence of U.S. troops in Haiti failed to find an approving majority.

was slightly weaker, and as a result, public support, while still high, was somewhat lower than that observed for Afghanistan. Bipartisan consensus on postconflict stability operations in Iraq, however, now appears elusive at best.

It is still too early to say whether or how this breakdown in consensus might color support for other military actions taken under the banner of the GWOT. Nevertheless, it raises the specter that as a result of the reappearance of leadership divisions, future operations in the GWOT also may suffer from the much lower and more highly conditional support that was associated with the peace operations of the 1990s.

While national leaders argue their differences on national security, they need to remain mindful that a failure to agree on the ends, ways, and means for ensuring the nation's security in the face of these new threats to the nation can actually weaken the credibility of deterrence and coercive diplomacy—and beliefs in the United States' ability to stay the course in its war on terrorism—and ultimately encourage the nation's enemies.

The United States has always been a noisy democracy when it comes to issues of war and peace—witness the sharp partisan divisions over the peace operations of the 1990s. But although the U.S. stakes in those operations were relatively modest, the outcome of the GWOT matters greatly. The only way to sustain the public's long-term support for this war—a necessary requirement to sustain the war on terrorism itself—will be for national leaders to find common ground and forge policies that reflect a durable consensus.

APPENDIX

Casualties and Consensus, Revisited

When RAND published its last major report on the subject of casualties and public support,[1] the conventional wisdom was that Americans would no longer accept casualties in military operations, i.e., that Americans had become casualty averse or "casualty-phobic." The 1996 study, which examined public support and the role of casualties in that support in a wide range of wars and military operations, including World War II, the Korean War, the Vietnam War, Panama, the Gulf War, and Somalia, suggested a very different perspective.

That study showed that the willingness to tolerate casualties can be high or low depending on the perceived merits of each case, but a tolerance for casualties historically has hinged on beliefs that the stakes involved in the operation are important, and that the outcome of the operation is likely to be successful. The result was that majorities of the public could be said to be casualty-tolerant when large percentages subscribe to these beliefs, and casualty-intolerant when they don't. It was unclear at the time, however, whether beliefs about the stakes or the prospects for success were more important in determining the tolerance for casualties in military operations.

The 1996 report included a plot of support against the log of actual or prospective casualties for a large number of operations. Although presenting the data in such a manner can be somewhat misleading because it masks other factors (not shown in the chart) that also influence the willingness to tolerate casualties, when this figure is

[1] RAND also published an earlier report on the subject, Lorell, Kelly, and Hensler (1984).

updated with data from the more recent cases, some very interesting patterns emerge (see Figure A.1).[2]

Support in peace operations such as the Dominican Republic, Lebanon, Somalia, Bosnia, and Kosovo suggested a rather low tolerance for casualties: they all are found in the bottom left-hand quadrant of the figure.[3] On the other hand, major wars that involved important U.S. stakes such as Korea, Vietnam, the 1991 Gulf War, and the 2003 war in Iraq presented somewhat higher tolerance for losses: these lines are above and to the right of the peace operations, and they show much more gradual declines as the casualties increase. "Quick and decisive" operations like Panama and Grenada (not shown) were successfully concluded too quickly for casualties to become an issue.

As hypothesized in the 1996 study, and confirmed in the present one, the reason is that Americans never had particularly favorable beliefs about the importance of the stakes or prospects for success of these peace operations, and accordingly they have been reluctant to place U.S. servicemen in harm's way in such situations. While there can be substantial support for the participation of U.S. troops in humanitarian or peace operations in a permissive environment, most Americans appear to draw the line short of ground combat, whether characterized as "peace enforcement" or some other term of art.

The present work casts doubt on those who have argued that Americans' unwillingness to tolerate casualties in peace operations is a "myth";[4] as one scholar of public opinion described Somalia: "In essence, when Americans asked themselves how many American lives

[2] The solid lines are for actual support for the operation given actual casualties, and the dashed lines are for questions that asked about prospective support given various hypothesized numbers of casualties.

[3] Although there didn't appear to be any questions that asked about the willingness to accept specific numbers of casualties in Haiti, a majority of those polled agreed that the intervention was not worth the loss of a single life.

[4] See Steven Kull and Clay Ramsay, "The Myth of the Reactive Public: American Public Attitudes on Military Fatalities in the Post–Cold War Period," at http://www.pipa.org, accessed May 2004.

Figure A.1
Relationship Between Support and Prospective U.S. Deaths

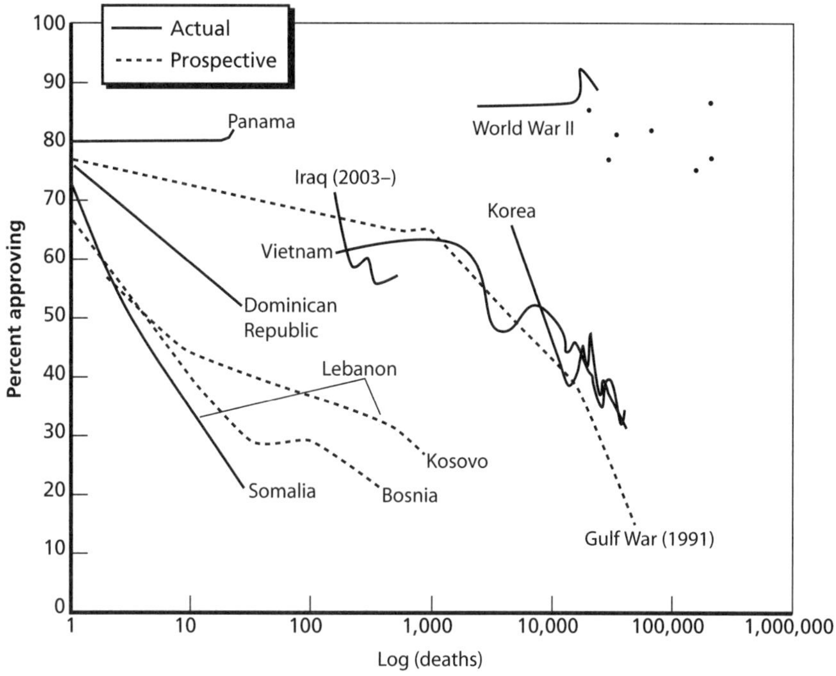

RAND *MG231-A-A.1*

peace in Somalia was worth, the answer came out rather close to zero."[5] As described in the case studies and summarized in Figure A.1, a lower willingness to accept casualties in peace operations is in fact no myth.

It also casts doubt on the assertion that the determining factor in the public's tolerance for casualties is whether or not they believe that the operation has good prospects for success:[6] in virtually every case,

---

[5] John E. Mueller, "Public Support for Military Ventures Abroad: Evidence From the Polls," in John Norton Moore and Robert F. Turner (eds.), *The Real Lessons of the Vietnam War: Reflections Twenty-Five Years After the Fall of Saigon,* Durham, NC: Carolina Academic Press, 2002, pp. 173–219.

[6] Ibid.

our respondent-level modeling suggested that the perceived stakes were a more important predictor of support than beliefs about the prospects for success. In fact, the case of Iraq provides what is perhaps the definitive counterexample to this assertion: to date, support for Iraq has held up in the face of growing casualties *in spite of* a greatly diminished belief in the prospects for the mission's success; in fact, it is only the widespread belief in the importance of the U.S. stakes there that has buoyed support for the mission in the face of mounting casualties. The policy implications are clear: in the face of casualties it will be harder to sustain support for peace operations, which generally do not involve compelling stakes, than for operations involving more important stakes.

The case of Iraq also clears up one other ambiguity: Are questions that ask respondents whether they would support a military operation given various hypothesized casualty levels good predictors of actual sentiment on the matter? The United States' relatively low-casualty experience in military operations over the last dozen or so years has meant that the predictive accuracy of these questions has never actually been tested. As shown in Figure A.2, however, the case of Iraq suggests that these questions provide valuable insights into casualty tolerance.

The figure reports the results of three public opinion questions, two of which were prospective questions that asked respondents whether they would still support war if it meant various hypothesized numbers of American casualties, and the third of which asked respondents whether they thought entry into the war had been a mistake. In the case of the prospective questions, the percent approving is plotted against the hypothesized number of casualties, whereas for the "mistake" question, the percentage saying that entry into the war was not a mistake is plotted against the total number of casualties that had actually been incurred by the end of the month in which the poll was done.

As shown, between mid-December 2002 and early April 2003, there was a fairly dramatic increase in the percentage who said they were willing to support a war involving hundreds or thousands of

Figure A.2
Casualties and Prospective and Actual Support for Iraq

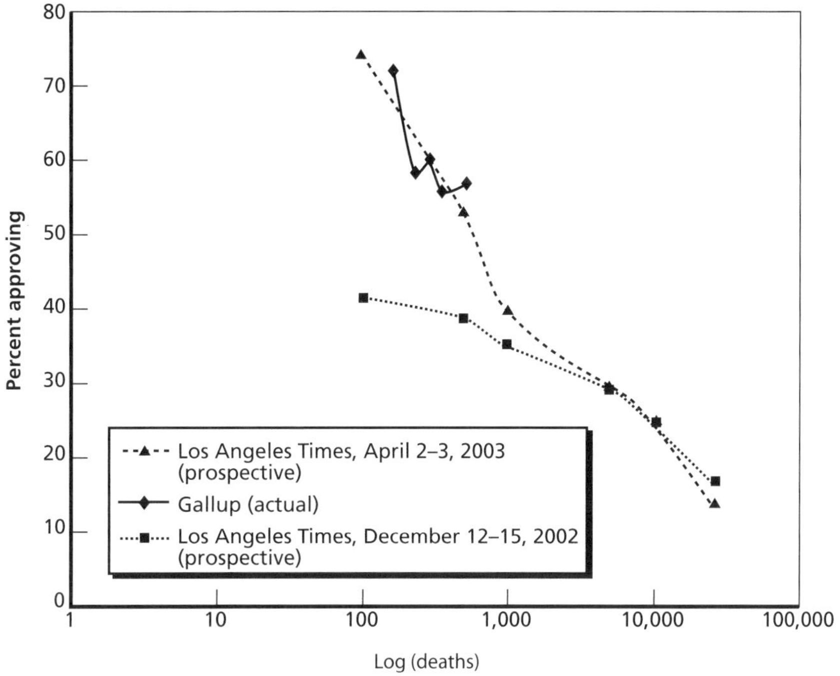

RAND *MG231-A-A.2*

NOTE: Question wordings were as follows. L.A. Times, December 12–15, 2002: "The number of possible casualties in a ground war with Iraq has been estimated at between 100 American soldiers, if the Iraqi military offers little resistance, to as many as 5,000 American soldiers if the Iraqi Republican Guard fight an effective urban defense. With this in mind . . . would you still support sending ground troops to fight in Iraq if it meant up to 100 American soldiers would be killed in battle, or not? (If Yes, ask:) Would you still support sending ground troops if up to 500 American soldiers were killed in battle, or not? (If Yes, ask:) Up to 1,000? (If Yes, ask:) Up to 5,000? (If yes, ask:) Would you say you would support sending ground troops to fight in Iraq no matter what it cost in American casualties, or not?"

L.A. Times, April 2–3, 2003: "Would you say the war in Iraq was successful if it removed Saddam Hussein from power and fewer than 100 American soldiers were killed in battle, or would you not say it was successful in that case? (If Yes, ask:) Would you still say it was successful if up to 500 American soldiers were killed in battle? (If Yes, ask:) Up to 1,000? (If Yes, ask:) Up to 5,000? (If Yes, ask:) Would you say that the military action against Iraq had been successful if Saddam Hussein was removed from power, no matter what it costs in American casualties?"

Gallup: "In view of the developments since we first sent our troops to Iraq, do you think the United States made a mistake in sending troops to Iraq, or not?"

U.S. military casualties. The figure also shows that the April 2003 hypothetical question did a fairly good job of predicting the percentage that approved of the war (i.e., those who said it was not a mistake) as casualties were actually incurred; the predictive power of polling suggesting that majority support would be lost somewhere between 500 and 1,000 combat deaths also seems to have been affirmed.

To emphasize, this is not to say that casualties were what lay behind declining support in the case of Iraq—in Somalia, for example, support seems to have declined primarily as a result of the change in objectives in the spring of 1993 and the deterioration of the situation over the following summer, a time in which few U.S. casualties were incurred. In Iraq, the contretemps over weapons of mass destruction, an Al Qaeda connection, and other matters began chipping away at Democratic support as early as the summer of 2003, and other developments, including the Abu Ghraib scandal, also appear to have eroded support.[7] And although casualties have grown, there has also been a declining belief in the prospects for success; it is only the continued strong belief in the importance of the United States' stakes there that has sustained support in the face of these unfavorable developments.

[7] Gallup's polling in April and May 2004 shows declines in the percentages approving of President Bush's handling of Iraq, and the belief that it was worth going to war. See Lydia Saad, "Public Remains Split on Iraq," Gallup Poll News Service, August 20, 2004.

Bibliography

"France's President Chirac Interviewed on Iraq Crisis," Paris France-2 Television in French, March 10, 2003.

"Nine Key Questions About Public Opinion on Iraq; Support for Invading Iraq Remains High—But With Conditions," The Gallup Organization, October 1, 2002.

"Public Backs Air Strike," *The Gallup Poll Monthly*, June 1993, pp. 23–25.

ABC News/Washington Post Poll, "Most Support Allied Attack Even Without U.N. Support," February 10, 2003.

———, "Support for War Spikes as Bush Sets a Deadline," March 18, 2003.

———, "Public Disquiet Grows with Casualties in Iraq," news release, June 23, 2003.

———, "Bush Faces Rising Public Doubts on Credibility and Casualties Alike," news release, July 11, 2003.

Ajzen, Icek, and Martin Fishbein, *Understanding Attitudes and Predicting Social Behavior*, Englewood Cliffs, NJ: Prentice-Hall, 1980.

Behr, R.L. and Shanto Iyengar, "Television News, Real-World Cues, and Changes in the Public Agenda," *Public Opinion Quarterly*, Vol. 49, 1985, pp. 38–57.

Bennett, Lance W., "Toward a Theory of Press-State Relations in the United States," *Journal of Communication*, Vol. 40, Spring 1990, pp. 103–125.

———, *The Politics of Illusion*, 3d edition, White Plains, NY: Longman, 1996.

———, and David L. Paletz, *Taken By Storm: The Media, Public Opinion, and U.S. Foreign Policy in the Gulf War*, Chicago: University of Chicago, 1994.

Bolton, John R., "Wrong Turn in Somalia," *Foreign Affairs*, January/February 1994.

Brody, Richard A., *Assessing the President: The Media, Elite Opinion, and Public Support*, Stanford: Stanford University Press, 1991.

Bueno de Mesquita, Bruce, and Randolph M. Siverson, "War and the Survival of Political Leaders: A Comparative Study on Regime Types and Political Accountability," *American Political Science Review*, Vol. 89, No. 4, December 1995, pp. 841–855.

Burbach, David T., "Presidential Approval and the Use of Force," Defense and Arms Control Studies Program, MIT Center for International Affairs, DACS Working Paper, May 1994.

Burk, James, "Public Support for Peacekeeping in Lebanon and Somalia: Assessing the Casualties Hypothesis," *Political Science Quarterly*, Vol. 114, No. 1, Spring 1999, pp. 53–78.

Bush, George W., "Remarks by the President After Two Planes Crash Into World Trade Center," September 11, 2001.

———, "Remarks by the President Upon Arrival at Barksdale Air Force Base," September 11, 2001.

———, "Statement by the President in His Address to the Nation," September 11, 2001.

———, "President's Remarks at the United Nations General Assembly," September 12, 2002.

———, "Radio Address of the President to the Nation," September 15, 2001.

———, "Remarks by the President to the Warsaw Conference on Combating Terrorism," November 6, 2001.

———, "President's Remarks at the United Nations General Assembly," September 12, 2002.

———, "State of the Union Address," January 28, 2003.

———, "President Says Saddam Hussein Must Leave Iraq Within 48 Hours," March 17, 2003.

———, "President Bush Addresses the Nation," March 19, 2003.

———, "President Bush Announces Major Combat Operations in Iraq Have Ended," May 1, 2003.

Byman, Daniel, Matthew C. Waxman, and Eric V. Larson, *Air Power as a Coercive Instrument*, Santa Monica, CA: RAND Corporation, MR-1061-AF, 1999.

Carlson, Darren K., "Americans Expected Postwar Military Deaths," The Gallup Organization, July 15, 2003a.

———, "Public Concern About Terrorist at Post-9/11 Low," The Gallup Organization, July 29, 2003b.

———, "Should the U.S. Keep the Peace in Liberia?" August 5, 2003c.

Carroll, Joseph, "Americans on Iraq: Military Action or Diplomacy?" The Gallup Organization, October 8, 2002.

Churchman, C.W., and R.L. Ackoff, "An Approximate Measure of Value," *Journal of Operations Research Society of America*, Vol. 2, No. 2, May 1954.

Clinton, William J., "Remarks to the 48th Session of the United Nations General Assembly in New York City," September 27, 1993.

———, "Address to the Nation on Somalia," October 7, 1993.

———, "President's Somalia Message to Congress," October 13, 1993.

———, "Remarks by the President in Television Address to the Nation," September 15, 1994.

———, "Remarks by the President in Television Address to the Nation," September 18, 1994.

———, "Address to the Nation on Implementation of the Peace Agreement in Bosnia-Herzegovina," November 27, 1995.

———, "Radio Address of the President to the Nation," November 25, 1995, and "Address to the Nation on Implementation of the Peace Agreement in Bosnia-Herzegovina," November 27, 1995.

———, "Statement by the President on Kosovo," March 24, 1999, and "Statement by the President to the Nation," March 24, 1999.

Commission on America's National Interests, *America's National Interests: A Report from the Commission on America's National Interests,* Cambridge,

MA: Center for Science and International Affairs, John F. Kennedy School of Government, Harvard University, 1996.

Cohen, Bernard C., *The Press and Foreign Policy*, Princeton: Princeton University Press, 1963.

Congressional Quarterly, "Administration Struggles With Bosnia Policy," *1993 CQ Almanac*, Washington, D.C.: CQ Press, 1994, pp. 493–499.

———, "Clinton, Congress Struggle To Define U.S. Interests; With Framework Imposed by the Cold War Gone, Focus Shifts From One Crisis to the Next," Washington, D.C.: CQ Press, 1994, pp. 445–446.

———, "Hill Demands Early '94 Somalia Withdrawal," *1993 CQ Almanac*, Washington, D.C.: CQ Press, 1994, pp. 486–493.

———, "U.N. Peacekeeping Proves Risky; Congress, Clinton Administration Grow Cautious About Providing Troops for Multinational Efforts," *1993 CQ Almanac*, Washington, D.C.: CQ Press, 1994, pp. 483–493.

———, "Bosnian War Remains Intractable," *1994 CQ Almanac*, Washington, D.C.: CQ Press, 1995, pp. 446–449.

———, "Clinton's Haiti Gamble Pays Off," *1994 CQ Almanac*, Washington, D.C.: Congressional Quarterly Press, 1995, pp. 449–451.

———, "Bosnian War Sparks Conflict at Home," *1995 CQ Almanac*, Washington, D.C.: CQ Press, 1996, pp. 10-10 to 10-15.

———, "As Crisis Escalates, Lawmakers Reconsider Use of Ground Troops," *1999 CQ Almanac*, Washington, D.C., 2000, pp. 14-22 to 14-24.

———, "House Votes in Support of U.S. Troops in Kosovo," *1999 CQ Almanac*, Washington, D.C., 2000, pp. 14-20 to 14-22.

———, "Kosovo Policy Gets Medley of Complaints," *1999 CQ Almanac*, Washington, D.C., 2000, pp. 14-19 to 14-20.

———, "Republicans Warn Clinton on Use of U.S. Peacekeepers in Kosovo," *1999 CQ Almanac*, Washington, D.C., 2000, p. 14-19.

———, "Senate Kills 'All Necessary Force' Resolution," *1999 CQ Almanac*, Washington, D.C., 2000, pp. 14-25 to 14-26.

———, "War Powers Act Forces House Vote; Senate Buys More Time," *1999 CQ Almanac*, Washington, D.C., 2000, p. 14-24.

———, "Concerns Linger for Lawmakers Following Difficult Vote for War," *CQ Weekly*, October 12, 2002, pp. 2671–2678.

Converse, Philip, "The Nature of Belief Systems Among Mass Publics," in D. Apter (ed.), *Ideology and Discontent*, New York: Free Press, 1964, pp. 206–261.

———, and Howard Schuman, "'Silent Majorities' and the Vietnam War," *Scientific American*, June 1970, pp. 17–25.

Crabtree, Steve, "Americans See More Military Action Coming," The Gallup Organization, June 17, 2003.

Department of Defense, *Quadrennial Defense Review*, Washington, D.C., September 30, 2001.

———, Washington Headquarters Services, Directorate for Information Operations and Reports, "War on Terrorism—Casualty Summary—Operation Enduring Freedom, as of October 22, 2003."

———, Washington Headquarters Services, Directorate for Information Operations and Reports, "War on Terrorism—Operation Iraqi Freedom—By Casualty Category, as of October 22, 2003."

Devroy, Ann, and Julia Preston, "Clinton Seeks Shift of Focus on Somalia," *Washington Post*, September 29, 1993, p. A1.

Downs, Anthony, *An Economic Theory of Democracy*, New York: Harper and Row, 1957.

Downs, George W., and David M. Rocke, "Conflict, Agency, and Gambling for Resurrection: The Principal-Agent Problem Goes to War," *American Journal of Political Science*, Vol. 38, May 1994, pp. 362–380.

Edwards, George C., III, with Alec M. Gallup, *Presidential Approval: A Sourcebook*, Baltimore: The Johns Hopkins University Press, 1990.

Feaver, Peter D., and Christopher Gelpi, "A Look at Casualty Aversion: How Many Deaths Are Acceptable? A Surprising Answer," *The Washington Post*, November 7, 1999, p. B3.

Ferejohn, John A., and James H. Kuklinski, *Information and Democratic Processes*, Urbana: University of Illinois Press, 1990.

Friedman, Milton, "The Methodology of Positive Economics," in *Essays in Positive Economics*, Chicago: University of Chicago Press, 1953, pp. 3–43.

Gallup, George, Jr., and Frank Newport, "Americans Support Military Action in Iraq," The Gallup Poll Monthly, July 1992, p. 50.

——— and ———, "Support Strong for U.S. Bombing Raid on Iraq," The Gallup Poll Monthly, January 1993, p. 7.

The Gallup Organization, "Poll Topics & Trends: Kosovo," The Gallup Organization, available at http://www.gallup.com/poll/topics/kosovo.asp.

The Gallup Organization, "Poll Topics and Trends: Iraq; Bush Approval Also Drops to Term Low," available at http://www.gallup.com/poll/topics/iraq2.asp.

Gamson, William, and Andre Modigliani, "Knowledge and Foreign Policy Opinion," *Public Opinion Quarterly*, Vol. 30, 1966, pp. 187–199.

Gelpi, Christopher, "Democratic Diversions: Governmental Structure and the Externalization of Domestic Conflict," *The Journal of Conflict Resolution*, Vol. 41, No. 2, April 1997, pp. 255–282.

Gillespie, Mark, "Support Grows for Kosovo Mission, But Public Still Divided," The Gallup Organization, March 26, 1999.

———, "Support for Mission Holds Steady, But Skepticism Grows," The Gallup Organization, April 2, 1999.

———, "Crisis in Kosovo: Questions and Answers About American Public Opinion," The Gallup Organization, April 16, 1999.

———, "Support for NATO Air Strikes Hold Steady in Wake of Embassy Attack," The Gallup Organization, May 11, 1999.

Hamilton, Richard F., "A Research Note on the Mass Support for 'Tough' Military Initiatives," *American Sociological Review,* Vol. 33, No. 3, June 1968, pp. 439–445.

Hastie, Reid, "A Primer of Information-Processing Theory for the Political Scientist," in Richard R. Lau and David O. Sears (eds.), *Political Cognition*, Hillsdale, NJ: Lawrence Erlbaum Associates, 1986, pp. 11–39.

Hendrickson, Ryan C., *The Clinton Wars*, Nashville: Vanderbilt University Press, 2002, pp. 51–56 and 65–67.

Huddy, Leonie, Nadia Khatib, and Theresa Capelos, "The Polls—Trends; Reactions to the Terrorist Attacks of September 11, 2001," *Public Opinion Quarterly*, Vol. 66, 2002, pp. 418–450.

Hyde, Charles K., "Casualty Aversion: Implications for Policymakers and Senior Military Officers," *Essays 2000*, Chairman of the Joint Chiefs of Staff Strategy Essay Competition, Washington, D.C., 2000.

International Institute for Strategic Studies, "War in Afghanistan," *Strategic Survey 2001/2001*, Oxford: Oxford University Press, 2002.

Iyengar, Shanto, *Is Anyone Responsible?* Chicago: University of Chicago, 1991.

Jeffords, Susan, and Lauren Rabinovitz, *Seeing Through the Media*, New Brunswick: Rutgers University Press, 1994.

Jentleson, Bruce, "The Pretty Prudent Public: Post Post-Vietnam American Opinion on the Use of Military Force," *International Quarterly*, Vol. 36, 1992, pp. 49–74.

———, and Rebecca Britton, "Still Pretty Prudent: Post–Cold War American Public Opinion on the Use of Military Force," *Journal of Conflict Resolution*, Vol. 42, No. 4, August 1998, pp. 395–417.

Jones, Jeffrey M., "Support Remains High Even If Military Action Is Prolonged, Involves Casualties; Support Lowest If War Lasted Several Years or Resulted in American Casualties," The Gallup Organization, October 4, 2001.

———, "Support for Military Effort Remains High; Americans Less Positive in their Assessment of Progress in War on Terrorism," The Gallup Organization, March 12, 2002.

———, "Removing Saddam Considered an Important Foreign Policy Goal; Majority Favors Sending U.S. Troops to Overthrow Iraqi President," The Gallup Organization, June 21, 2002.

———, "Americans Distrust Iraq but Favor Giving U.N. Inspectors More Time; Support for Invasion at Lowest Point Since Last Summer, But Opinions Not Firmly Held," The Gallup Organization, January 27, 2003.

———, "Speech Watchers Believe Iraq Victory Aids U.S. in War on Terrorism; Many Still Reluctant to Say Iraq War is Over," The Gallup Organization, May 2, 2003.

———, "Half of Americans Continue to Say Iraq War 'Worth It'; One in Four Cite Situation in Iraq as Most Important Problem Facing Country," Gallup News Service, May 7, 2004.

Kagay, Michael R., "Variability Without Fault: Why Even Well-Designed Polls Can Disagree," in Thomas E. Mann and Gary R. Orren (eds.), *Media Polls in American Politics*, Washington, D.C.: The Brookings Institution, 1992, pp. 95–124.

Kahneman, Daniel, Paul Slovic, and Amos Tversky (eds.), *Judgment Under Uncertainty: Heuristics and Biases*, Cambridge: Cambridge University Press, 1982.

Kernell, Samuel, *Going Public: New Strategies of Presidential Leadership*, 2d edition, Washington, D.C.: Congressional Quarterly Press, 1993.

Klarevas, Louis J., "The Polls—Trends: The United States Peace Operation in Somalia," *Public Opinion Quarterly*, Vol. 64, 2000, pp. 523–540.

———, "The 'Essential Domino' of Military Operations: American Public Opinion and the Use of Force," *International Studies Perspectives*, Vol. 3, 2002, pp. 417–437.

———, and Daniel O'Connor, "At What Cost? American Mass Public Opinion and the Use of Force Abroad, paper presented at the International Studies Association Annual Meeting, March 1994.

Kull, Steven, and Clay Ramsay, "The Myth of the Reactive Public: American Public Attitudes on Military Fatalities in the Post–Cold War Period," available at http://www.pipa.org.

———, and I.M. Destler, *Misreading the Public: The Myth of a New Isolationism*, Washington, D.C.: The Brookings Institution, 1999.

Larson, Eric V., *Casualties and Consensus: The Historical Role of Casualties in Domestic Support for U.S. Military Operations*, Santa Monica, CA: RAND Corporation, MR-726-RC, 1996a. Available for download at http://www.rand.org/publications/MR/MR726/.

———, *Ends and Means in the Democratic Conversation: Understanding the Role of Casualties in Support for U.S. Military Operations*, Santa Monica, CA: RAND Corporation, RGSD-124, 1996b.

———, "Putting Theory to Work: Diagnosing Public Opinion on the U.S. Intervention in Bosnia," in Miroslav Nincic and Joseph Lepgold (eds.), *Being Useful: Policy Relevance and International Relations Theory*, Ann Arbor, MI: University of Michigan Press, 2000, pp. 174–233.

———, David T. Orletsky, and Kristin Leuschner, *Defense Planning in a Decade of Change: Lessons from the Base Force, Bottom-Up Review, and Quadrennial Defense Review*, Santa Monica, CA: RAND Corporation, MR-1387-AF, 2001.

Lasswell, Harold, *A Pre-View of the Policy Sciences,* New York: American Elsevier, 1971.

Leeds, Brett Ashley, and David R. Davis, "Domestic Political Vulnerability and International Disputes," *Journal of Conflict Resolution*, Vol. 41, 1997, pp. 814–834.

Levy, Jack, "The Diversionary Theory of War: A Critique," in Manus Midlarsky (ed.), *Handbook of War Studies*, Ann Arbor: University of Michigan Press, 1993, pp. 259–288.

Lewis, Paul, "U.N. Will Increase Troops in Somalia," *The New York Times*, March 27, 1993, p. 3.

Lorell, Mark A., Charles Kelly, and Deborah Hensler, *Casualties, Public Opinion, and Presidential Policy During the Vietnam War*, Santa Monica, CA: RAND Corporation, R-3060-AF, 1984.

MacKuen, Michael B., "Exposure to Information, Belief Integration, and Individual Responsiveness to Agenda Change," *American Political Science Review*, Vol. 78, 1984a, pp. 372–391.

———, "Reality, the Press, and Citizens' Political Agendas," in Charles F. Turner and Elizabeth Martin (eds.), *Surveying Subjective Phenomena*, New York: Russell Sage Foundation, 1984b, pp. 443–473.

———, and Steven L. Coombs, *More Than News: Media Power in Public Affairs*, Beverly Hills: SAGE Publications, 1981.

Maren, Michael, "Somalia: Whose Failure?" *Current History*, May 1996, pp. 201–205.

Martinez, Gebe, "Concerns Linger for Lawmakers Following Difficult Vote for War," *CQ Weekly*, October 12, 2002, pp. 2671–2678.

Mason, Heather, "Public's Partisanship Evident on Terror Issue," The Gallup Organization, June 3, 2003.

———, "Assessing Threat Levels: Saddam or Bin Laden," The Gallup Organization, August 19, 2003.

McClosky, Herbert, "Consensus and Ideology in American Politics," *American Political Science Review*, Vol. 58, 1964, pp. 361–382.

Meernik, James, "Presidential Decision Making and the Political Use of Military Force," *International Studies Quarterly*, Vol. 38, 1994, pp. 121–138.

———, and Peter Waterman, "The Myth of the Diversionary Use of Force by American Presidents," *Political Research Quarterly*, Vol. 49, No. 3, September 1996, pp. 573–590.

Menkhaus, Ken, with Louis Ortmayer, *Key Decisions in the Somalia Intervention*, Pew Case Study in International Affairs, no. 464, Washington, D.C.: Georgetown University, Institute for the Study of Diplomacy, 1995.

Mermin, Jonathan. "Television News and American Intervention in Somalia: The Myth of a Media-Driven Foreign Policy," *Political Science Quarterly*, Vol. 112, 1997, pp. 385–403.

Milstein, Jeffrey S. *Dynamics of the Vietnam War,* Columbus: Ohio State University Press, 1974.

Modigliani, Andre, "Hawks and Doves, Isolationism and Political Distrust: An Analysis of Public Opinion on Military Policy," *American Political Science Review*, Vol. 66, 1972, pp. 960–978.

Moore, David W., "Public: 'Get Out of Somalia,'" *The Gallup Poll Monthly*, October 1993, pp. 23–24.

———, "Public Supports Stronger Stand Against Iraq; Gives Clinton High Marks for Actions So Far," The Gallup Organization, November 6, 1997.

———, "Americans Divided On U.S. Troops In Bosnia," The Gallup Organization, December 24, 1997.

———, "Support Increasing For Military Action Against Iraq; Men in Favor, Women Opposed," The Gallup Organization, February 5, 1998.

———, "Public Ready For War With Iraq; Support Wavers If Substantial U.S. Military Casualties," The Gallup Organization, February 18, 1998.

———, "Public Backs Attack on Iraq," The Gallup Organization, December 19, 1998.

———, "Attitudes About Kosovo Not Highly Partisan; Unless Clinton Specifically Mentioned," The Gallup Organization, The Gallup Organization, May 4, 1999.

———, "Americans See Terrorist Attacks as 'Act of War'; But Want Culprits Clearly Identified Before United States Retaliates," The Gallup Organization, September 12, 2001.

———, "Support for War on Terrorism Rivals Support for WWII; Vietnam War Received Least Support," The Gallup Organization, October 3, 2001.

———, "Public Overwhelmingly Backs Bush in Attacks on Afghanistan; Expects New Terrorist Attacks," The Gallup Organization, October 8, 2001.

———, "Public Optimistic on Progress of War on Terrorism; Willing to See War Expanded to Other Countries," The Gallup Organization, January 25, 2002.

———, "Americans Dubious About Progress in War on Terrorism; But Widespread Support for U.S. Troops in Afghanistan," The Gallup Organization, June 27, 2002.

———, "Public Uncertain About Success of War in Afghanistan; Half of All Americans Say Success Depends on Capturing Osama bin Laden," The Gallup Organization, July 11, 2002.

———, "Majority of Americans Favor Attacking Iraq to Oust Saddam Hussein: But Support Has Declined to pre-9/11 level; Four in 10 Now Opposed," The Gallup Organization, August 23, 2002.

———, "Support for Invasion of Iraq Remains Contingent on U.N. approval; Most Americans Doubt Saddam Hussein Will Comply With U.N. Resolutions," The Gallup Organization, November 12, 2002.

———, "Public Taking Wait-and-See Attitude on U.N. Inspections; Two in Three Americans Say Support for War Will Depend on What Happens in Iraq in Next Couple of Weeks," The Gallup Organization, December 12, 2002.

———, "Public Rallying Around Bush's Call for War; But Less Than Majority Support War Without New U.N. Vote," The Gallup Organization, February 11, 2003.

———, "Little Concern About Lack of WMD in Iraq; Public Rejects Charges of Deliberate Deception by Bush Administration," The Gallup Organization, June 4, 2003.

———, "Fewer Say Iraq Worth Going to War Over; Failure to Find Weapons of Mass Destruction, Continuing Conflict Appear to Have Major Impact," The Gallup Organization, July 1, 2003.

———, "Americans Favor U.S. Peacekeeping Force in Liberia; Still Strong Support for U.S. Troops in Iraq," The Gallup Organization, July 11, 2003.

———, "Iraq War Rally Effect Has Disappeared; Bush's Ratings Essentially the Same as Before the War Began," The Gallup Organization, July 22, 2003.

———, "Public Steady About Iraq, Could Waver as U.S. Casualties Increase; More Confident Saddam Will be Killed or Captured After Death of Sons," The Gallup Organization, July 29, 2003.

———, and Lydia Saad, "After Clinton Speech: Public Shifts In Favor of Haiti Invasion," *The Gallup Poll Monthly*, September 1994, pp. 16–17.

——— and ———, "Public Supports Actions Against Iraq," *The Gallup Poll Monthly*, October 1994, pp. 14–15.

Mueller, John E., *War, Presidents and Public Opinion*, New York: Wiley, 1973.

———, "Changes in American Public Attitudes Toward International Involvement," in Ellen Stern (ed.), *The Limits of Military Intervention,* Beverly Hills, CA: Sage, 1977.

———, *Policy and Opinion in the Gulf War*, Chicago: Chicago University Press, 1994.

———, "Public Support for Military Ventures Abroad: Evidence From the Polls," in John Norton Moore and Robert F. Turner (eds.), *The Real Lessons of the Vietnam War: Reflections Twenty-Five Years After the Fall of Saigon*, Durham, NC: Carolina Academic Press, 2002, pp. 173–219.

Neuman, Johanna, *Lights, Camera, War: Is Media Technology Driving International Politics?* New York: St. Martin's Press, 1996.

Neustadt, Richard E., *Presidential Power and the Modern Presidents,* New York: Free Press, 1990.

Newman, W. Russell, *The Paradox of Mass Politics: Knowledge and Opinion in the American Electorate*, Cambridge, MA: Harvard University Press, 1986.

Newport, Frank, "Foreign Affairs Erodes Public's Confidence in Clinton," *The Gallup Poll Monthly*, October 1993, pp. 29–31.

———, "Americans Still Cautious About U.S. Involvement in Bosnia," *The Gallup Poll Monthly,* December 1995, pp. 31–33.

———, "Majority of Americans Want U. S. Troops Out of Bosnia," The Gallup Organization, July 25, 1997.

———, "Public Support for U.S. Involvement in Yugoslavia Lower Than for Gulf War, Other Foreign Engagements," The Gallup Organization, March 30, 1999.

———, "Despite Skepticism, Support Grows for U.S. Involvement in Kosovo Crisis," The Gallup Organization, April 8, 1999.

———, "Gradual Increase in American Support for Kosovo Involvement Continues," The Gallup Organization, April 16, 1999.

———, "Public Support for U.S. Involvement in Kosovo Diminishing," The Gallup Organization, April 29, 1999.

———, "Support for U.S. Kosovo Involvement Drops; Americans Strongly Favor Cease-Fire in Order to Negotiate Peace; Clinton Approval Drops to Lowest Level in Three Years," The Gallup Organization, May 26, 1999.

———, "Americans Endorse Idea of Peace Plan, But Remain Skeptical of Serb Compliance," The Gallup Organization, June 7, 1999.

———, "New Poll on Kosovo Finds an Underwhelmed Public," The Gallup Organization, June 11, 1999.

———, "Americans Hesitant to Give Clinton Credit for Kosovo Peace," The Gallup Organization, June 15, 1999.

———, "East Timor Has Yet to Register on Americans' Consciousness; But Majority Says a Peaceful Solution Is at Least Somewhat Important to U.S.," The Gallup Organization, October 4, 1999.

———, "Retaliation; Americans Continue to Be Strongly Behind Retaliatory Military Actions," The Gallup Organization, September 24, 2001.

———, "Americans Remain Strongly in Favor of Military Retaliation; Nine Out of 10 Support Military Action Against Those Responsible for Terrorist Attacks," The Gallup Organization, September 27, 2001.

———, "Retaliation; Nine in 10 Americans Support Military Retaliation for Attacks, With Most Favoring Specific Action Against Afghanistan," The Gallup Organization, October 3, 2001.

———, "Support For Military Action Remains Strong; Eight Out of 10 Americans Also Support the Use of Ground Troops," The Gallup Organization, October 24, 2001.

———, "Overwhelming Support for War Continues; Americans Have Also Become More Likely to Support Long-Term War Against Global Terrorism," The Gallup Organization, November 29, 2001.

———, "Taking the War Beyond Afghanistan: Americans Generally Support Military Action in Iran, Iraq, and the Philippines," The Gallup Organization, February 4, 2002.

———, "Americans Still Consider Sept. 11 Most Tragic Event of Their Lives," The Gallup Organization, March 11, 2002.

———, "Public Wants Congressional and U.N. Approval Before Iraq Action; Majority Support for Removing Saddam Hussein Remains, but Many Feel President Bush Needs to Do Better Job of Explaining Rationale for Such Action," The Gallup Organization, September 6, 2002.

———, "Public Supports Bush Positions on U.N. Involvement in Iraq," The Gallup Organization, September 18, 2002.

———, "Should Bush Be Reading the Polls?" The Gallup Organization, March 5, 2003.

———, "Seventy-Two Percent of Americans Support War Against Iraq; Bush Approval Up 13 Points to 71%," The Gallup Organization, March 24, 2003.

———, "Americans Still Think Iraq Had Weapons of Mass Destruction Before War; Only a Third Believe Bush Administration Deliberately Misled American Public," The Gallup Organization, June 16, 2003.

Newport, Frank, and Leslie McAneny, "Haiti Yields Clinton Small 'Rally Effect,'" *The Gallup Poll Monthly,* September 1994, pp. 18–19.

Nincic, Donna, and Miroslav Nincic, "Commitment to Military Intervention: The Democratic Government as the Economic Investory," *Journal of Peace Research,* Vol. 32, No. 4, November 1995, pp. 413–426.

Nincic, Miroslav, "Loss Aversion and the Domestic Context of Military Intervention," *Political Research Quarterly,* Vol. 50, March 1997, pp. 97–120.

Nincic, Miroslav, and Donna Nincic, "Race, Gender, and War," *Journal of Peace Research,* Vol. 39, No. 5, 2002, September 2002, pp. 547–568.

Oneal, John R., Brad Lian, and James H. Joyner, Jr., "Are the American People 'Pretty Prudent'? Public Responses to U.S. Uses of Force, 1950–1988," *International Studies Quarterly*, Vol. 40, No. 2, June 1996, pp. 261–279.

Ostrom, Charles, and Brian Job, "The President and the Political Use of Force," *The American Political Science Review*, Vol. 80, No. 2, June 1986, pp. 541–566.

Petty, R.C., and J.T. Cacioppo, *Attitudes and Persuasion: Classic and Contemporary Approaches*, Dubuque, IA: William C. Brown Company, Publishers, 1981.

Pew Research Center, "Bush Engages and Persuades Public on Iraq," polling report, September 19, 2002.

Pfiffner, James P., *The Strategic Presidency*, 2d edition, Leavenworth, KS: University of Kansas Press, 1996.

Popkin, Samuel L., *The Reasoning Voter*, Chicago: Chicago University Press, 1994.

Powell, Colin L., Interview with French television channel TF-1, January 29, 2003.

———, "Remarks to the United Nations Security Council," February 5, 2003, U.S. State Department website, http://www.state.gov/secretary/rm/2003/17300.htm, accessed August 22, 2003.

Rasinski, Kenneth A., Jennifer Berktold, Tom W. Smith, and Bethany L. Albertson, *America Recovers: A Follow-Up to a National Study of Public Response to the September 11th Terrorist Attacks,* Chicago: National Opinion Research Center, August 7, 2002.

Richman, Alvin, "The American Public's 'Rules of Military Engagement' in the Post Cold War Era," paper prepared for the 1994 annual meeting of the American Political Science Association, 1994.

———, "When Should We Be Prepared to Fight?" *The Public Perspective,* April/May 1995, pp. 44–49.

Russett, Bruce, "Doves, Hawks, and U.S. Public Opinion," *Political Science Quarterly*, Vol. 105, No. 4, 1990–91, pp. 515–538.

Saad, Lydia, "'Operation Restore Hope' Gets Public's Blessing," *The Gallup Poll Monthly,* December 1992, pp. 18–20.

———, "Americans Hesitant, As Usual, About U.S. Military Action in the Balkans," The Gallup Organization, March 24, 1999.

———, "Americans Clearly Support a Military Response to Terrorist Assault," The Gallup Organization, September 13, 2001.

———, "Fewer Americans Perceive Anti-Terror War as Successful; But Americans' Fear of Being a Victim Holds Steady," The Gallup Organization, June 7, 2002.

———, "Do Americans Understand Bush Rationale for Striking Iraq? Fear of Weapons and Terrorism Are Paramount Reasons Given," The Gallup Organization, August 12, 2002.

———, "Top Ten Findings About Public Opinion and Iraq; Public Still Supportive of Iraq Invasion, But With Reservations," The Gallup Organization, October 8, 2002.

———, "Preventing Terrorism and Securing Energy Supplies Top Americans' Foreign Policy Concerns; Building Democracy Abroad Ranks Last Among Nine Possible Goals," The Gallup Organization, February 20, 2003.

———, and Frank Newport, "Americans Grow More Doubtful About Iraq War," The Gallup Organization, September 23, 2003.

———, "Public Remains Split on Iraq; No Indication That Early Fighting in Najaf Soured Attitudes," Gallup Poll News Service, August 20, 2004.

Schuman, Howard, "Two Sources of Antiwar Sentiment in America," *American Journal of Sociology*, Vol. 78, No. 3, 1972, pp. 513–536.

Seelye, Katherine Q., "Balkan Accord: In Congress, Anguished Senators Vote to Support Bosnia Mission; Clinton Off to Paris Signing," *The New York Times*, December 14, 1995, p. 1.

Skowronek, Stephen, *The Politics Presidents Make: Leadership from John Adams to George Bush*, Cambridge, MA: Balknap Press, 1993.

Sloyan, Patrick J, "Somalia Mission Control: Clinton Called the Shots in Failed Policy Targeting Aidid," *Newsday*, December 5, 1993a.

———, "Hunting Down Aidid; Why Clinton Changed His Mind," *Newsday*, December 6, 1993b.

———, "Full of Tears and Grief; For Elite Commandos, Operation Ended in Disaster," *Newsday*, December 7, 1993c.

———., "A Tough Encounter with Policy Survivors," *Newsday*, December 8, 1993d.

Smith, Tom W., Kenneth A. Rasinski, and Marianna Toce, *America Rebounds: A National Study of Public Response to the September 11th Terrorist Attacks; Preliminary Findings*, Chicago: National Opinion Research Center, October 25, 2001.

Sobel, Richard, "A Report: Public Opinion About United States Intervention in El Salvador and Nicaragua," *Public Opinion Quarterly*, Vol. 53, No. 1, Spring 1989, pp. 114–128.

———, "U.S. and European Attitudes Toward Intervention in the Former Yugoslavia: Mourir pour la Bosnie?" in Richard Ullmann (ed.), *The World and Yugoslavia's Wars*, New York: Council on Foreign Relations, 1996, pp. 145–181.

———, "The Polls—Trends: United States Intervention in Bosnia," *Public Opinion Quarterly*, 1998, Vol. 62, pp. 250–278.

Strobel, Warren P., *Late-Breaking Foreign Policy: The News Media's Influence on Peace Operations*, Washington, D.C.: U.S. Institute of Peace, 1997.

Wheeler, C. Gray, and David W. Moore, "Clinton's Foreign Policy Ratings Plunge," *The Gallup Poll Monthly*, October 1993, pp. 25–28.

White House, "List of Members of Congress Attending Meeting With The President on Somalia," October 7, 1993.

———, "Administration Policy on Reforming Multilateral Peace Operations (PDD-25)," May 5, 1994.

———, "Press Briefing by National Security Advisor Tony Lake and Director for Strategic Plans and Policy General Wesley Clark," May 5, 1994.

———, *A Decade of Deception and Defiance*, Washington, D.C., September 12, 2002.

Wittkopf, Eugene, *The Faces of Internationalism: Public Opinion and American Foreign Policy*, Durham, NC: Duke University Press, 1990.

———, "When Should We Be Prepared to Fight?" *The Public Perspective*, April/May 1995, pp. 44–49.

Yankelovich, Daniel, *Coming to Public Judgment: Making Democracy Work in a Complex World*, Syracuse, NY: Syracuse University Press, 1991.

Zaller, John R., *The Role of Elites in Shaping Public Opinion,* Ph.D. dissertation, University Microfilms, 1984.

———, *The Nature and Origins of Mass Opinion*, Cambridge: Cambridge University Press, 1992.

———, "Elite Leadership of Mass Opinion: New Evidence from the Gulf War," in Lance W. Bennett and David L. Paretz (eds.), *Taken By Storm: The Media, Public Opinion, and U.S. Foreign Policy in the Gulf War*, Chicago: University of Chicago Press, 1994, pp. 186–209.

Datasets

ABC News. ABC News "Nightline" Somalia Poll, October 5, 1993 [Computer File]. ICPSR version. Radnor, PA: Chilton Research Services [producer], 1993. Ann Arbor, MI: Inter-university Consortium for Political and Social Research [distributor], 1997.

ABC News. ABC News "Nightline" Haiti Poll, October 12, 1993 [Computer file]. ICPSR version. Radnor, PA: Chilton Research Services [producer], 1993. Ann Arbor, MI: Inter-university Consortium for Political and Social Research [distributor], 1997.

ABC News/The Washington Post. ABC NEWS/WASHINGTON POST TERRORIST ATTACK POLL #3, SEPTEMBER 2001 [Computer file]. ICPSR version. Horsham, PA: Taylor Nelson Sofres Intersearch [producer], 2001. Ann Arbor, MI: Inter-university Consortium for Political and Social Research [distributor], 2001.

ABC News/The Washington Post. ABC NEWS/WASHINGTON POST WAR POLL #2, NOVEMBER 2001 [Computer file]. ICPSR version. Horsham, PA: Taylor Nelson Sofres Intersearch [producer], 2001. Ann Arbor, MI: Inter-university Consortium for Political and Social Research [distributor], 2002.

ABC News/The Washington Post. ABC NEWS/WASHINGTON POST WAR POLL #1, MARCH 2003 [Computer file]. ICPSR version. Horsham, PA: Taylor Nelson Sofres Intersearch [producer], 2003. Ann Arbor, MI: Inter-university Consortium for Political and Social Research [distributor], 2003.

ABC News/The Washington Post. ABC NEWS/WASHINGTON POST WAR POLL #2, MARCH 2003 [Computer file]. ICPSR version. Horsham, PA: Taylor Nelson Sofres Intersearch [producer], 2003. Ann Arbor, MI: Inter-university Consortium for Political and Social Research [distributor], 2003.

ABC News/The Washington Post. ABC NEWS/WASHINGTON POST WAR POLL #3, MARCH 2003 [Computer file]. ICPSR version. Horsham, PA: Taylor Nelson Sofres Intersearch [producer], 2003. Ann Arbor, MI: Inter-university Consortium for Political and Social Research [distributor], 2003.

ABC News/The Washington Post. ABC NEWS/WASHINGTON POST WAR POLL #1, APRIL 2003 [Computer file]. ICPSR version. Horsham, PA: Taylor Nelson Sofres Intersearch [producer], 2003. Ann Arbor, MI: Inter-university Consortium for Political and Social Research [distributor], 2003.

CBS News. CBS NEWS MONTHLY POLL #1, OCTOBER 2001 [Computer file]. ICPSR version. New York, NY: CBS News [producer], 2001. Ann Arbor, MI: Inter-university Consortium for Political and Social Research [distributor], 2002.

CBS News. CBS NEWS MONTHLY POLL #2, MARCH 1999 [Computer file]. ICPSR version. New York, NY: CBS News [producer], 1999. Ann Arbor, MI: Inter-university Consortium for Political and Social Research [distributor], 1999.

Gallup. Gallup/CNN/USA Today Poll: Haiti/Honesty and Ethical Standards, September 23–25, 1994 [Computer File]. Roper version. The Gallup Organization [producer], 1994. Storrs, CT: The Roper Center for Public Opinion Research [distributor], 1994.

Gallup. Gallup/CNN/USA Today Poll: Bosnia Speech, November 27, 1995 [Computer File]. Roper version. The Gallup Organization [producer], 1995. Storrs, CT: The Roper Center for Public Opinion Research [distributor], 1995.

Gallup. Gallup/CNN/USA Today Poll: Congress/War on Terrorism/North Korea/2004 Presidential Election/Economy/Title Nine, January 3–5, 2003 [Computer File]. Roper version. The Gallup Organization [producer], 2003. Storrs, CT: The Roper Center for Public Opinion Research [distributor], 2003.

Pew Research Center. Kosovo News Interest Index, April 15–18, 1999 [Computer File]. Washington, D.C.: The Pew Research Center for the People and the Press [producer and distributor], 1999.

Pew Research Center. May News Interest Index, May 12–16, 1999 [Computer File]. Washington, D.C.: The Pew Research Center for the People and the Press [producer and distributor], 1999.

Pew Research Center. Early October 2002 Election Study, October 2–10, 2002 [Computer File]. Washington, D.C.: The Pew Research Center for the People and the Press [producer and distributor], 2003.